IMAGES
of America

HORICON AND HORICON MARSH

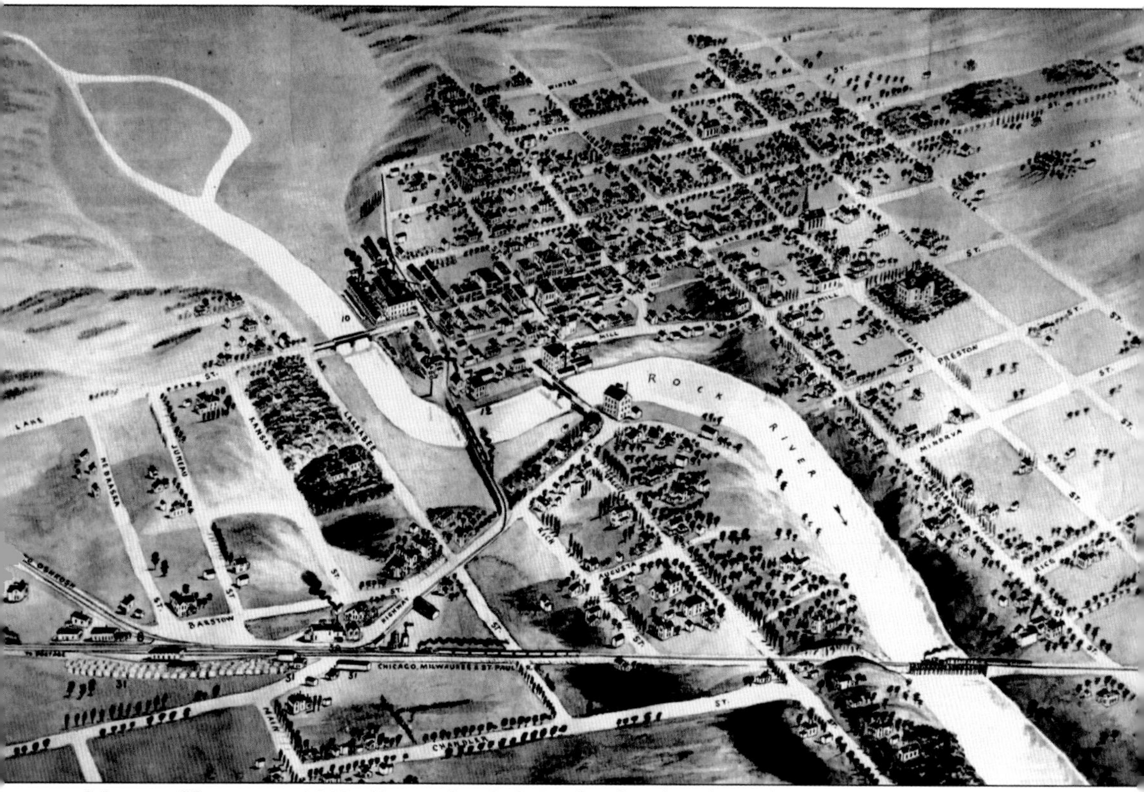

MAP OF HORICON, 1892. Drawn by C. J. Pauli of Milwaukee, this overhead view provides a good perspective of the town. Even in Horicon's early days, religion played an important civic function as the city boasted five churches around 1900. Much of the manufacturing, including the Van Brunt Manufacturing Company and the Kalies Windmill Factory, was located along the banks of the Rock River. (Courtesy Horicon Reporter.)

On the cover: **HORICON REPORTER, 1898.** The staff of the *Horicon Reporter*, when it was located at the northwest corner of the Lake and Vine Streets intersection in what would later become the tavern of Marsh Lanes Bowling Alley, stops work to strike a pose. Pictured are, from left to right, William Powell and Art Showers, owners, and Art Getchel, an employee. (Courtesy Horicon Reporter.)

IMAGES
of America

Horicon and Horicon Marsh

Susan Brunner and Jennee Harmuth

ARCADIA
PUBLISHING

ISBN 978-0-7385-6135-6

Published by Arcadia Publishing
Charleston SC, Chicago IL, Portsmouth NH, San Francisco CA

Printed in the United States of America

Library of Congress Catalog Card Number: 2008935485

For all general information contact Arcadia Publishing at:
Telephone 843-853-2070
Fax 843-853-0044
E-mail sales@arcadiapublishing.com
For customer service and orders:
Toll-Free 1-888-313-2665

Visit us on the Internet at www.arcadiapublishing.com

"Man can learn nothing except by going from the known to the unknown."

—Claude Bernard

This book is dedicated to the seekers.

CONTENTS

ACKNOWLEDGMENTS

As with any endeavor spanning the centuries, it is vital when telling a story through pictures to obtain the entire community's participation. Their ability to provide photographs and to share their family stories presents the true perspective of a town. Residents of the city of Horicon opened their homes and invited us in to gather historical memories passed down through generations. We thank all of them for their warm acceptance of our inquisitiveness.

Without the assistance of the following volunteers, we most definitely would not have a book: Andrew Johnson, publisher of the *Horicon Reporter*; Ed Knop; Don Miescke; Geri Pyrek; and Buzz Vanderhei. The Horicon Historical Society was invaluable for the information in its archives and photographic collections. A very special thank-you to Bill Volkert, wildlife educator/naturalist for Wisconsin Department of Natural Resources, for his tireless efforts in keeping us on track with the history of the Horicon Marsh.

Susan is grateful to her husband, Patrick, for without him, she may have never known of this magnificent location—his hometown; to her father, Edwin Boehm, for encouraging her and loving her unconditionally no matter what she attempted; to brother Christopher, for smiling on the other side; and to Karen Olson, who believes in her many adventures. A special thanks goes to Joan Schwantes Hansen.

Jennee is indebted to her dad, Dale Lindenberg, for living his life as an example that all things are possible; her mom, Judy, for always being Mom; Judy Billington for the pockets full of sunshine along the way; her children Courtney, Hailey, and Noah, who give life its melody each day; and finally God, her family at MarshView Ministries, and her husband Tory, all of whom fill her life with so much beauty and love.

We hope this book spurs your interest in Horicon and the Horicon Marsh and encourages you to delve into history and research further into what we trust has peaked your curiosity. As with any writing, any errors are ours alone. Unfortunately, many photographs have been lost to time and tragedy and could not be included.

INTRODUCTION

Over the course of the thousands of years spanning the ice ages when glaciers shaped the plains of Wisconsin into the land we see today, the city of Horicon and the Horicon Marsh have evolved several times over. When the glaciers receded, the Horicon area became hunting grounds for early nomads. These people left evidence of their existence through recordings in carved rock and cave paintings. More than 50 sites of these renderings have been discovered in Wisconsin and are today protected by archaeologists who continue studying the depictions of animals and hunters to better understand the culture.

Between AD 800 and AD 1,200, the late Woodland culture, or effigy mound builders, began creating animal- and earthen-shaped mounds, some of which can still be seen today at the Nitschke Mounds County Park, located just a few miles west of the city of Horicon. Effigy mound builders typically buried their dead in small pits or laid them on carefully prepared surfaces. Mounds were then constructed over them like modern-day grave markers. An effigy, a representation or sculptured image, was the way of honoring their dead at the time. Mounds were created in the shapes recognizable as animals, such as a bird, bear, deer, or turtle, to name but a few, or alternatively as linear- or dome-shaped creations. Horicon itself was built upon these Native American mounds, with Increase Lapham, a surveyor, having charted approximately 90 formations here. His 1851 survey provided evidence of what, at the time, were the most complicated and intricate mounds discovered in Wisconsin.

Since the time of the Woodland tribes, inhabitants of the Horicon Marsh area have been tied to the land. For those early settlers, this tie meant hunting and gathering, living and coexisting with everything wild on the great marsh. When the white man entered the area around 1830, the Winnebago, the most prominent tribe in the area, had been living off the land, fishing in the bountiful Rock River, and hunting the local wetlands for generations. Freezing of the river in the winters allowed the Native Americans to ice fish, while their summers consisted of harvesting wild rice, the roots of water lilies, and bulrushes. They were a peaceful tribe, yet the white man persuaded them to move to Minnesota in exchange for annuities. Many returned to Horicon not long after, realizing either that they had not made such a good trade or because enemy tribes made life uncomfortable in the Minnesota area. In 1850, the Winnebago were moved to Dakota County, Nebraska, a destination farther away, but a few drifted back and camped along the Rock River. Around 1880, the government once more moved them from the area with Red Wolf, a Kickapoo Native American, and his family being the last Native Americans to live in the vicinity. Red Wolf's daughter Mendota was the last Native American to graduate from Horicon High School, having done so in 1920.

When pioneer Satterlee Clark first entered the noted Winnebago village in 1830, there were approximately 2,000 inhabitants who called the place Maunk-shak-ah, meaning "white breast." Over the next 16 years, the village was known successively as Elk Village (in 1832), Doty's Grove (in 1838), Indian Ford and then Hubbard's Rapids (in 1839), and finally as Horicon (in 1846). In some reference material, the names Indian Ford and Hubbard's Rapids may have referred to a small portion of land, not the entire village, which was later sold by Henry Hubbard Jr. for town and water site purposes. Named by Charles Larrabee after Lake Horicon in New York (later Lake George), Horicon means "pure and clear water."

With the growth of the town, transportation of goods and passengers became vital. The railroad was an important part of the city, and in 1852, the Milwaukee and Horicon Railroad Company was chartered. On December 25, 1855, the first freight train arrived in town, and on January 2, 1856, the first passenger train entered Horicon from Milwaukee. By 1858, logs by the thousands entered Horicon by railroad and were dumped into the Rock River and driven to southern markets. That spring, several million feet of logs were rafted on the river. Horicon boasted a depot and restaurant to greet visitors to the town, as well as those who came to enjoy the hunting and fishing on Lake Horicon. With the railroads expanding, additional capital was needed for the growth. Area farmers were talked into taking second mortgages on their properties, with many subsequently losing them when the local railroads went under financially. Those who were able to hold on recovered their money when the local railroad was bought and became part of the Milwaukee and St. Paul Railroad. Notably, Maurice Whitty and his wife, Hazel, worked for the railroad for more than 80 years combined. Whitty Park is named in their honor for their many contributions to the community.

An elevator was built near the depot by Jonas Schoenman in 1869 to hold wheat for shipment. It changed hands several times over the years, was purchased by Hugo Henkel in 1938, and was later expanded. He also built a large grain and feed business, which was located near the depot.

While the number of inhabitants grew, so too did the business sector. Banks, hotels, restaurants, and dry goods stores sprang to life. Many people of Irish and German ancestry moved into the area, as did the Hungarians. Mill Street was known for its large population of Hungarians, and residents dubbed it "Hunk Hill," a name still in use today. South Hubbard Street boasted three breweries in the mid-1800s, with the underground cellars still in existence, although closed to those wishing to explore.

Prior to the dawn of the 20th century, with the Rock River and the marsh as its backdrop, Horicon grew and became a draw for other enterprises. Lumber and gristmills sprang up along the riverbanks, small mom-and-pop shops opened in town, and churches opened their doors to parishioners throughout the community.

With the railroad moving passengers into and out of town and the advent of the automobile, living in Horicon and working in neighboring cities became easier. As larger conglomerations built their enterprises, the mom-and-pop shops could no longer compete and folks began shopping in outlying cities. Over the past 100 years, the town has evolved from a booming business arena to a wonderful bedroom community in which to raise a family.

When Daniel Van Brunt first settled in nearby Mayville, he opened a wagon and blacksmith business. By 1861, Daniel and his brother George had patented an experimental seeder and manufactured their first product at the Mayville shop. That same year they moved their business to Horicon and found their niche manufacturing grain drills. The company had several owners and changed names many times over the next several years until a purchase agreement was reached in 1911 with Deere and Company but not without conditions set by Willard Van Brunt. The factory was to remain in Horicon, and employees were to be retained by Deere and Company. With all conditions met, Deere and Company expanded, adding a new shop building, warehouse, and two-story building. Van Brunt remained as president of the company until November 1917, when John Bodden was named president. In 1920, with housing a serious issue for employees, the company started a building program. With employees providing 10 percent down and 1 percent of the balance each month, several homes were built in the city. Years later, during World War II, the company supported its country by producing $212 million of equipment for the United States War and Navy Departments, including tank transmissions, ammunition, trailers, and aircraft parts. Utility trailers were made for the U.S. Army Corps of

Engineers, as well as pilothouses and other ship assemblies. The company's name changed many times, always retaining the Van Brunt name. In 1953, the Van Brunt name no longer showed up on the hoppers. Grain boxes were now green and yellow, rather than the traditional red of the Van Brunt wooden boxes. By 1956, the company began manufacturing lawn and garden tractors. Today, known as John Deere Horicon Works, the company is the largest manufacturer of those distinctive green and yellow lawn tractors.

On November 1, 1928, Clarence Gardner incorporated Gardner Manufacturing after acquiring the IDEAL Barn Equipment Company. By 1937, the company had formed three product divisions—barn equipment, sheet metal fabrication, and insect electrocutor (commercially sold as the Bug Zapper). In 1980, Gardner Manufacturing was sold to John S. Jones who, in 1981, built a new metal fabrication facility at the Horicon Industrial Park. In 1985, the barn equipment division was sold, and in 1992, an environmental products division was added. The business continues to thrive today.

The Horicon Plant of the Columbus Canning Company building was erected in 1920 as a branch of the Columbus Food Corporation. The factory, located on the banks of the Rock River on South Hubbard Street, canned both peas and corn. In 1945, the plant was purchased by Stokely Foods, and in the late 1940s, cranberries were canned in the facility. The factory remained in town for many years before finally closing its doors in 1976.

The Horicon Iron and Manufacturing Company was chartered in 1846 to provide waterpower for milling and the manufacture of iron. The dam raised the level of water over the marsh more than nine feet. The energy generated by the waterpower supplied several businesses, including a sawmill, two gristmills, a sash-and-door factory, and an ironworks shop. Previously known as the Winnebago Marsh, with the construction of the dam, the waters were renamed Lake Horicon, which at the time was touted as the largest man-made lake in the world. Steamboats made their way through the waters, carrying passengers to the many nearby islands and resorts that sprang up along the banks. In 1852, the dam collapsed from heavy rains and caused damage to surrounding farms. Within six weeks, the dam was functioning again, but farmers whose land adjacent to the marsh had been compromised because of the raised water level filed suit for damages and won. The court, in 1869, ordered the dam removed. With the dam gone, the land reverted to its former marshland state.

In 1930, a new dam, still in operation today, was built to help restore the marsh to its original level following the drainage effort.

With the original dam removed, native plant life rapidly returned, drawing waterfowl back to the fold, thus beginning the era of the hunting clubs in the 1880s. The Diana Shooting Club (so named after the Roman goddess of the hunt), the Horicon Shooting Club, and the Chicago Shooting Box (founded by a group of men from Chicago) were notable organizations for those interested in hunting, fishing, and trapping. In addition to the private hunting clubs, market hunters also plied the marsh, slaughtering birds en masse in order to sell them as food in the larger cities of Milwaukee and Chicago. Birds were so plentiful that entire freight cars, packed with 200 birds to a barrel, were shipped for sale. It was the unregulated hunting of the market hunters that devastated the waterfowl. With the ducks nearly gone, others tried to utilize the marsh by draining it and attempting to convert the acreage to cropland.

In an attempt to change the marsh into viable cropland, dredging began in 1910. The dredging destroyed ponds, and where once birds migrated to the area, water was no longer in abundance for their nesting grounds. By 1916, it was hoped to be the most fertile farmland in the upper Midwest. "Onions and Independence" was a great sales pitch told by Ed Oliver, encouraging ownership of marshlands and the bounty of food to be gotten in the agricultural "farmland." Many hoping to cash in on this venture purchased land and planted root crops. This, of course, was not to occur, as the land would not properly drain for the successful planting and harvesting of onions or any other vegetables.

When the soil was tilled and the underlying peat exposed, it dried and rotted during the summer months, eventually catching fire and burning for years. Utilizing the land for farming was not viable, but farmers found that cutting the marsh hay and shipping it to markets around the world was a profitable venture.

Muskrat harvesting was also profitable on the marsh during the early 20th century, with more than 50,000 muskrats being trapped each year. Steamboat Island and Fourmile Island were popular places for skinning the muskrats and hanging the hides to dry.

Following the destruction of the marsh as a result of drainage and the resultant peat fires, conservationists, led by Louis "Curley" Radke, were finally able to convince the state to establish the Horicon Marsh State Wildlife Area after the passage of the Horicon Wildlife Refuge Bill of 1927. This bill provided money to buy land and construct the dam that still regulates the marsh water levels today. Radke spent years working to support the restoration of the marsh to bring the wildlife back into the fold. One historic event to encourage folks to think of the marsh as a wildlife area was Duck Liberation Day in 1935. People could purchase ducks for $1 and release them at the marsh. For many years, the marsh provided a wonderful venue for hunting waterfowl as a main source of nourishment, especially during the Depression years. Palmer Miescke, a lifelong resident of Horicon, recalled that in 1938 he would hunt ducks and sell them for $5 each to earn money for necessities. Hunting to sell the fowl at market was illegal at that time; however, many did so in order to feed their own families. Other later restrictions were put in place to preserve the wildlife.

Conservationists worked hard to make the waters pure and clear for generations to come, and those efforts have paid off over the years. Established in 1927, the Horicon Marsh State Wildlife Area is a complex of 11,000 acres of wetlands and uplands managed by the Wisconsin Department of Natural Resources. This area comprises the southern one-third of the Horicon Marsh. Dike Road separates the state-run southern one-third of the marsh from the federally run northern two-thirds of the marsh. The victory of the Horicon Wildlife Refuge Bill paved the way for the creation of the Horicon Marsh National Wildlife Refuge on July 16, 1941. The 21,000-acre refuge was established to protect migratory birds, and today the marsh in its entirety plays host to the largest migratory flock of Canada geese in the world. The Horicon Marsh is the largest freshwater cattail marsh in the nation, measuring nearly 14 miles long by 5 miles wide.

Designated as a "Wetland of International Importance" under the Ramsar Convention in 1991, visitors can tour the distinguished Horicon Marsh throughout the year. Those who make the trip will not be disappointed as they can enjoy many nature-centered activities, including hiking, biking, driving, fishing, hunting, trapping, hiking, snowshoeing, cross-country skiing, and canoeing. Bird-watching and taking in the peace and serenity of what Mother Nature has provided makes for a wonderful day as well. The newly opened Horicon Marsh International Educational Center, located on State Highway 28 between the cities of Horicon and Mayville, provides tours, field trips, and other special events throughout the year.

Join us as we take a trip through the past to explore the history of this wonderful little city and wildlife refuge. We, along with the generations of Horiconites who have come before, are sure you will be as entranced by the beauty of the city of Horicon and the Horicon Marsh as the residents and visitors are today.

One

The Early Years

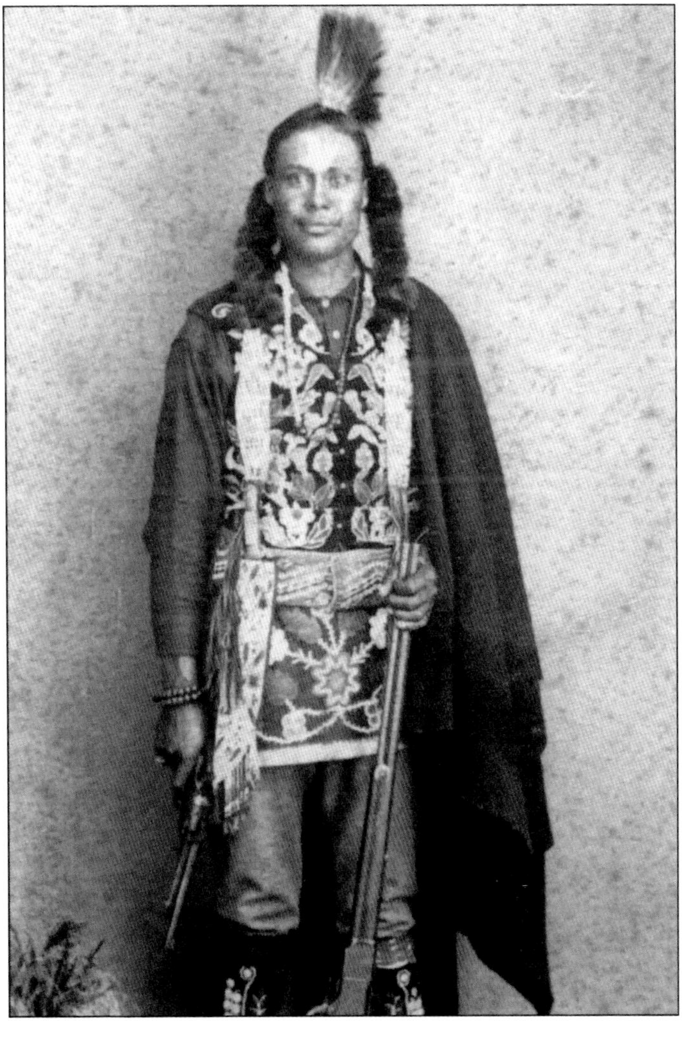

Red Wolf, 1890. Born in 1853 in Kentucky of Kickapoo ancestry, Red Wolf is in full Native American dress in this photograph. As one of the last Native Americans to call the Horicon area home, Red Wolf trapped on the marsh and assisted farmers with thrashing of wheat and cutting of marsh hay. This historic figure is buried west of the city at Stone Cemetery overlooking Nitschke Mounds County Park. (Courtesy Horicon Reporter.)

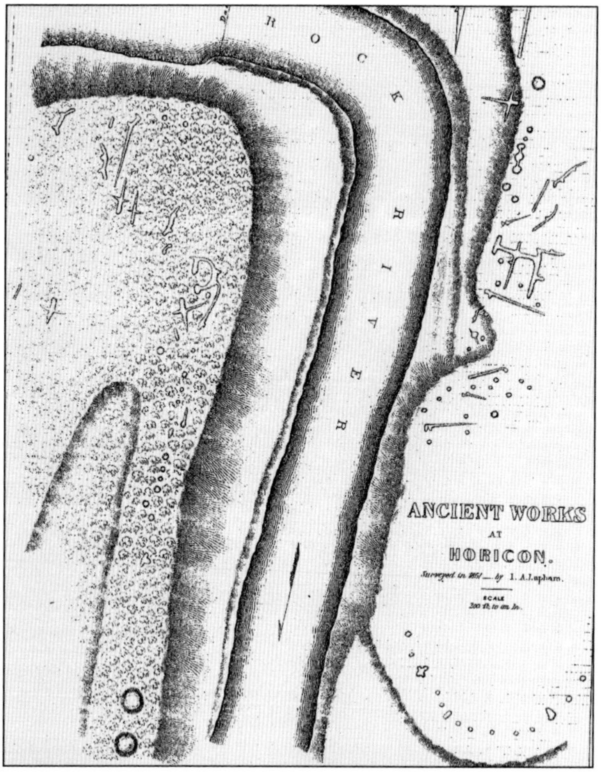

I. A. LAPHAM'S SURVEY, 1851. Increase Allen Lapham surveyed Horicon and mapped hundreds of Native American mound formations in town. Approximately 90 such structures were identified throughout the town along the Rock River. Not surprisingly, many home owners found human remains when digging basements. When Lapham began mapping the mounds in 1851, he noticed they were shaped mimicking animals. Most effigy mounds fell into the realms of air, earth, or water and oftentimes were oriented toward a spring or water source. Once opened, it was typical to locate the burial of remains in the heart of the animal shape. Today one can visit Nitschke Mounds County Park just a few miles west of town to learn more about this mound-building culture. (Courtesy Don Gehrke.)

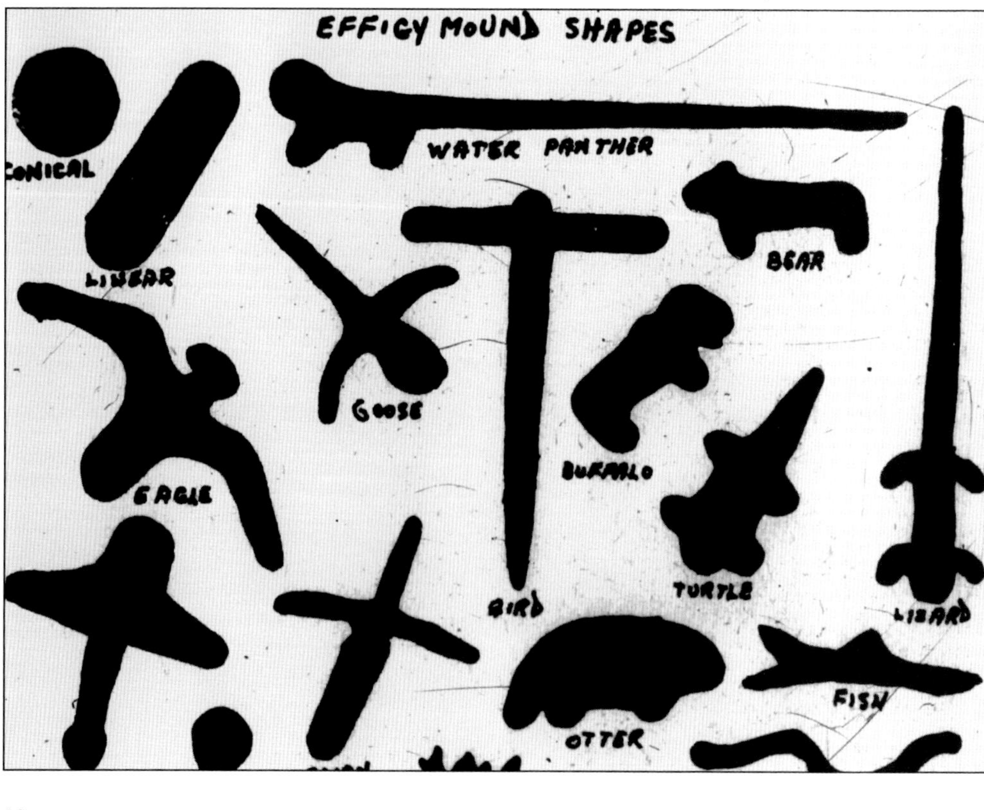

SATTERLEE CLARK. Born in 1817, Satterlee Clark, considered one of the city's founding fathers, first moved to Green Bay from Washington, D.C. At the age of 23, Pres. Andrew Jackson assigned him to Fort Winnebago, located at modern-day Portage. Clark later settled in Horicon, where he worked as a lawyer and was active in politics, serving in both the Wisconsin senate and the state assembly. (Courtesy Horicon Historical Society.)

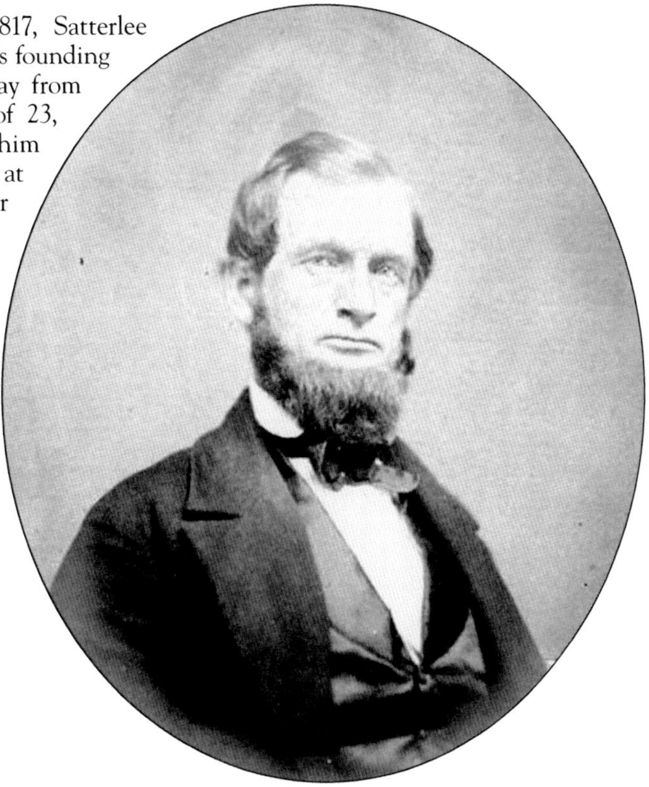

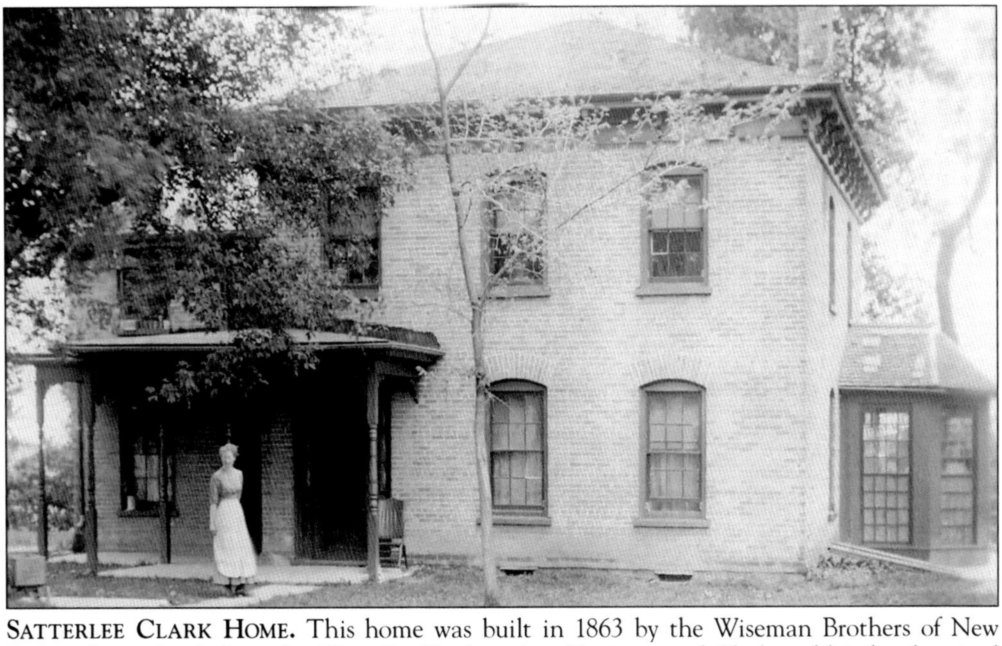

SATTERLEE CLARK HOME. This home was built in 1863 by the Wiseman Brothers of New York utilizing brick from the Chandler Brickyard in Horicon, and Clark and his family raised pedigreed horses and dogs on the Winter Street property. Today the home is a museum containing thousands of items, many donated by city residents, as well as the meeting place of the Horicon Historical Society. (Courtesy Horicon Historical Society.)

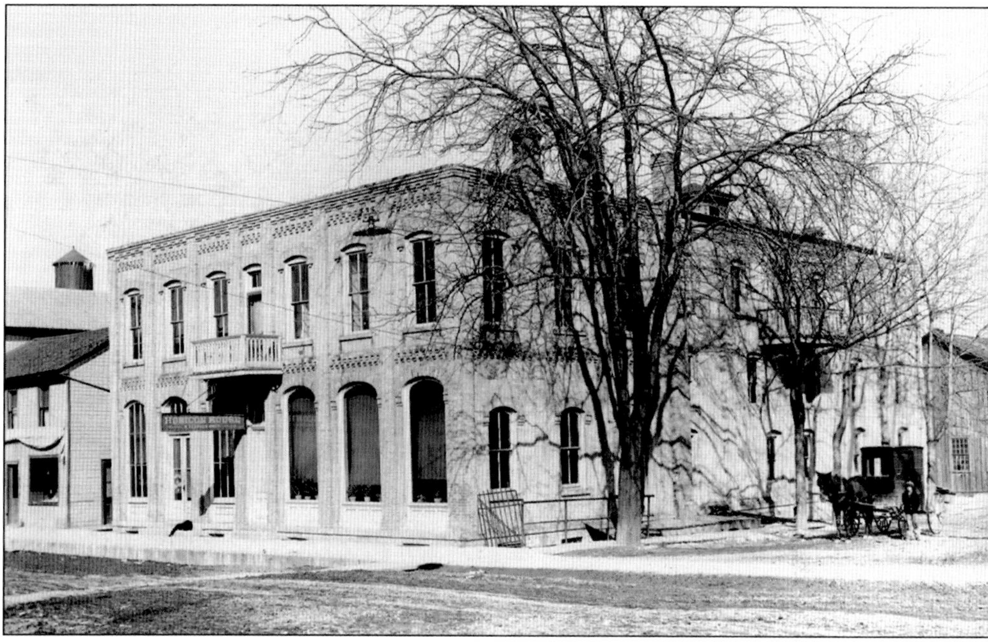

WINTER HOUSE. Built in 1855 by Peter Winter, the hotel was later owned and operated by the Bossman family and known as the Bossman House from 1898 to 1903. Later the establishment was known as Horicon Hotel and was a fixture at the corner of East Lake and Hubbard Streets. It remained until 1964, when it was razed to make way for the Horicon Federal Building. (Courtesy Horicon Historical Society.)

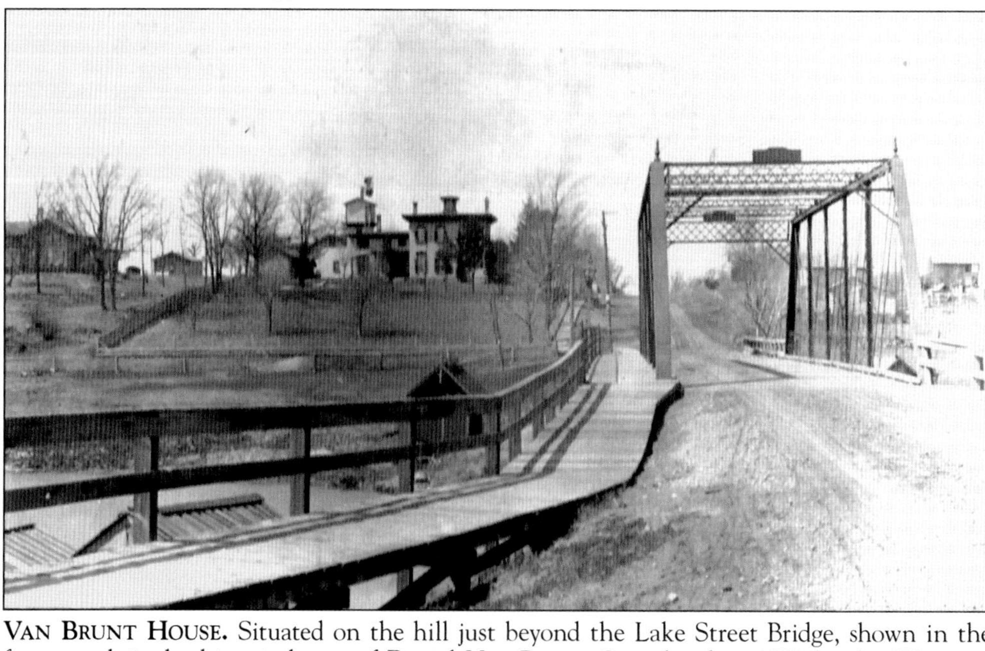

VAN BRUNT HOUSE. Situated on the hill just beyond the Lake Street Bridge, shown in the foreground, is the historic home of Daniel Van Brunt. Completed in 1858 by the Wiseman Brothers using Chandler brick, the home is of Italianate design. Built for William Decker, the town's first dentist, and his wife, Julia, the home was owned by several others before Van Brunt moved in on May 16, 1868. (Courtesy Horicon Historical Society.)

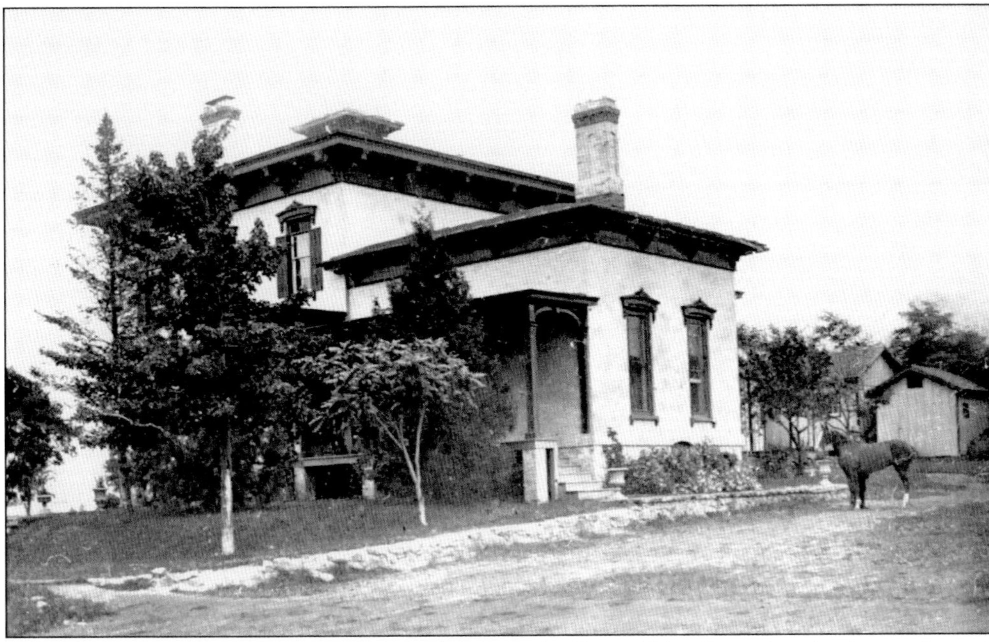

Van Brunt House, Late 1800s. Once home to the Daniel Van Brunt family, the residence is now privately owned and on the National Register of Historic Places. Although not built by Van Brunt, he lived in the home from 1868 until his death in 1901. From 1922 until the 1960s, the home was used by the community pursuant to the wishes of Martha Moore Van Brunt, widow of Daniel. (Courtesy Donna Ronzani.)

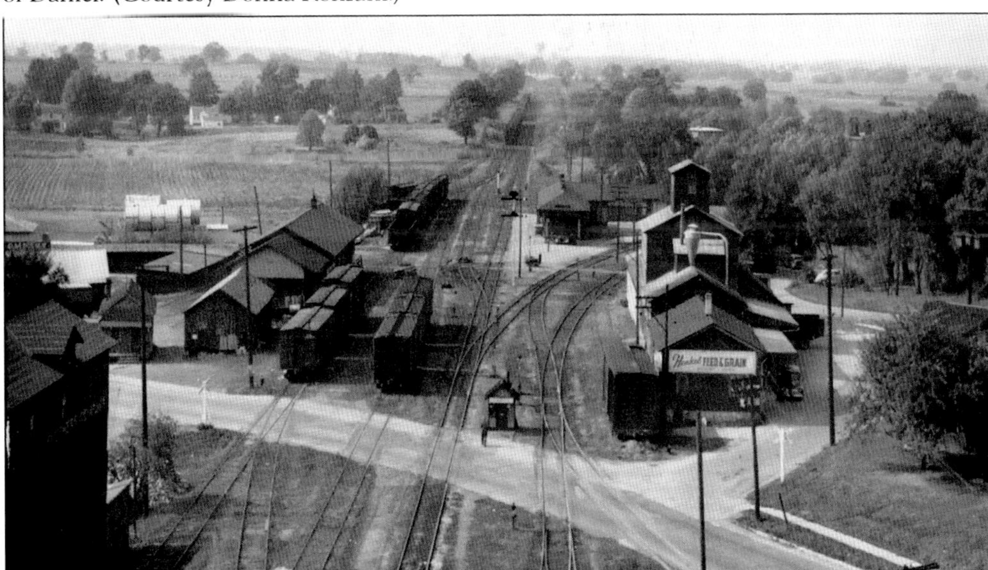

Train Depot. The railway forged its way into Horicon on December 25, 1855, with the first freight train arrival. On January 2, 1856, the first passenger train entered the city from Milwaukee on the Milwaukee and Horicon Railroad Company line later absorbed by the La Crosse-Milwaukee Railroad. Horicon's historic depot stands today on the grounds of what is now the Wisconsin and Southern Railroad Company, located off Barstow Street in the heart of the city. (Courtesy Marge Anfinson.)

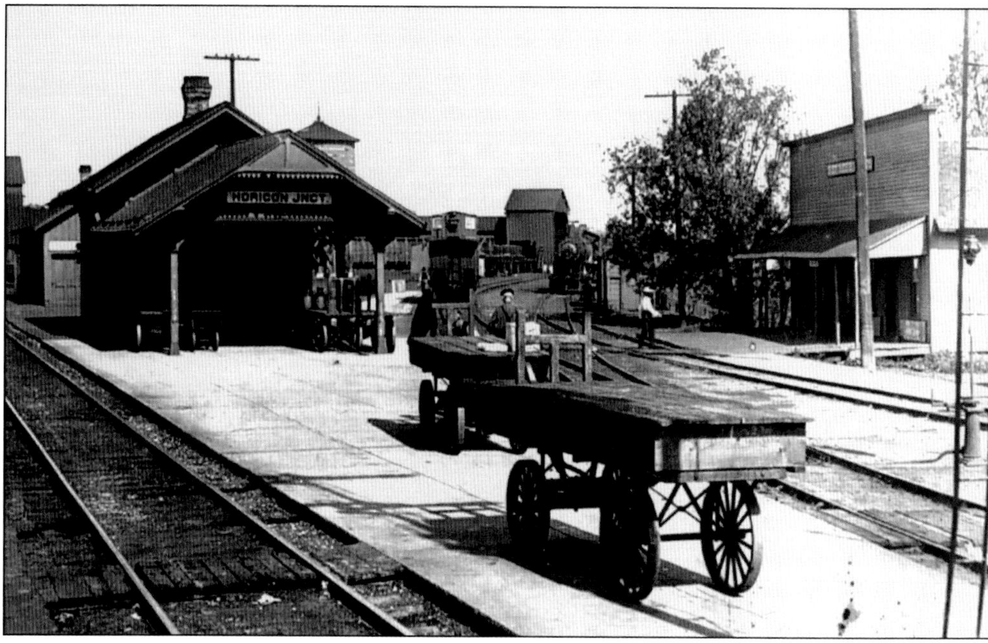

HORICON JUNCTION. The La Crosse-Milwaukee Railroad came into Horicon in 1856, and auxiliary buildings to accommodate passengers and workers were constructed. Depot buildings originally sat on the east side of the river, and a roundhouse was completed in 1857 for housing and switching locomotives. Railroad car and repair shops were constructed in 1861, and large numbers of passenger and freight cars were manufactured over the next two years. The Chicago, Milwaukee and St. Paul Railroad line took control in 1863, and a new depot building was erected on the west side of the river. With railroad transportation establishing Horicon as a center of commerce, a grain building was constructed near the depot. Horicon was proclaimed a wheat market by the *Horicon Argus* in August 1858 with prices of 91¢ per bushel. (Courtesy Frank Owens.)

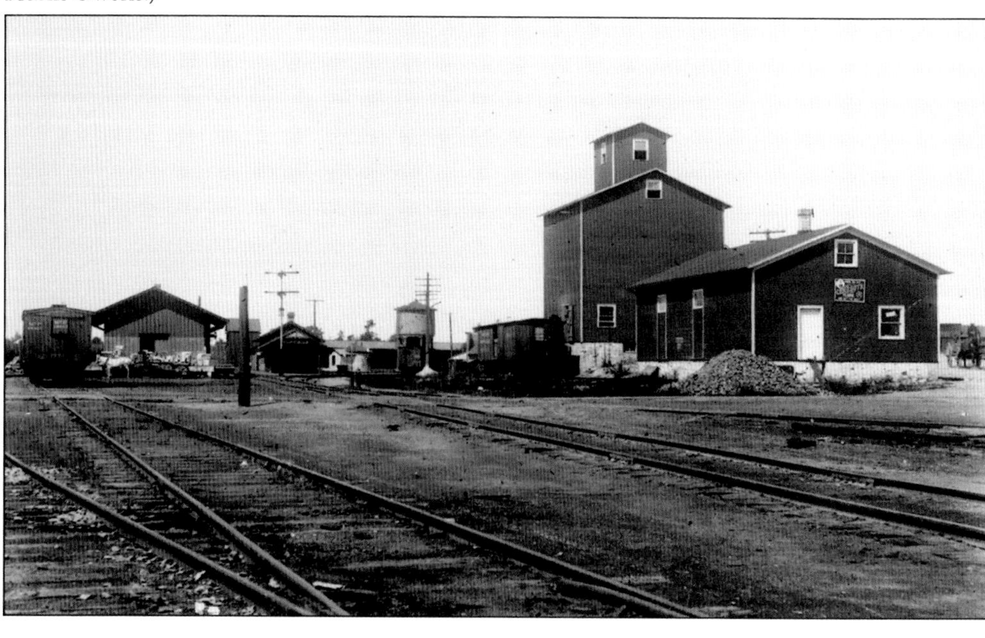

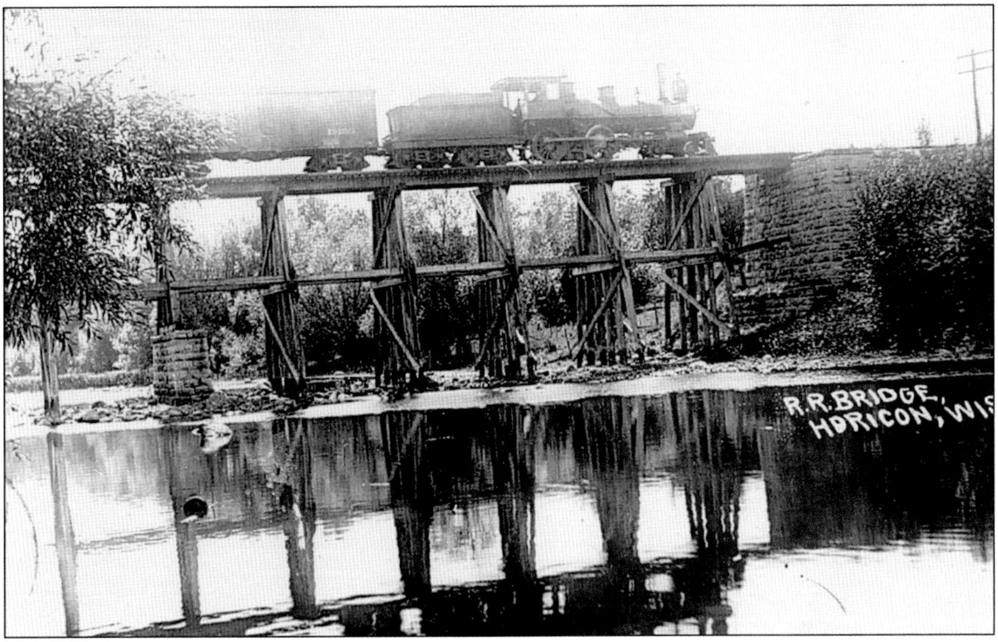

RAILROAD BRIDGE AND COAL TOWER. When the Milwaukee and Horicon Railroad Company was chartered in 1852, construction of railroad bridges was also planned. A pile bridge was built in 1855 and was in use until 1912, when a concrete bridge was erected. Earlier years of wood-burning engines brought wood for the Horicon line from Germantown and Richfield. Averaging 200 cords per trainload, a wood supply train typically consisted of 25 flatcars with a crew of approximately 30 men. The last wood-burning engine ran through the area around 1888, when coal-burning engines were then instituted. The photograph at right shows the coal tower that sat south of Barstow Street and southeast of the present crossing. (Courtesy Frank Owens.)

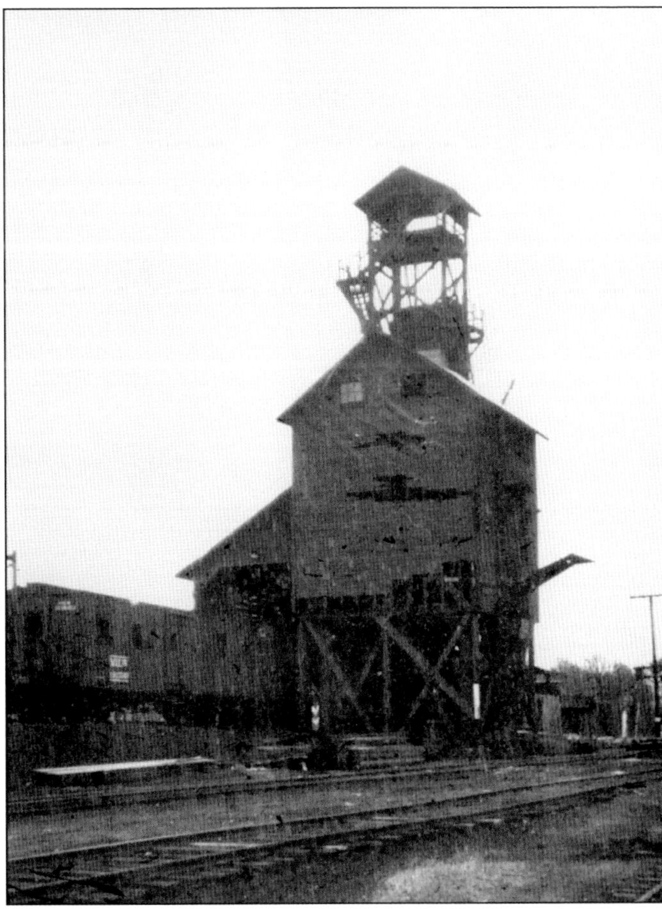

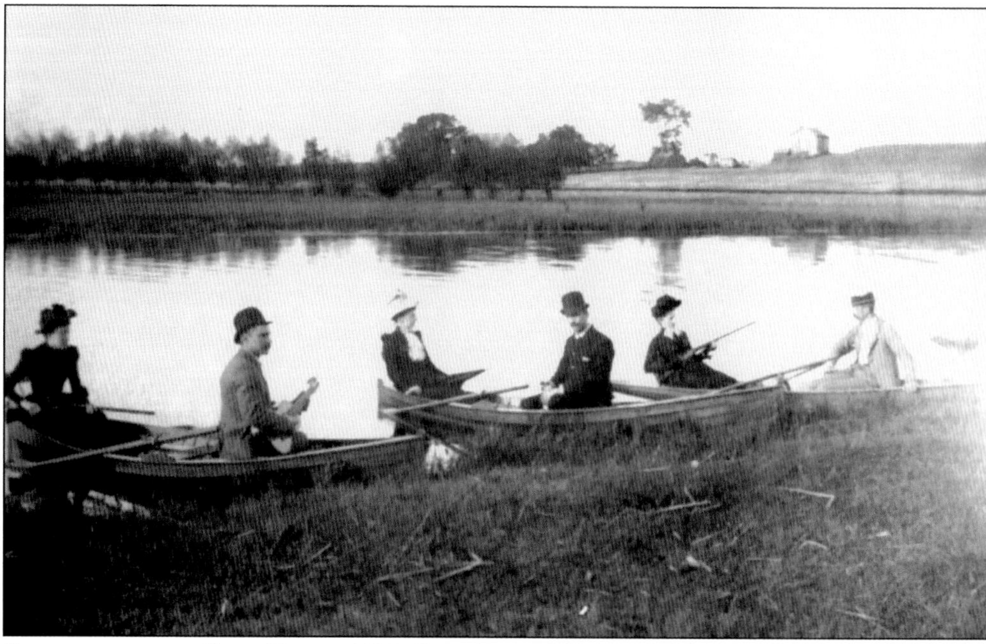

Canoeing on the Rock River, 1890. Spending an afternoon with one's hoped-to-be-betrothed are, from left to right, an unidentified Elliott (who is known to have later married Herb Freeman) and H. F. Krueger; Jessie Stacks and John Bodden, a couple who married that same year; and Alma Krause and Frank Forbes, who married at a later time. (Courtesy Horicon Reporter.)

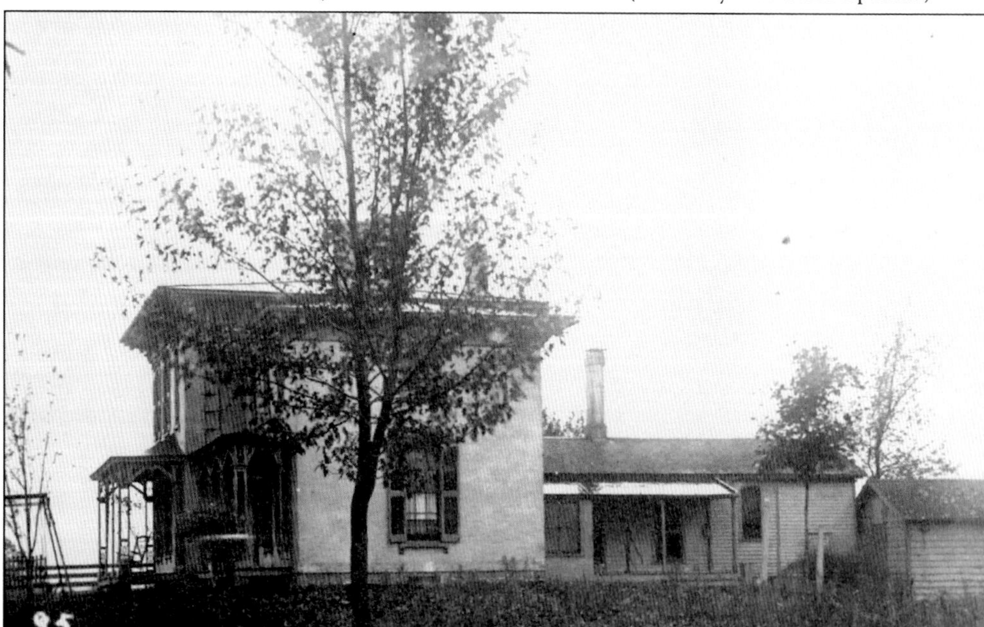

Stacks Home. Mary Sullivan recalls visiting her grandparents Jessie Stacks Bodden and John Bodden at their home located at 112 Kansas Street. Jessie's parents, John Stacks and Lydia Ellen Stacks, moved to Horicon on August 2, 1882, when Jessie was 16 years old. The historic home was built prior to 1873 and continues to shine as one of the city's best examples of the Italianate building style. (Courtesy Mary Sullivan.)

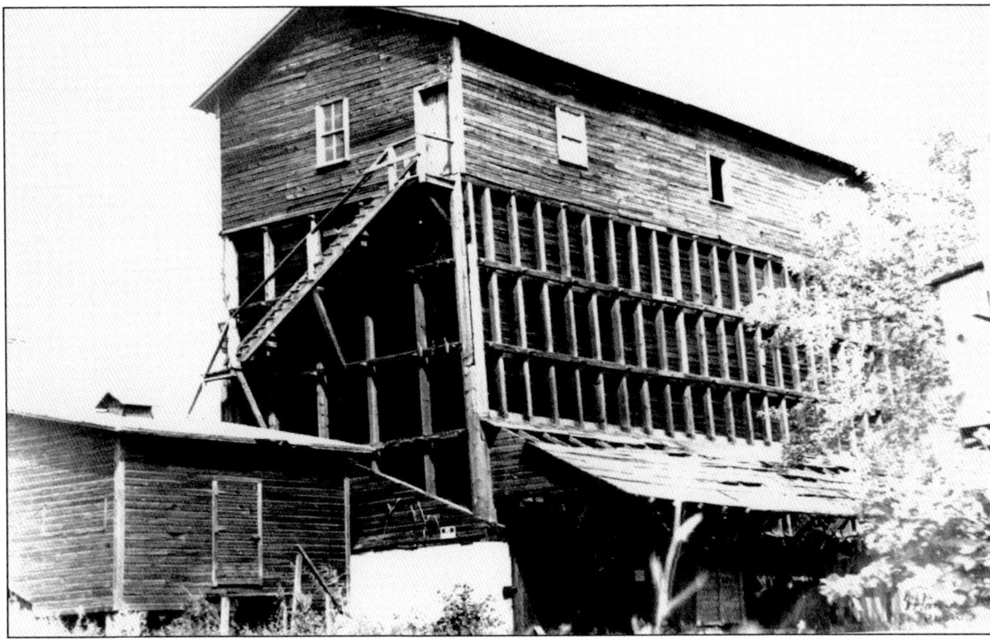

BODDEN BROTHERS COMPANY, 1895. Located on the west side of Vine Street, brothers Frank, John, and Henry began business in 1895 and remained working in the lumberyards for more than 50 years. Frank was among the organizers of the Horicon Chamber of Commerce, the Horicon Telephone Company, and the Oak Hill Cemetery Association. Today the John Deere Horicon Works occupies the property on which the yard once stood. (Courtesy Keith Pahl.)

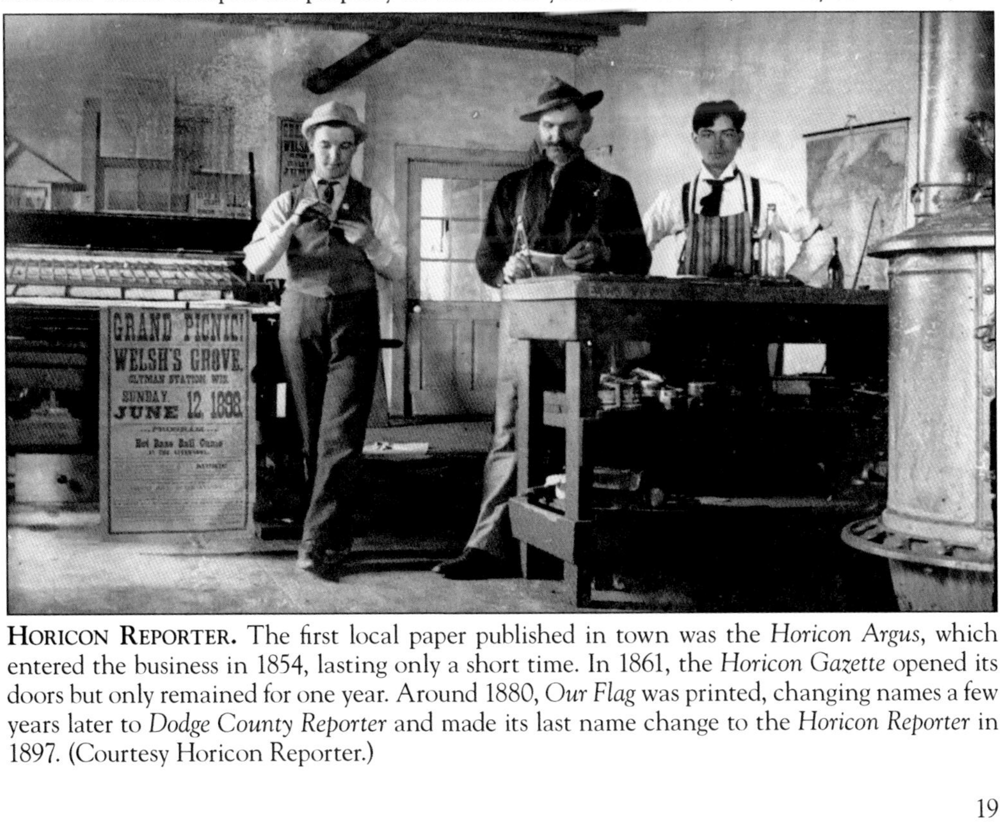

HORICON REPORTER. The first local paper published in town was the *Horicon Argus*, which entered the business in 1854, lasting only a short time. In 1861, the *Horicon Gazette* opened its doors but only remained for one year. Around 1880, *Our Flag* was printed, changing names a few years later to *Dodge County Reporter* and made its last name change to the *Horicon Reporter* in 1897. (Courtesy Horicon Reporter.)

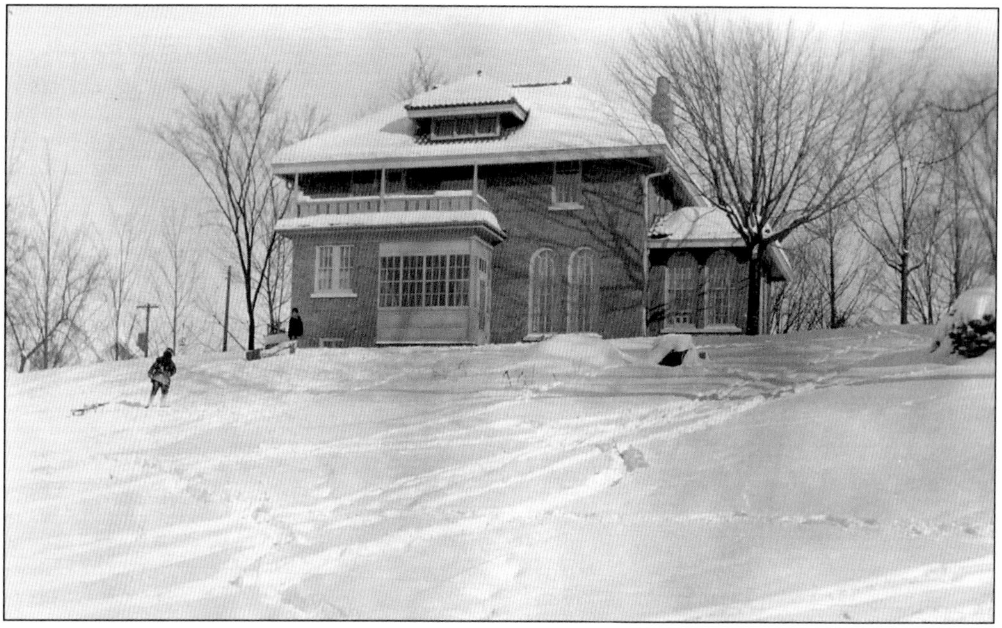

GARDNER RESIDENCE. Located at 106 Kansas Street, the backyard presented a wonderful play area for children with their sleds. The residence was built between 1925 and 1926 and was owned by Clarence Gardner, founder of Gardner Manufacturing, and his wife, Mildred Bodden Gardner. The home still stands and is a wonderful example of a home built in the Spanish Colonial/Mediterranean Revival style. (Courtesy Mary Sullivan.)

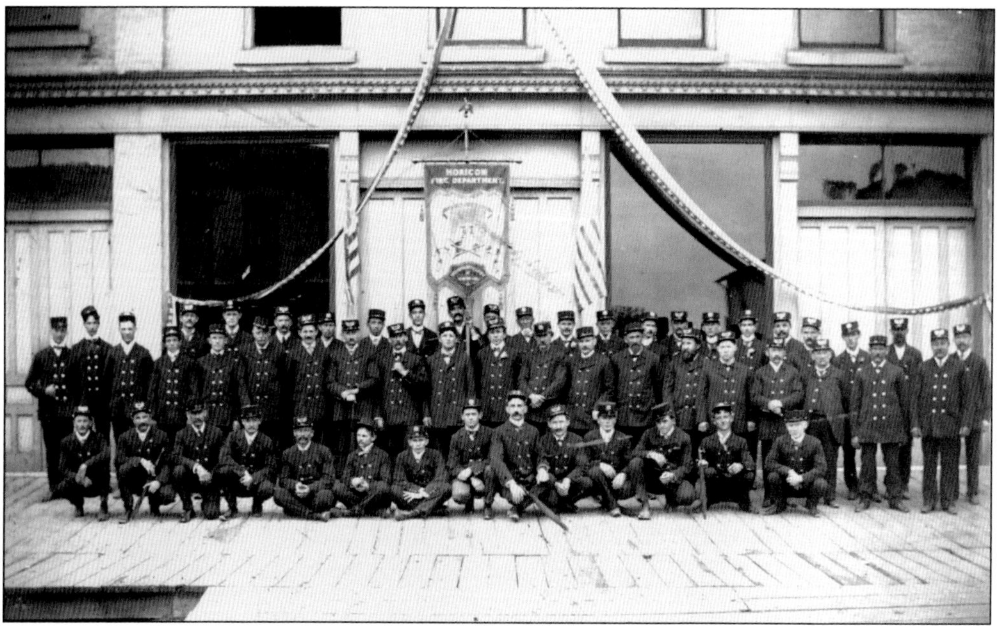

VOLUNTEER FIRE DEPARTMENT, 1900. Several fires ravaged Horicon in the mid-1800s, beginning with the gristmill fire in 1857. Nearly all the manufacturing businesses were destroyed in 1859. In 1863, the business portion of town was destroyed. In 1873, the north side of Main Street succumbed to fire, and in 1875, the south side was devoured. In 1877, that which burned in 1863 was taken again. (Courtesy Horicon Historical Society.)

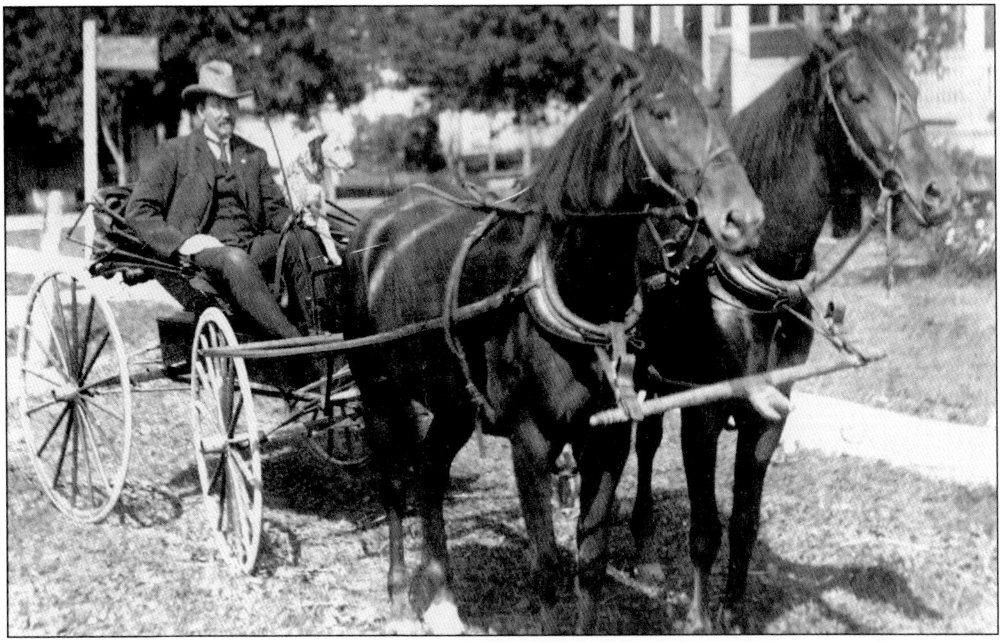

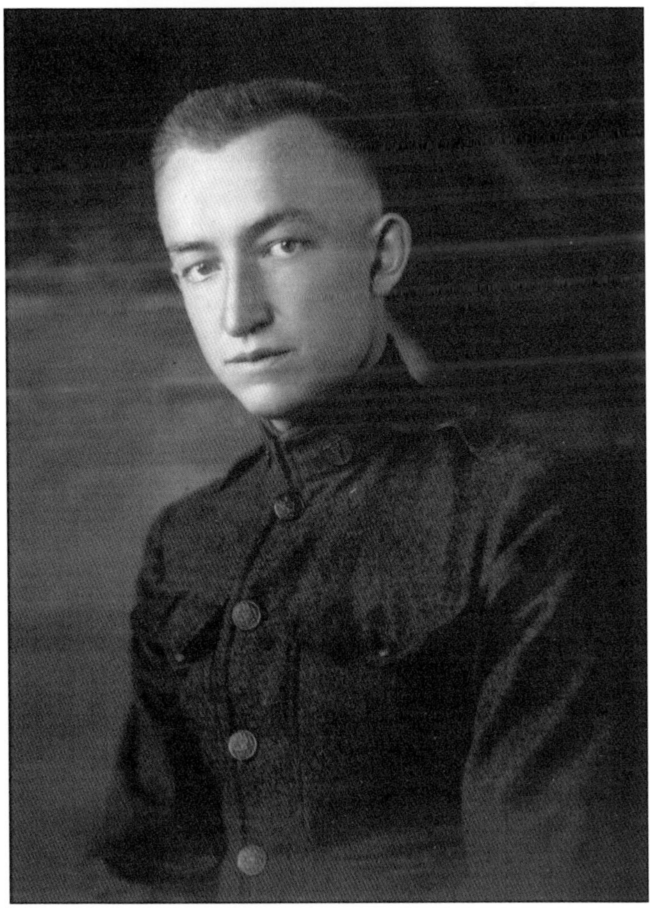

DOCTORS ADRIAN AND JOHN KARSTEN. Establishing his office in Horicon in 1893, Adrian "Old Doc" Karsten served the community for more than 25 years before he passed away in 1922. He would frequently traverse the city with his horse and buggy. His son John Karsten served in the medical corps in France in World War I and carried forth his father's practice upon his return to Horicon, being the second "Doc Karsten" to serve the city. John, shown at right in his World War I uniform, married Catherine Clausen, daughter of Eleanor and Frederick Clausen, president and manager of Van Brunt Company. John and Catherine's son Fred became the town's next doctor. Clarence Gardner and John were best friends, and they purchased property together on Raasch Hill Road that remains in the families today. (Courtesy John Karsten family.)

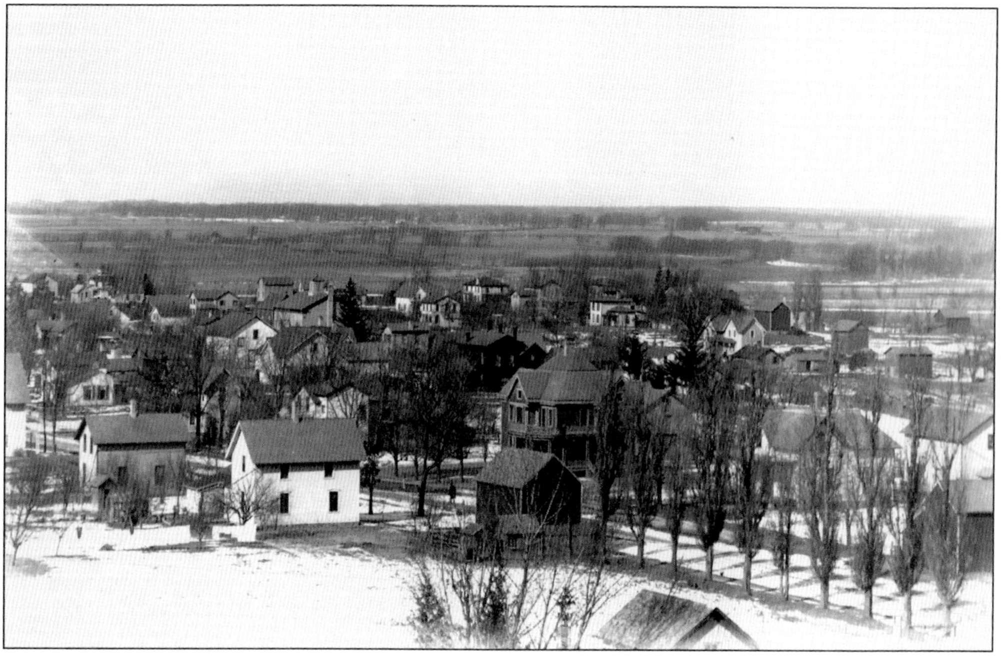

CITY VIEW, 1902. This photograph taken from north of Lake Street from atop Tower Hill Park depicts the beautiful landscape of the city in the foreground and the marsh in the distance. With the marsh providing fish and fowl to the inhabitants of town, food was plentiful. Many homes shown here still remain intact today. (Courtesy Horicon Historical Society.)

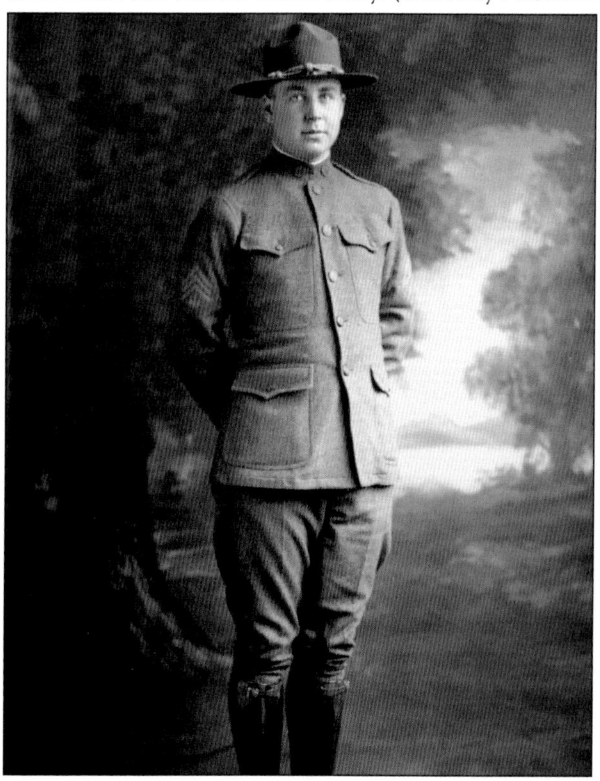

RUSSELL WILCOX, EARLY 1900S. Serving as chairman of the board for the Horicon State Bank in the late 1940s, Russell Wilcox was known to be fair. In 1933, he and his brother Howard issued scrip, which they personally guaranteed, when the national bank moratorium closed all banks for 10 days. Russell also served as the national regional rationing director for four years during World War II. (Courtesy Horicon Historical Society.)

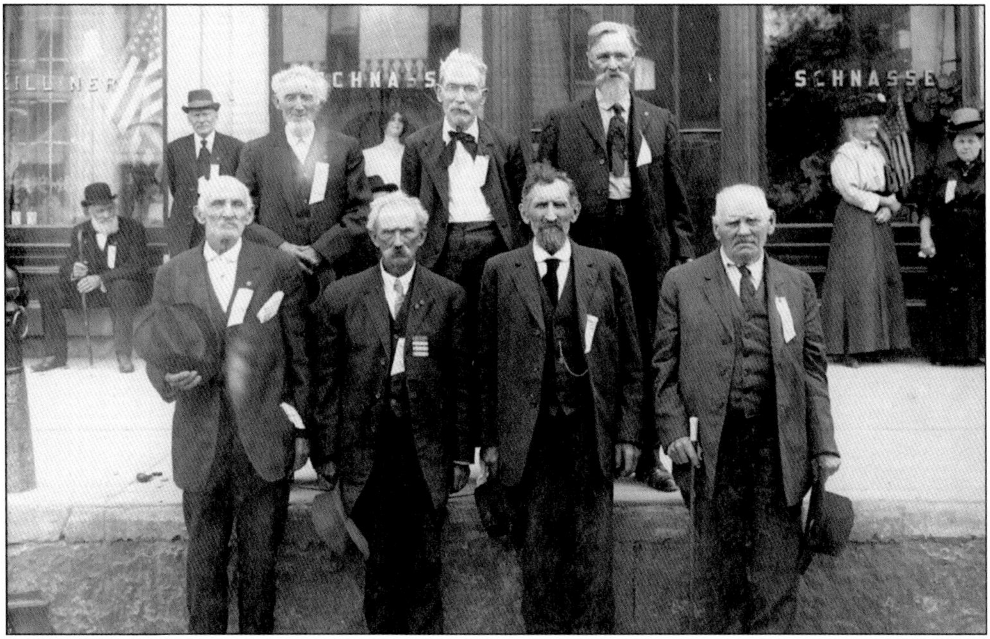

CIVIL WAR VETERANS. Union soldiers in the Civil War, hailing from the 29th Regiment, Wisconsin Volunteer Infantry (WVI), gathered for this reunion photograph in the early 1900s. Seen are, from left to right, (first row) two unidentified, Charles Discher, and J. Quick; (second row) Julius Beyer, unidentified, and Charles Ward. Among other battles, the 29th Regiment fought in the Vicksburg Campaign as well as the Red River Campaign. (Courtesy Horicon Historical Society.)

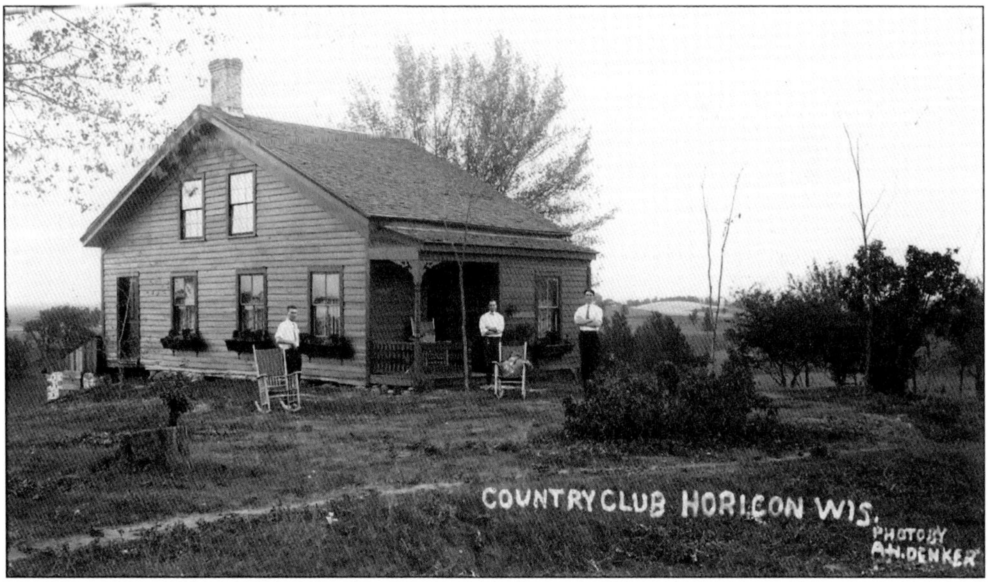

COUNTRY CLUB. Located on Raasch Hill Road, the Horicon Men's Country Club, which no longer exists, was a gathering place for those interested in the marsh, hunting, and fishing. In the background on the left is Palmatory Street, and on the right is Quick's Point, where the Department of Natural Resources' field station is currently located. (Courtesy Horicon Historical Society.)

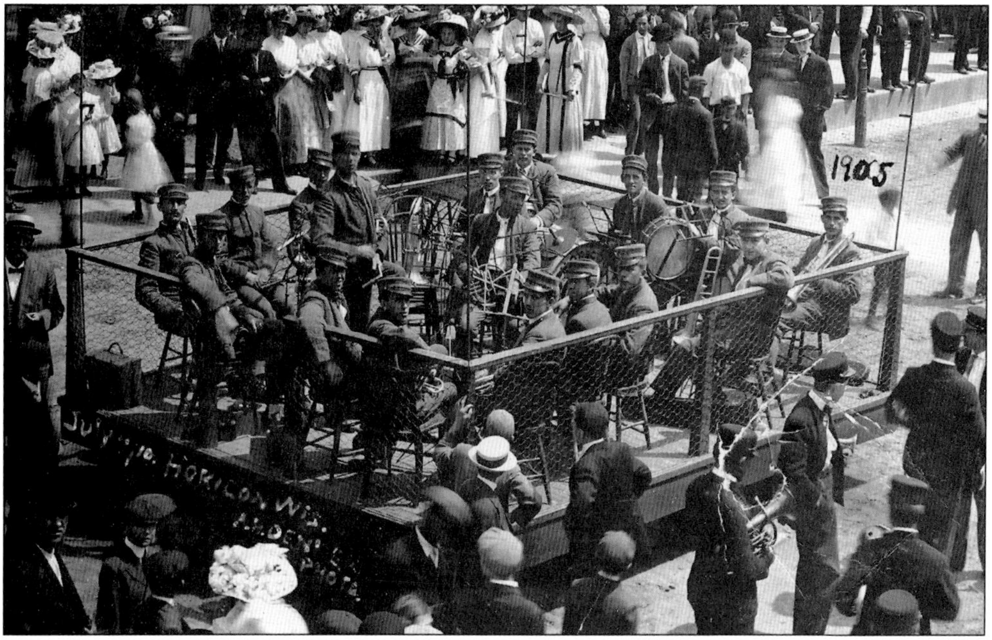

HORICON CITY BAND, 1905. Known as "Ye Old Band Wagon," the Horicon City Band used to play Saturday band concerts between Vine and Elm Streets on East Lake Street. Longtime Horicon resident Ed Knop recalls in the days before World War II that the bustling street, which also functions as State Highway 33, would be blocked off, much to the delight of the city's residents. (Courtesy Horicon Historical Society.)

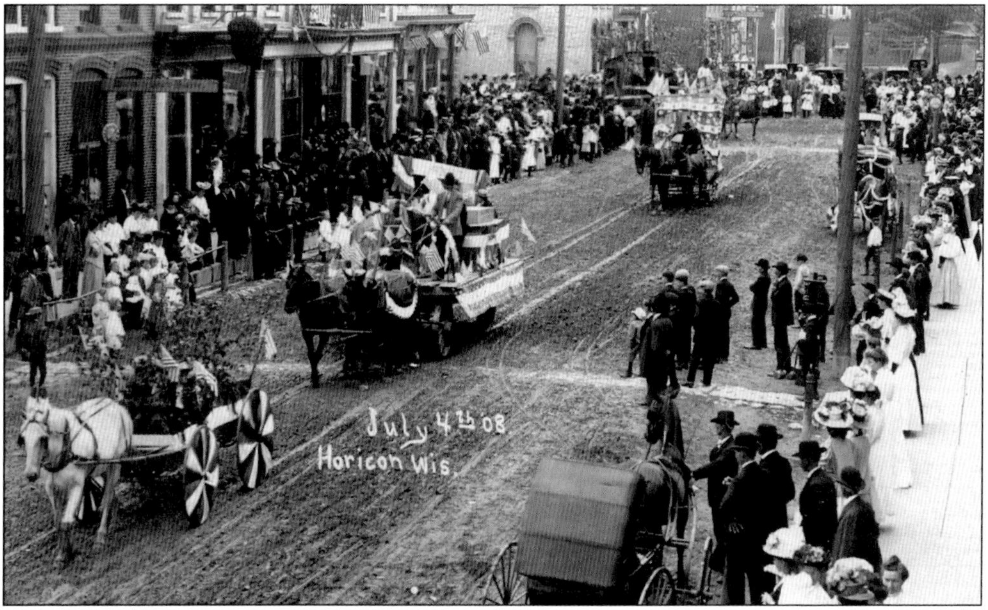

FOURTH OF JULY PARADE, 1908. Max Miescke married Esther Owen on July 8, 1894, and continued the family tradition of "truck farming," taking his produce door to door by horse and wagon. In 1895, they lived on the second floor or what was to become "Fat" Kasten's tavern and is now home to the Horicon Chamber of Commerce and Rehse Insurance Agency. Shown leading the holiday celebration in 1908 is the Miescke rig. (Courtesy Horicon Historical Society.)

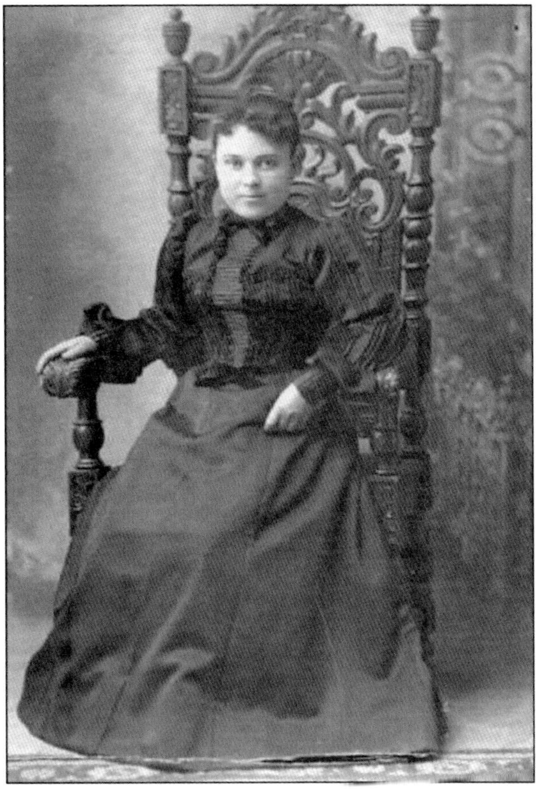

IDA VAN BRUNT AND CAMPBELL HOUSE. Ida Van Brunt, daughter of Daniel Van Brunt and Mary Wright, was born on July 18, 1854. In 1905, this gorgeous Victorian arts-and-crafts home on the corner of Walnut and Finch Streets was completed after three years of intensive labor for heiress Ida as a wedding gift from her husband, Stephen N. Campbell. Designed by architects Van Ryn and De Gallka of Milwaukee, this home was built at a cost of approximately $38,000, an unbelievable expenditure in 1908. This photograph shows the home when it was owned by its second owner, C. B. Cotton. For many years, Ida taught piano and was a musical leader in the city before moving to California in her retirement years. (Courtesy Barbara Ruka.)

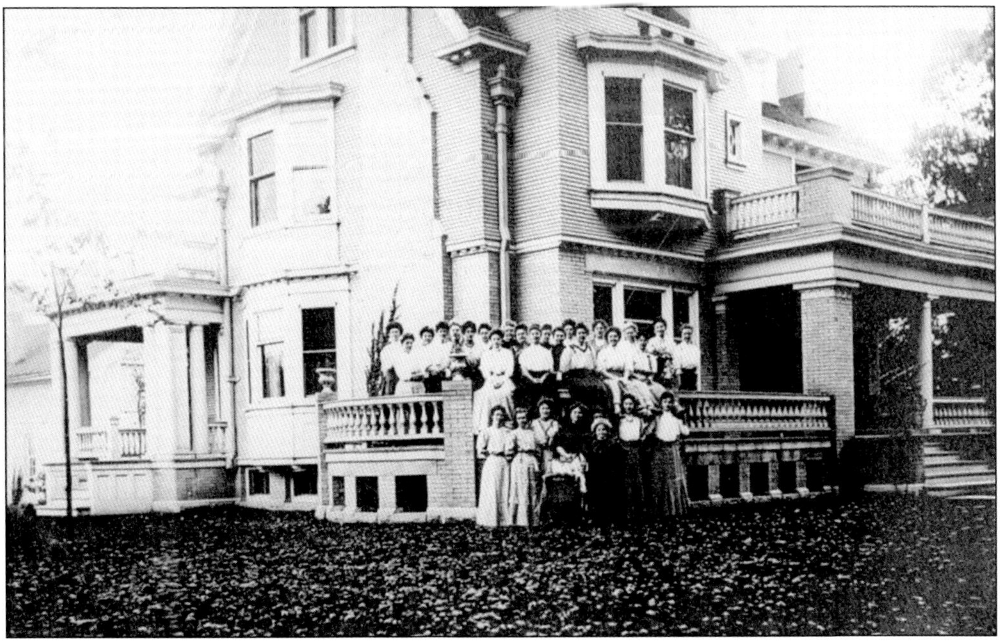

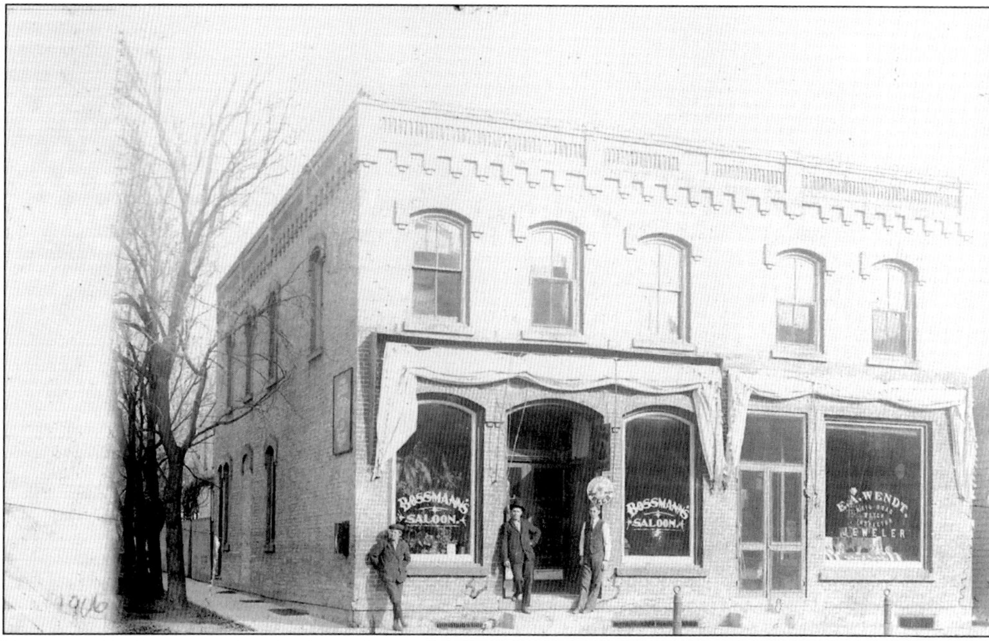

Bossman's Saloon, 1906. Frank Bossman ran his tavern at the corner of East Lake and Vine Streets for 37 years. During Prohibition, an ice-cream parlor was added, as was the restaurant. Next door was jeweler E. A. Wendt's shop, which provided services for more than 50 years. The saloon, later known as A and P Tavern, today is the site of Ginger's Hide Away. (Courtesy Paul Kruel.)

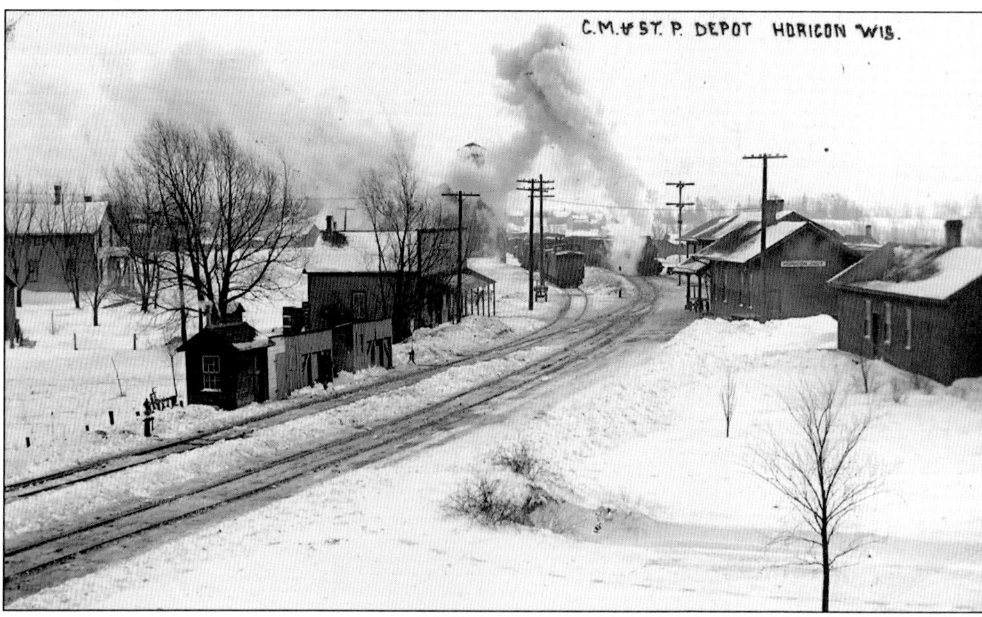

Horicon Junction, 1906. Taken from the back side of the depot building, what is clearly visible on the left is the two-story establishment run by Betsy Trumball, whose husband was killed working on the railroad. Originally serving meals, the facility took in lodgers for a number of years before becoming a restaurant and tavern. The original passenger depot, on right, served as the city's Methodist church for a time. (Courtesy Paul Kruel.)

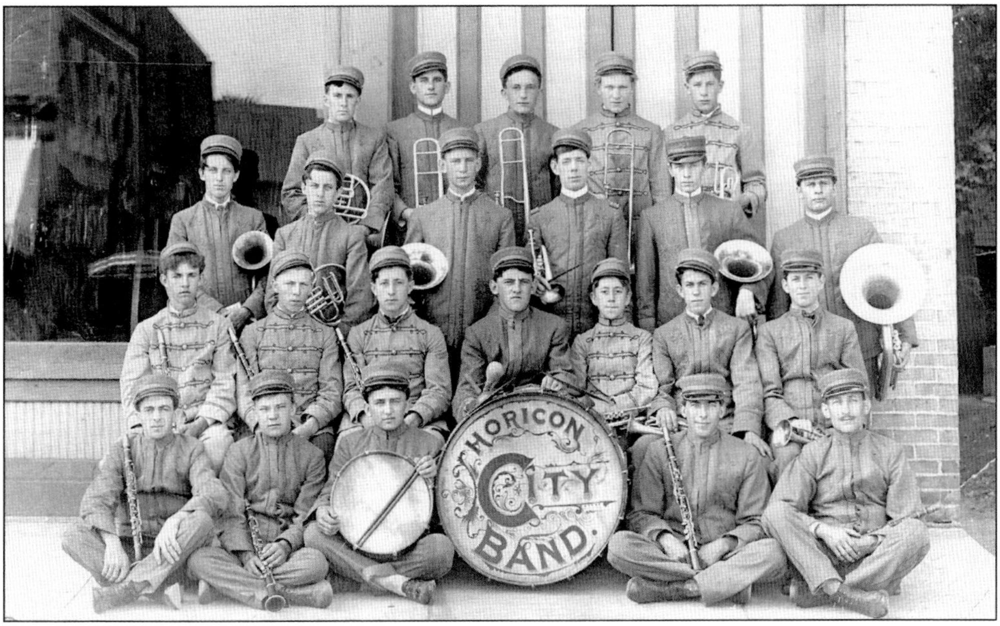

HORICON CITY BAND, 1906. The members are, from left to right, (first row) Henry Clausen, W. Schlicker, Herb Krueger, John Ehlert, and Joe Prindle; (second row) Ben Rave, John Frienwold, Herb Schilling, Ed Gadow, William Weinke, Bill Hoferman, and Tom Pluck; (third row) William Erdman, Rhienhold Erdman, Bill Schilling, Jack Freeman, Gus Diekleman, and Ed Matthes; (fourth row) Fred Dreckow, Art Firehammer, Louis Kross, Art Last, and Emil Simon. (Courtesy Buzz Vanderhei.)

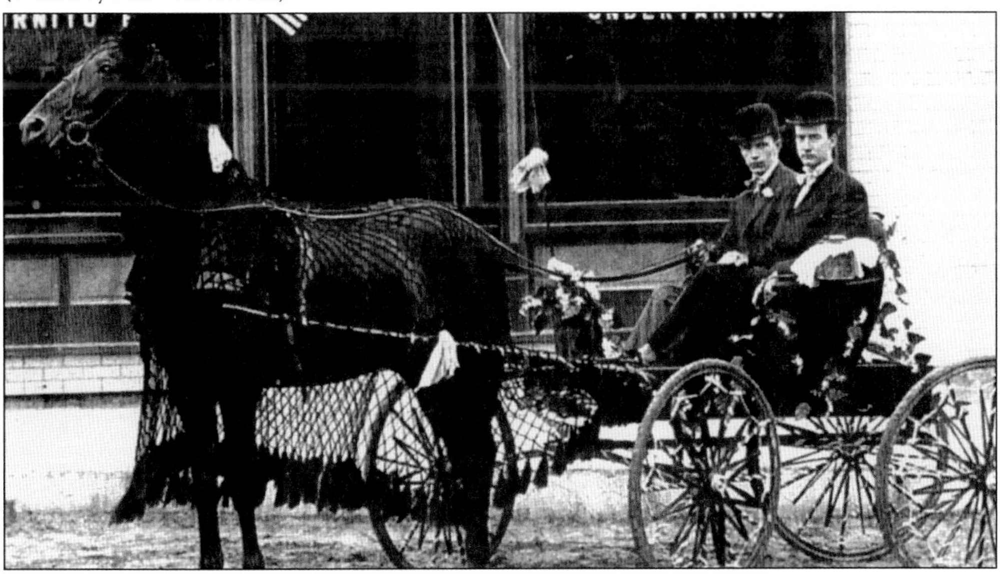

MANN-NEILL MORTUARY, 1906. George Neill and David Mann went into business in 1906, and the partnership continued until 1915. In 1923, Neill took George Ulmer under his wing and took him into partnership in 1938. Upon Neill's death in 1942, Ulmer bought out the business and served the community for years. Later it became Fat's Tavern and today is home to the Horicon Chamber of Commerce and the Rehse Insurance Agency. (Courtesy Horicon Historical Society.)

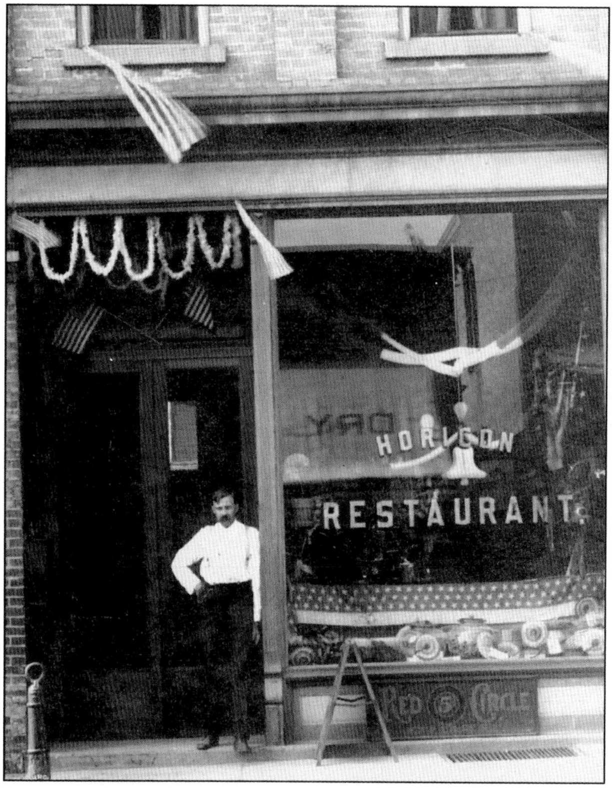

HORICON RESTAURANT, 1907. Otto Lehmann stands in the doorway of his East Lake Street restaurant, which was conveniently located next door to the tavern he ran for 31 years. After he retired, his son Alfred took over the management and ownership of the tavern, which was located east of the Odd Fellows building. (Courtesy Paul Kruel.)

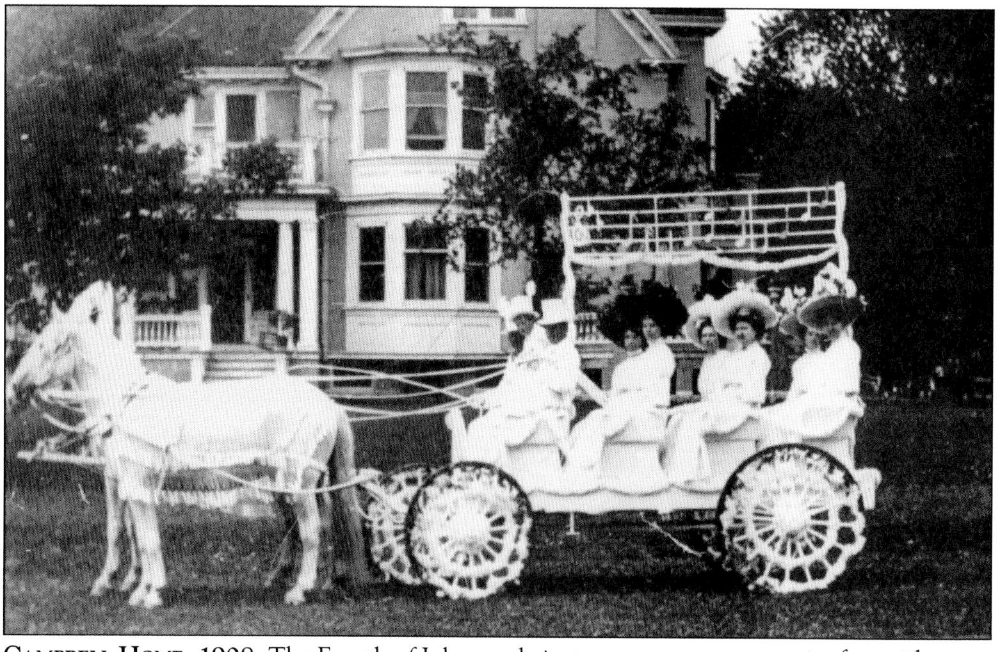

CAMPBELL HOME, 1908. The Fourth of July parade in town was an opportunity for residents to decorate their carriages and dress in their finest. This carriage sits before the Campbell home at 611 East Walnut Street at a time when Ida Van Brunt and her husband Stephen Campbell were still in residence. (Courtesy Horicon Historical Society.)

FISHING, C. 1910. Burn Johnson (left) and Lee Burrow took to fishing and hunting early in their lives. Burrow was later to become an instrumental part of the community, especially when folks were stranded or lost on the Rock River or in the marsh. The first call was typically to the authorities, and the second call was to Burrow, who saved many lives. (Courtesy Charlotte Burrow.)

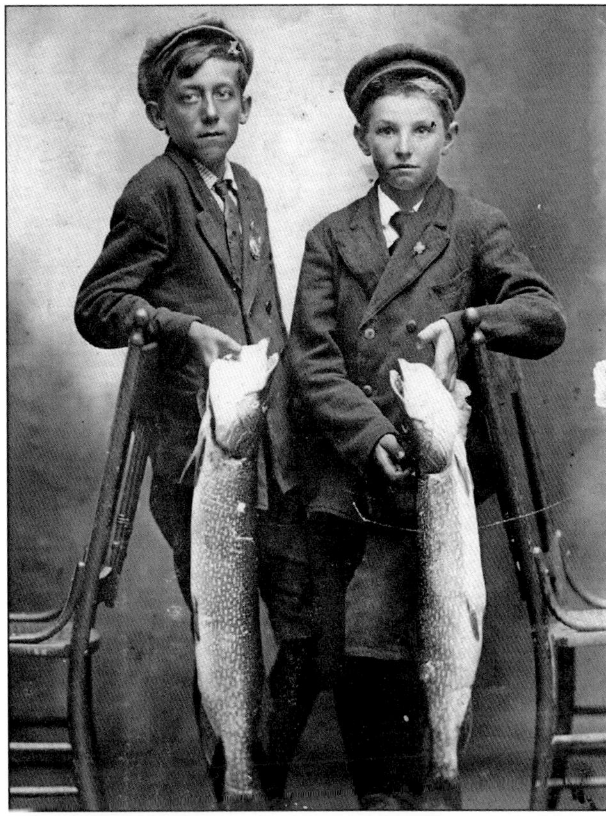

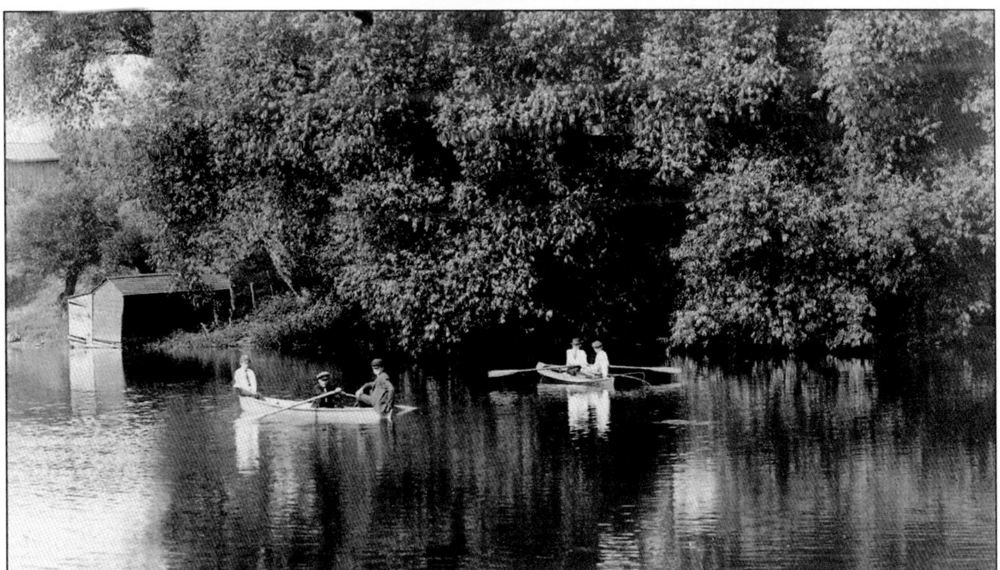

CANOEING, C. 1910. The Rock River provided not only bountiful fish but also an enjoyable way to stay cool in the hot summer months early in the last century. Prior to the river being dredged, there were large rocks and boulders in the water, causing rapids. Before the town was named Horicon by New Yorker Charles Larrabee, it was fittingly known as Hubbard's Rapids. (Courtesy Buzz Vanderhei.)

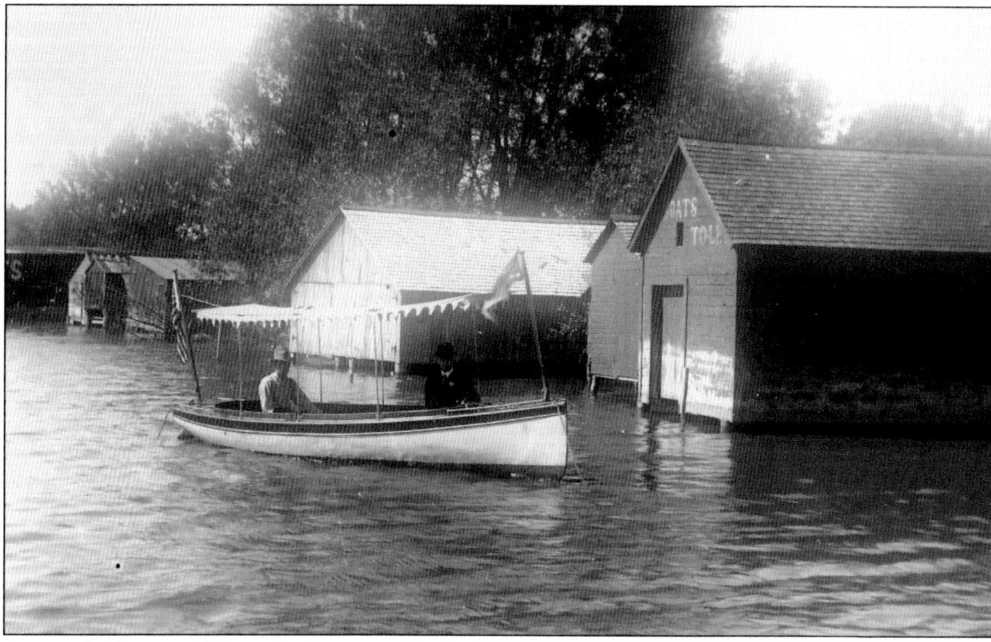

ARNDT'S DITCH. When dredging took place in the marsh starting in 1910, many owners of property along the banks paid to have ditches dug to their land. Several ditches became home to scores of boathouses over the years. The last to remain a boathouse haven for avid boaters is Arndt's Ditch, located on the west side of Horicon. (Courtesy Paul Kruel.)

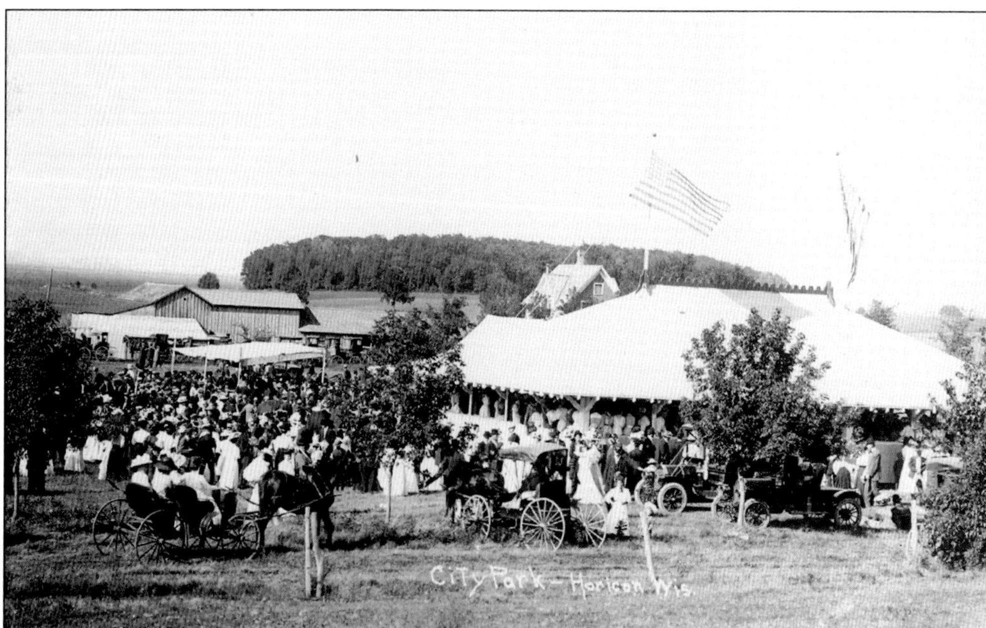

CITY PARK, 1910. Acquisition of the property that was City Park, now known as Discher Park, was made in 1900. On this date, a dedication of the pavilion at the park was held, and tents were used to shade the guests in attendance. A large dance hall was added in 1927 and continues to serve the community today. (Courtesy Horicon Historical Society.)

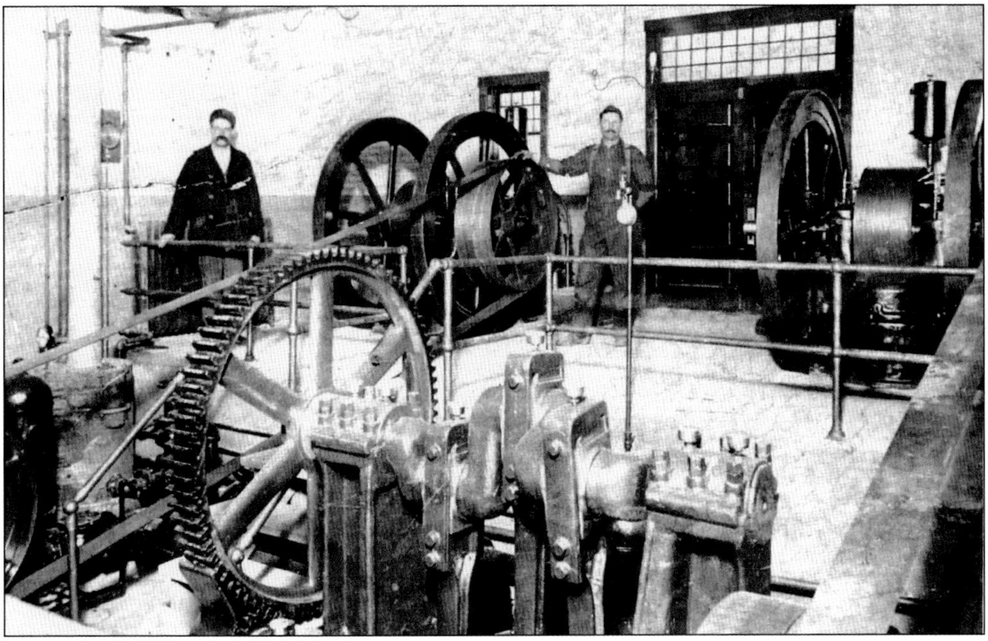

Booster Pumps, 1912. With the town's need for water, wells 1 and 2 were drilled on Mill Street. In 1913, Frank Martzhein, shown on right, was killed in an accident in the room next to the pump house. Both wells were shot with 154 pounds of dynamite in 1941 to increase the capacity of the wells. Today each well produces 250 gallons of water per minute for use by residents. (Courtesy Horicon Utility Department.)

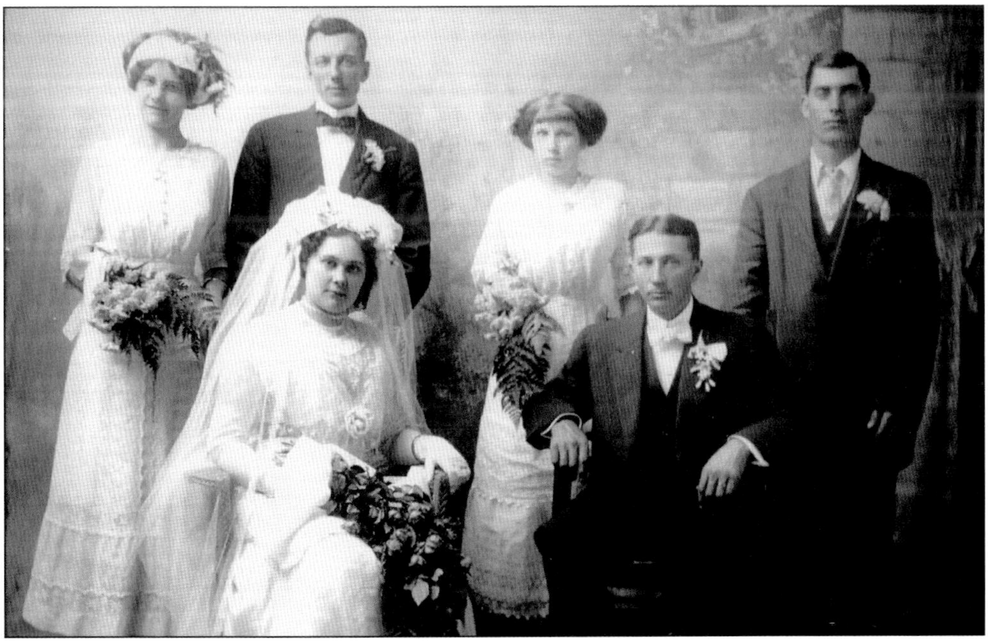

Miescke Wedding, 1912. Edward Miescke and Alma Lueck wed on September 19 and settled in Horicon. Edward had been a barber for more than 50 years and was an avid hunter and fisherman. Attendants for their nuptials were Louis A. Bossman, Rosy Miescke, Mamie Radke, and Gilbert Voigt. (Courtesy Palmer Miescke.)

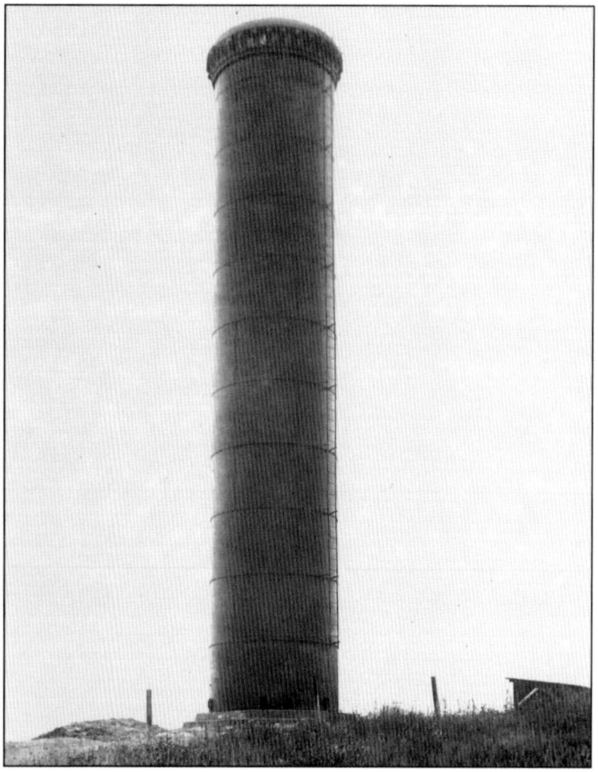

WATER TOWER, 1913. Tower Hill was so named as the city's original water tower stood on the east-side site. Once the city's second water tower was built on the west side of town, the historic tower was razed and a new one was constructed in its place. (Courtesy Paul Kruel.)

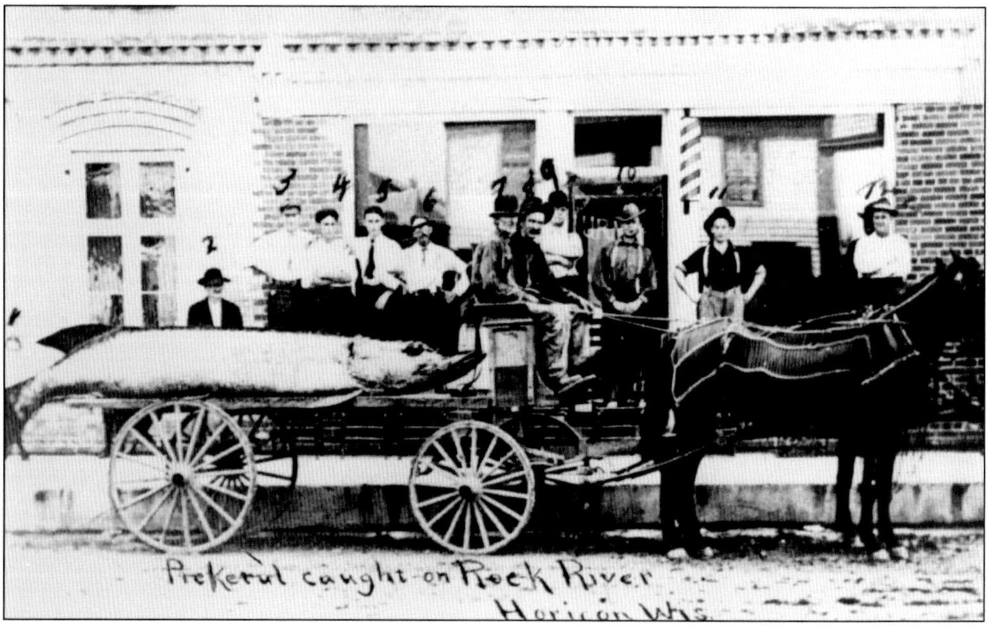

PICKEREL CATCH. This makes for one big fish story. Many postcards showing overly large fish or vegetables were produced, showing the sense of humor at the time. Those shown bringing their "catch" into town are, from left to right, Marg Westfall, Herman Kross, Ed Schwantes, Chief Harold Westfall, Armond Kross, Selby Rich, Jack Brunner, August Puls, ? Martzah, Charles Lauer, August Neitzel, and William Cummings. (Courtesy Horicon Historical Society.)

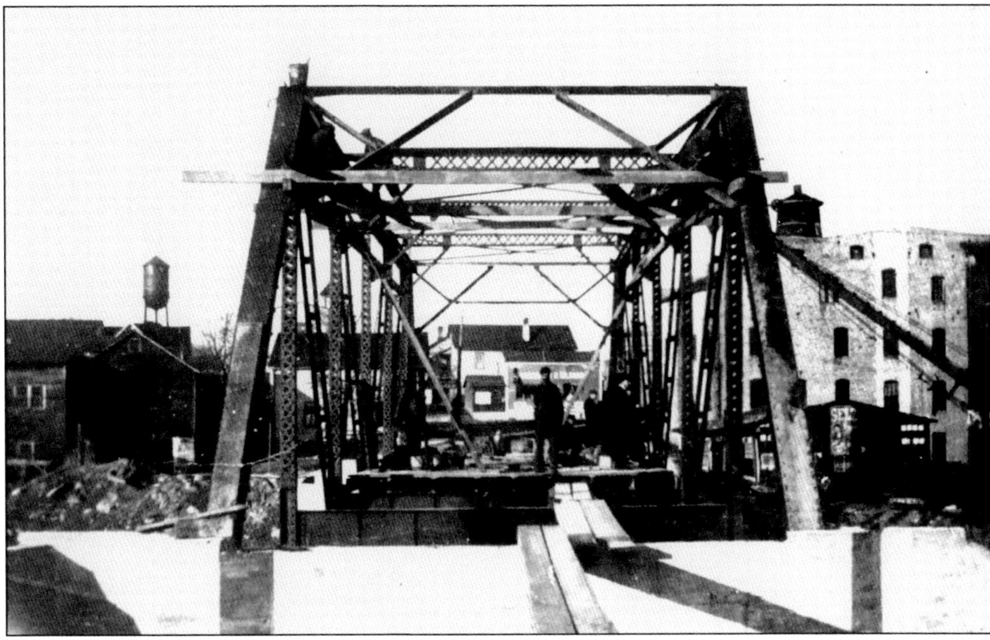

BARSTOW BRIDGE, 1913. Construction of the new bridge that crossed the Rock River on Barstow Street (now Vine Street/Highway 33) consisted of steel, replacing the old one. The old stone shop where Willard Van Brunt manufactured his "New Van Brunt" seeder in 1870 is on the right, and the lumberyard is on the left. Neither business exists today. While dredging the Rock River, deposits of dirt and silt were moved to the banks of the river with those deposits often becoming parks throughout the city. Replacement of the Short Bridge by the steel construction of the Barstow Street Bridge was welcomed by the residents. The newly constructed St. Malachy's Catholic Church can be seen on the right. (Courtesy Horicon Historical Society.)

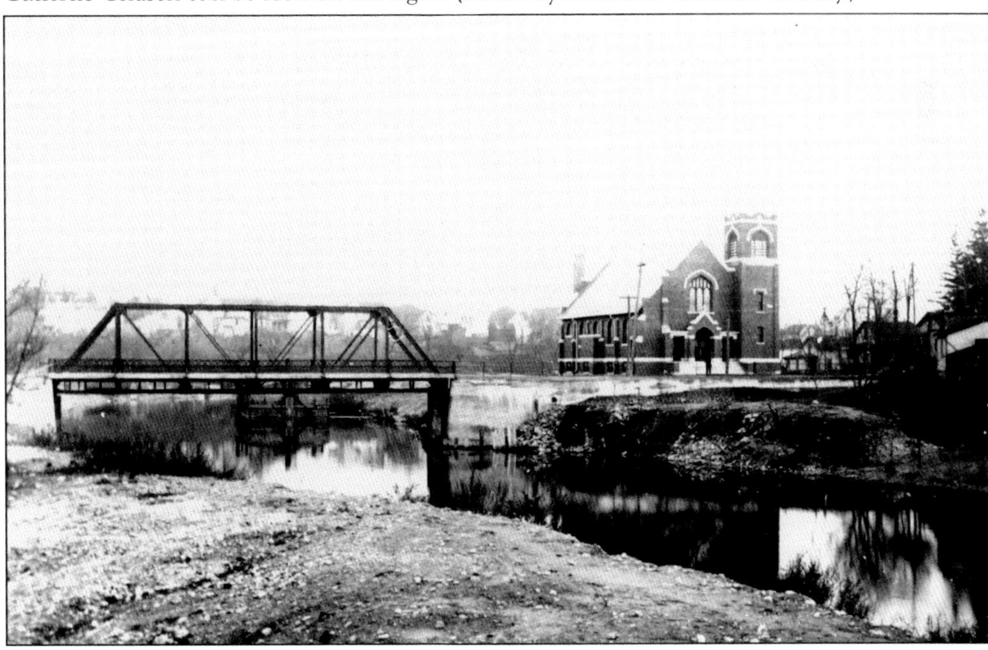

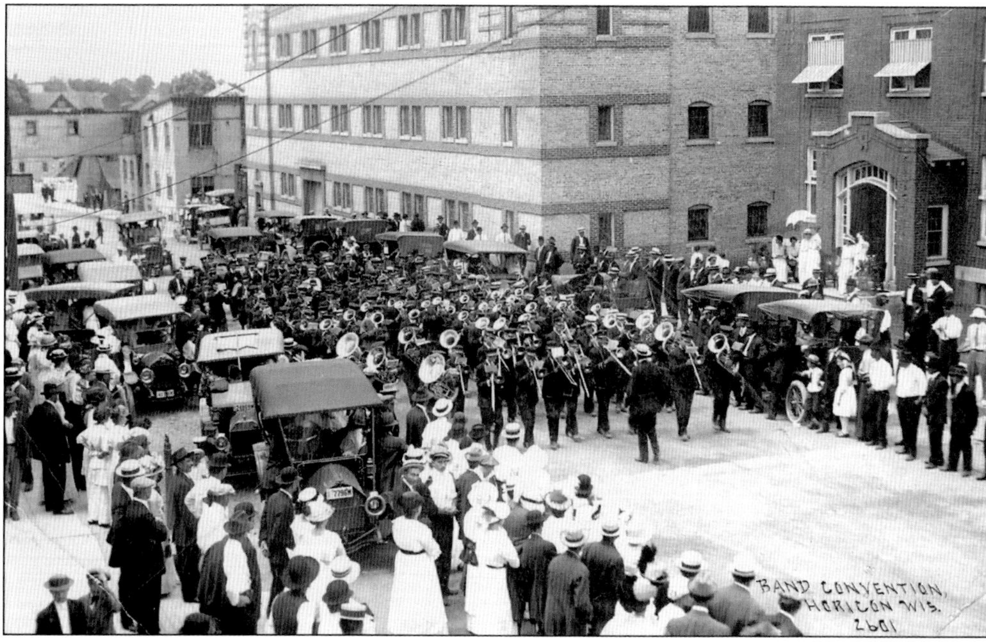

BAND CONVENTION, 1914. The Northwestern Band Convention was held in Horicon, and excursion trains were used to bring participants into the city. As its name implies, bands from all around participated in the event. An estimated 8,000 people descended upon the town, netting a profit of $1,100 for the local band and firemen. (Courtesy Horicon Historical Society.)

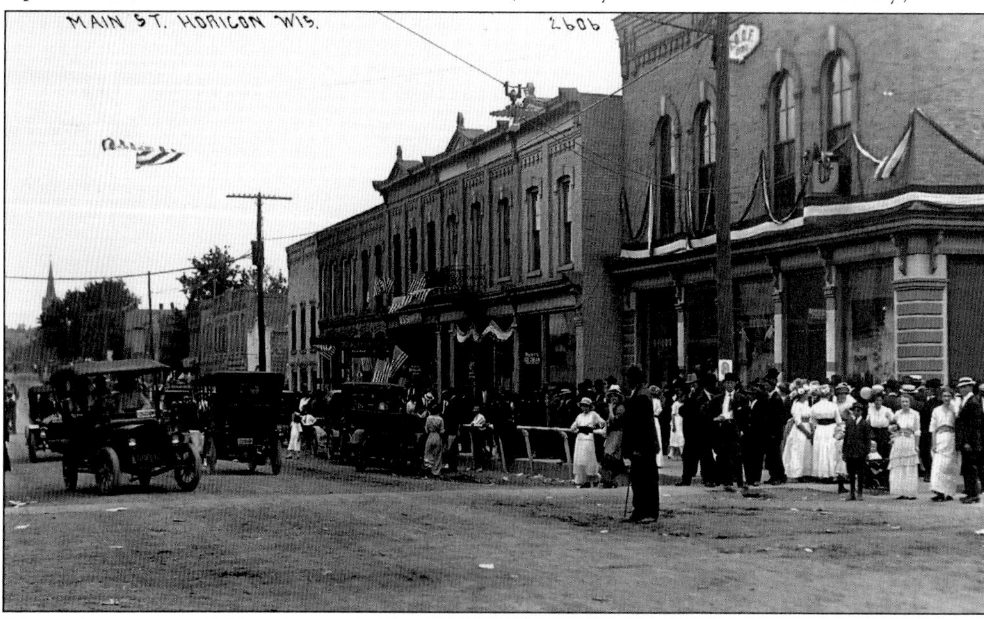

MAIN STREET, 1914. Residents who have called the city home for years report the downtown district being home to grocery, drug, and dry goods stores; meat markets; and dairies during their growing years. Although many buildings throughout the area have been demolished, the southeast corner of East Lake Street (formerly Main Street) and Vine Street has remained virtually unchanged since the time this early photograph was taken. (Courtesy Horicon Historical Society.)

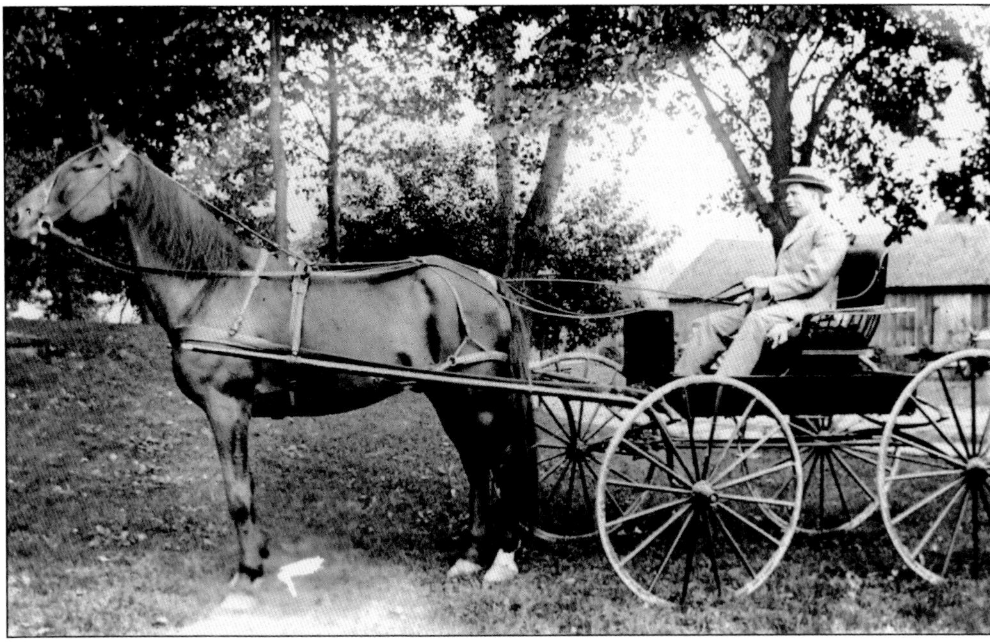

Edward Matthes. Appearing all over town, Edward Matthes sang in the Presbyterian Male Quartet, performed in plays, taught dance, played tuba, and was a member of the Milwaukee Shriners Band. He performed in the Horicon City Band for more than 50 years. (Courtesy Horicon Historical Society.)

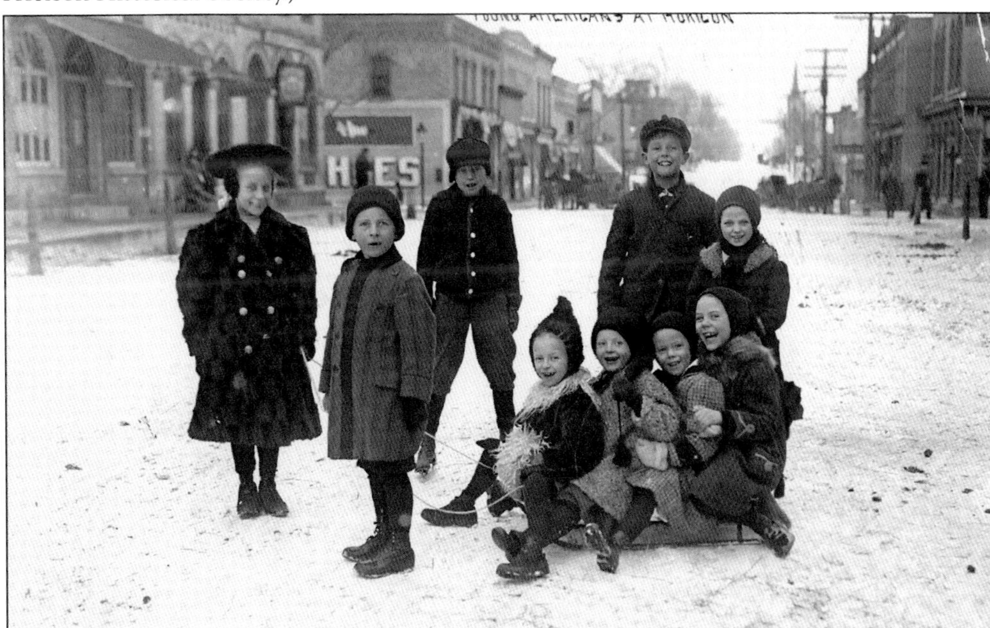

Young Americans At Horicon. This photograph was taken on Main Street (now Lake Street) when postcards were only 1¢ to mail. Standing in front of Dasenbrock's Store are, from left to right, Erma Dorve, Fred Westfall, Merlin Dasenbrock, ? Roberts, and Julia Dugan. Sitting on the sled are, from left to right, Viola Dorve, Alice Bossman, Catherine Clausen, and Margaret Clausen. (Courtesy Horicon Historical Society.)

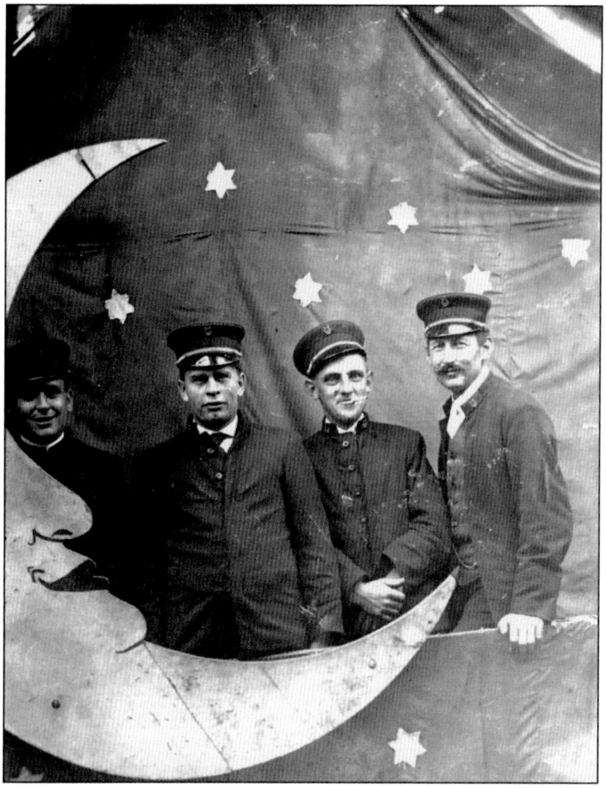

BAND MEMBERS. Bands typically would play in the center of town on a bandwagon and entertain the city residents. They would also perform in the theater located at the old city hall. Pictured are, from left to right, Maurice Whitty, Edward Matthes, Ed Gadow, and band director Joe Prindle. (Courtesy Horicon Historical Society.)

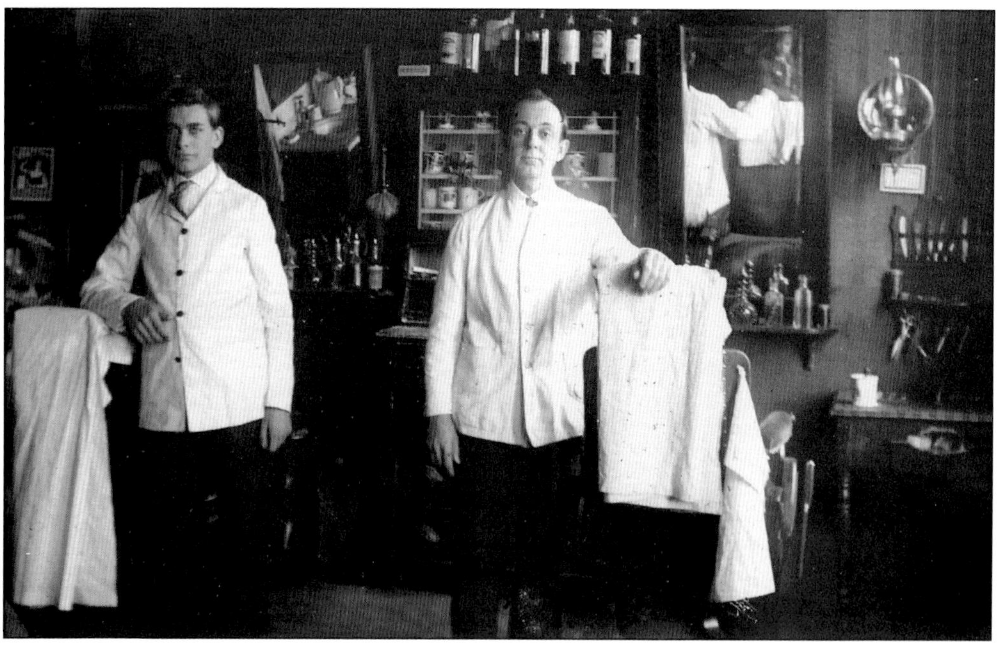

OTTO'S BARBERSHOP, 1915. Carl Otto, on left, and his father, Henry Otto, were fixtures in the community for more than 100 years. Henry began advertising haircuts in 1856, and each patron had a cup with his name in the shop. Carl continued on after his father's passing, and many in town still recall the 1950s and getting their hair cut by "Otto." (Courtesy Paul Kruel.)

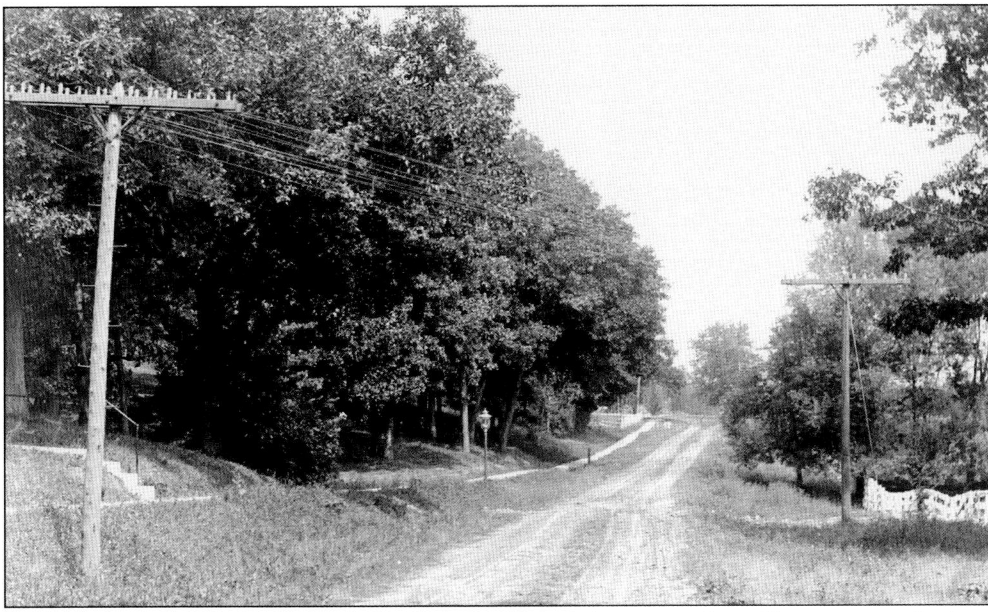

LOVER'S LANE. Larrabee Street, with Bowling Green Park on one side and houses sitting high on the hill overlooking what is now John Deere Horicon Works and the park on the other, provided an enchanting setting for young lovers to spend cool summer evenings. Trees still line the street, and the park offers a wonderful spot to enjoy a picnic. (Courtesy Horicon Historical Society.)

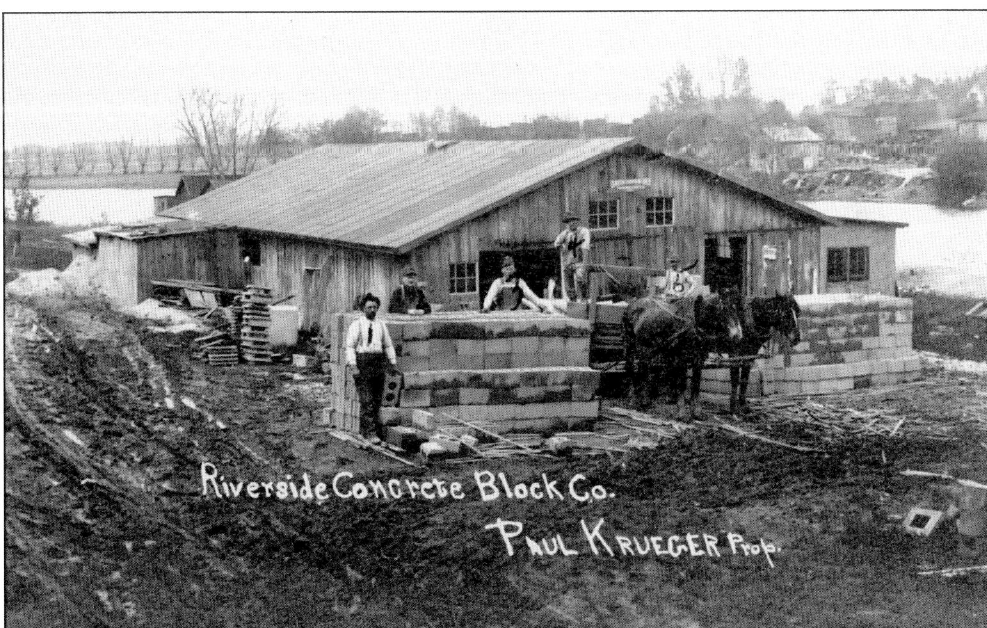

RIVERSIDE CONCRETE BLOCK COMPANY. Located on the Rock River west of the Van Brunt Manufacturing Company, proprietor Paul Krueger and employees George Waltzer, Frank Betke, Skinny Albert, and Eli Tyler built a 30-by-70-foot building and ran their block business for a number of years. Today the site is home to Rock River Tap. (Courtesy Paul Kruel.)

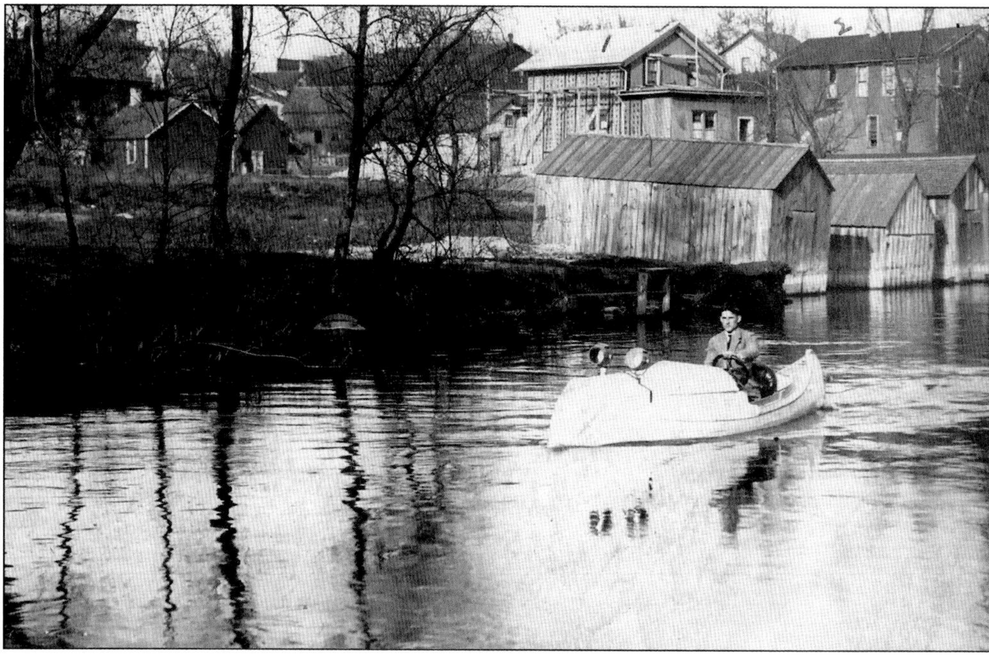

ROCK RIVER, SOUTH OF MILL STREET. Shown in the photograph is Forbes' Speed Canoe. This motorized version of the typical paddle canoe made travel up the river more time efficient. The homes on the hill are the Frank Schessow home on the left and the John Weiler home on the right. (Courtesy Paul Kruel.)

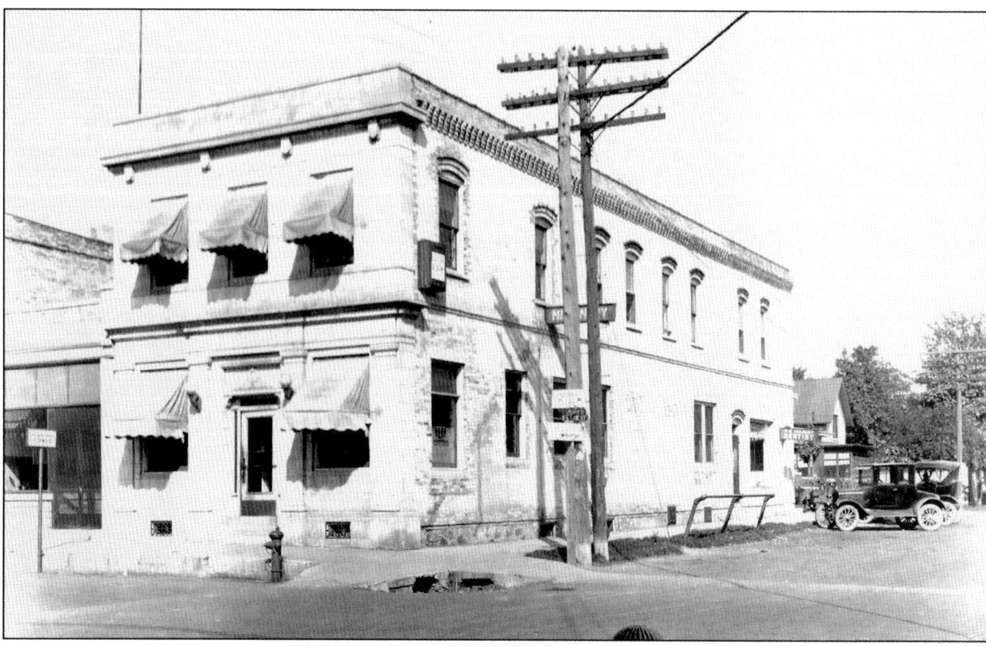

FIRST NATIONAL BANK. Organized in 1917, the bank stood at the northwest corner of East Lake and Vine Streets. Horicon State Bank had been organized in 1896 and was held in good stead by those in town. Unfortunately, the latter bank's success became the downfall of the First National Bank, as it closed its doors for good in 1932. (Courtesy Paul Kruel.)

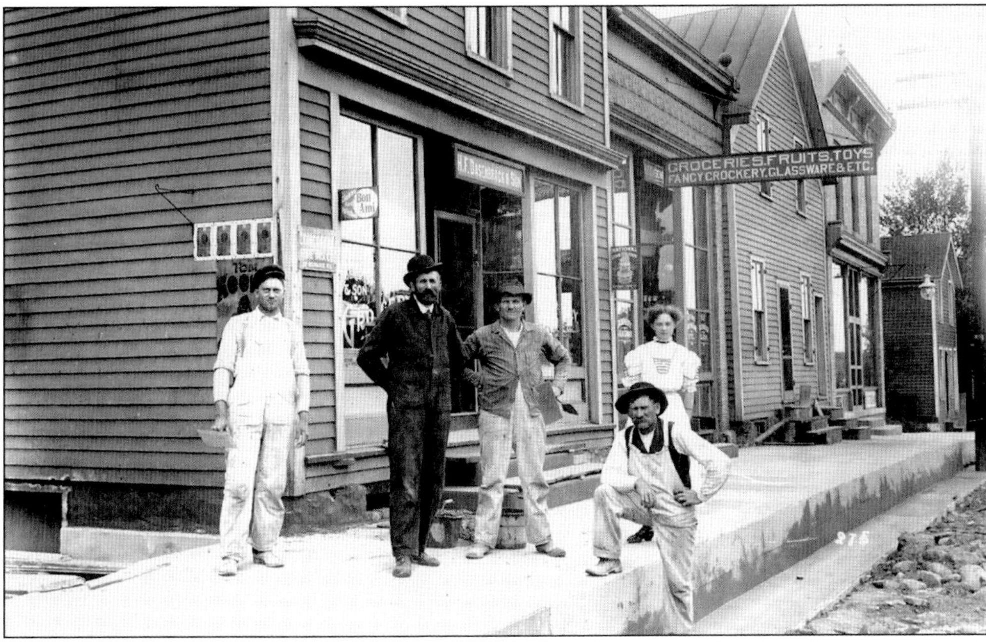

DASENBROCK GROCERY STORE. Workers from Waltzer Brothers take a break from laying the first cement sidewalk in Horicon in front of H. F. Dasenbrock and Son Grocery Store on Lake Street. H. F. Dasenbrock can be seen in the derby hat, and his daughter Eva poses along with the workmen. A few doors down was Port's Bakery, where fabulous baked goods of all kind could be found. The most exciting draw for the children in town, however, was the Dasenbrock Toy Store, seen below, located next to the grocery store. Children of all ages could find a myriad of toys in this wonderland. Dolls in their pushcarts and teddy bears were on display with gifts for good little boys and girls lining the shelves. (Courtesy Horicon Historical Society.)

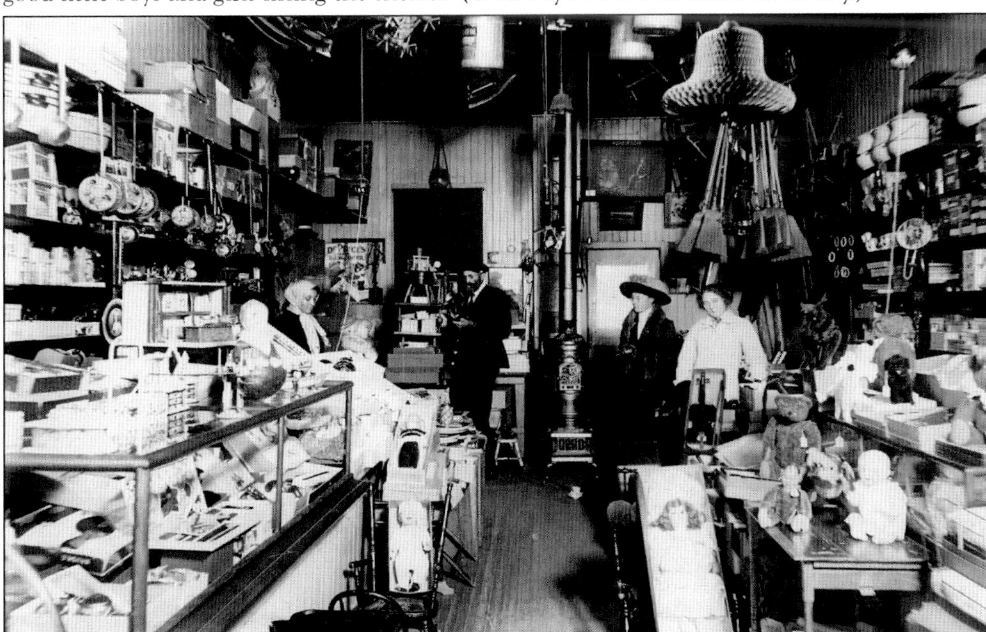

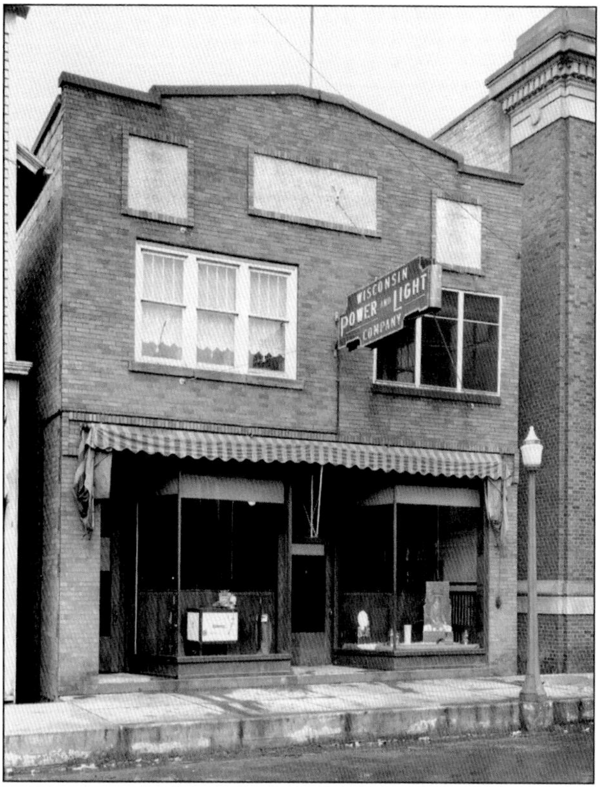

WISCONSIN POWER AND LIGHT. This undated photograph hails from the era when the power and light business was a local enterprise. Not only were offices housed on the first floor, appliances were sold from the storefront as well. The second floor was home to an apartment. As the automobile became prevalent during the mid-20th century, the building was razed to make way for Horicon State Bank's drive-thru. (Courtesy Horicon Historical Society.)

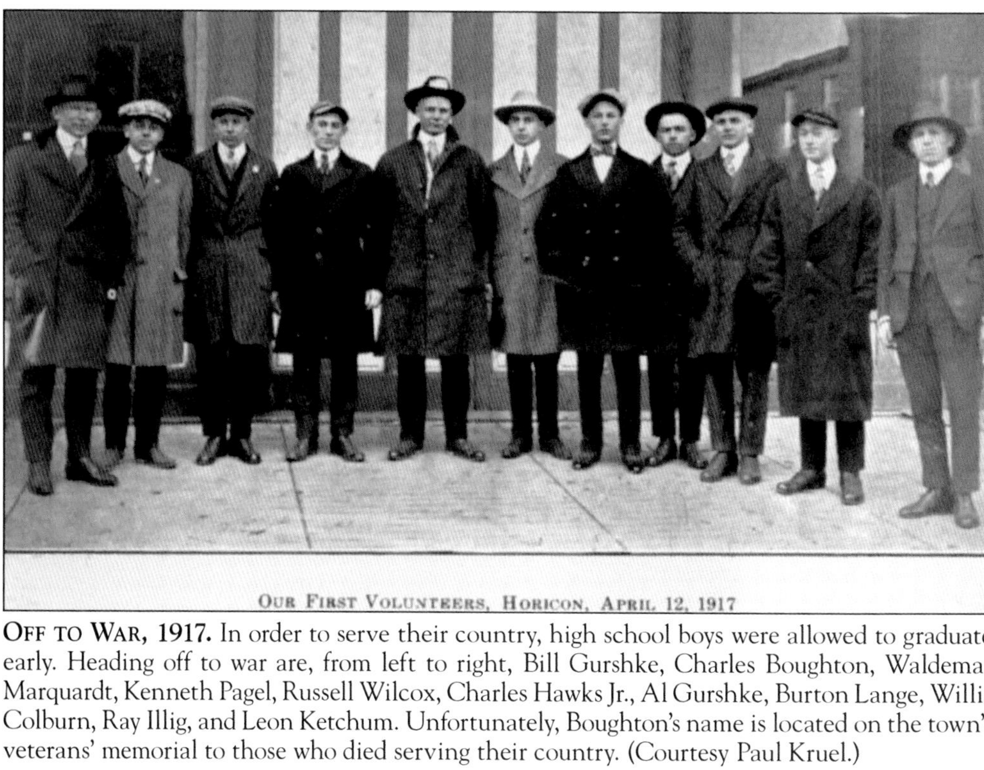

OFF TO WAR, 1917. In order to serve their country, high school boys were allowed to graduate early. Heading off to war are, from left to right, Bill Gurshke, Charles Boughton, Waldemar Marquardt, Kenneth Pagel, Russell Wilcox, Charles Hawks Jr., Al Gurshke, Burton Lange, Willis Colburn, Ray Illig, and Leon Ketchum. Unfortunately, Boughton's name is located on the town's veterans' memorial to those who died serving their country. (Courtesy Paul Kruel.)

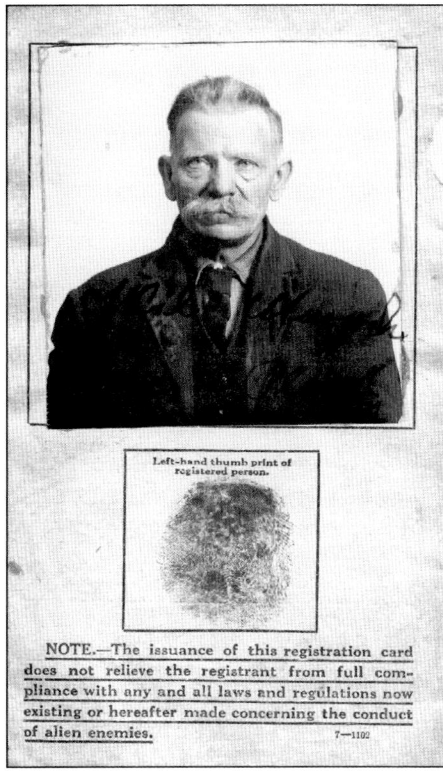

WILLIAM MAROCH REGISTRATION, 1918. In 1917 and 1918, William Maroch was one of more than 24 million men across the country required to register for the draft. This accounted for approximately 23 percent of the population at the time. However, not every man who registered served in the military and not every man in the military registered. On May 18, 1917, the Selective Service Act was passed authorizing the president to temporarily increase the military establishment of the United States. Maroch registered with the postmaster, Thomas D. Pluck, in Horicon on February 27, 1918. The signing of the armistice on November 11, 1918, curtailed the activities of the Selective Service System, and it was terminated on July 15, 1919. (Courtesy Horicon Historical Society.)

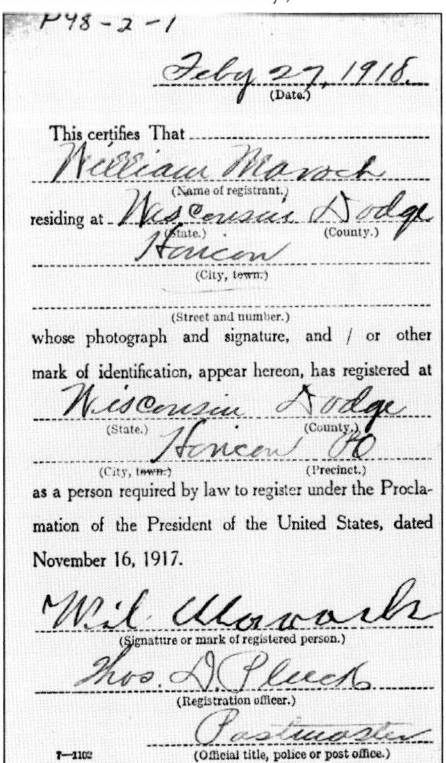
P48-2-1

Feby 27, 1918
(Date.)

This certifies That
William Maroch
(Name of registrant.)
residing at Wisconsin Dodge
(State.) (County.)
Horicon
(City, town.)

(Street and number.)
whose photograph and signature, and / or other mark of identification, appear hereon, has registered at
Wisconsin Dodge
(State.) (County.)
Horicon 1
(City, town.) (Precinct.)
as a person required by law to register under the Proclamation of the President of the United States, dated November 16, 1917.

Wil. Maroch
(Signature or mark of registered person.)
Thos. D. Pluck
(Registration officer.)
Postmaster
7—1102 (Official title, police or post office.)

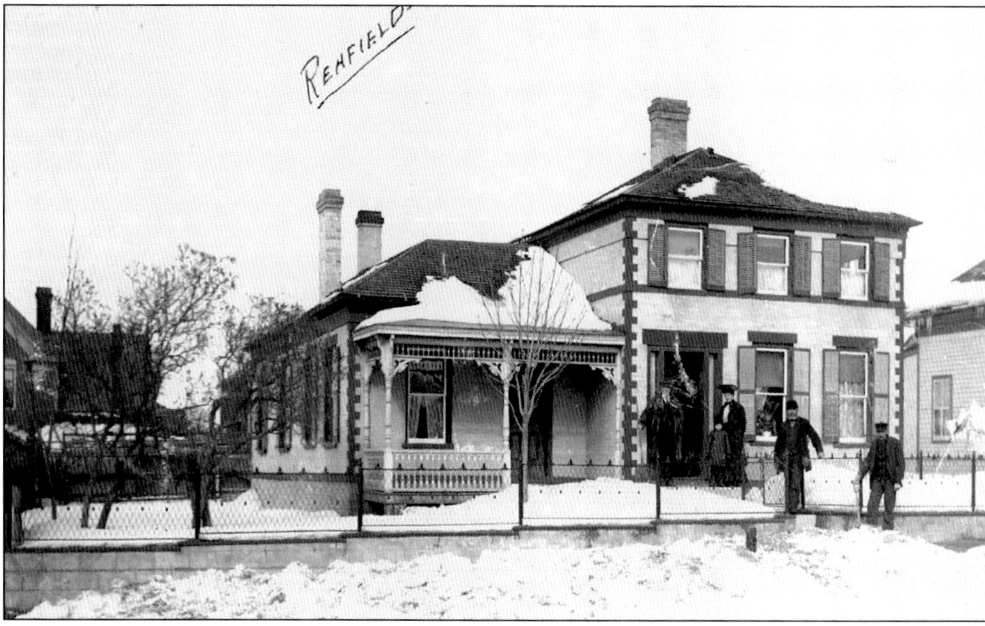

REHFELD HOME. This home at East Lake and Elm Streets was owned by C. W. Rehfeld, a Civil War veteran who was in the battles of Shiloh and Corinth, as well as many others. He was with Gen. William Sherman on his famous "march to the sea." Rehfeld was one of the first officers of Post No. 220 of the Grand Army of the Republic organized in Horicon on June 15, 1886. (Courtesy Paul Kruel.)

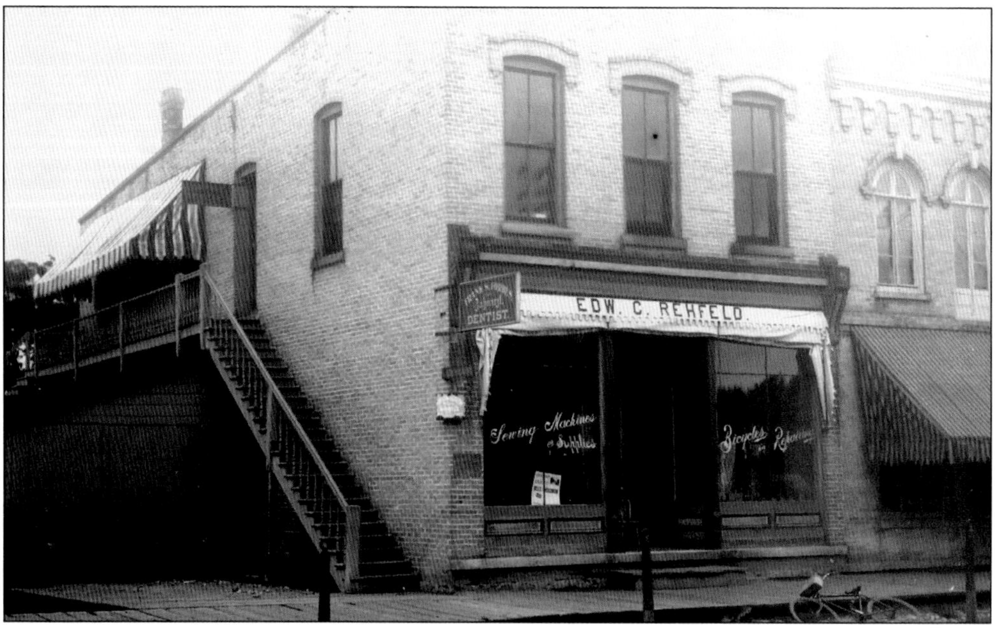

REHFELD STORE. After Rehfeld returned from service, he married Frederike Hochschild and sold sewing machines, farm equipment, and supplies in his store on East Lake Street. Bicycles were also sold and repaired in his shop, which his son Edward continued running after his father's death. Upstairs was the dental office of Frank Forbes. Today the building houses Horicon Bank offices west of the parking lot. (Courtesy Horicon Historical Society.)

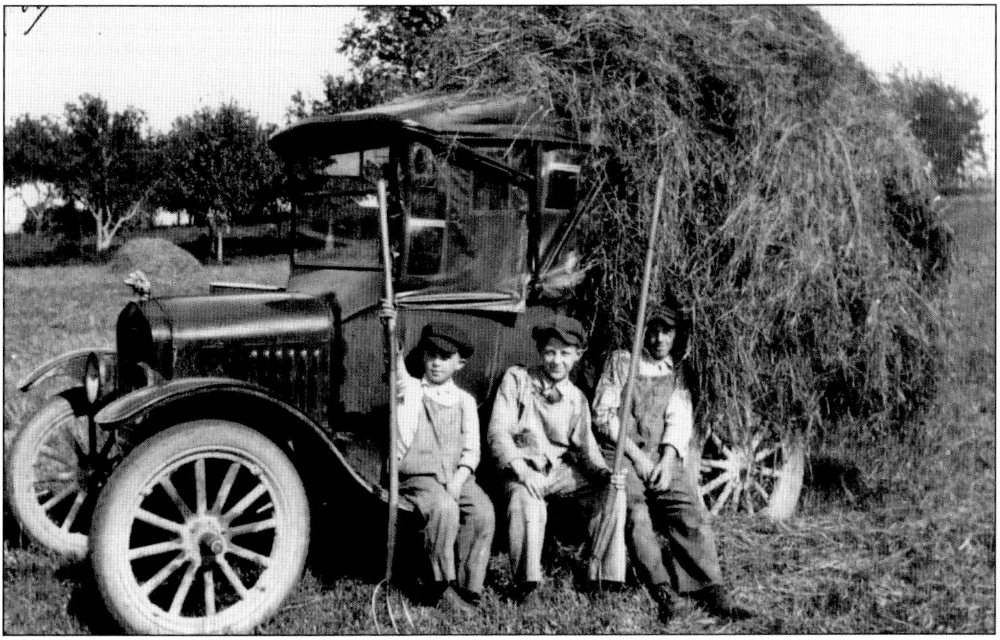

KRUEL BOYS, 1918. Paul, Eddie, and Fritz Kruel spent arduous days collecting hay. Haymaking had become a sizeable industry on the marsh, with many hauling it home in the winter. Hay was also used as packing for breweries and was shipped to South Africa during the Boer War to feed horses. (Courtesy Paul Kruel.)

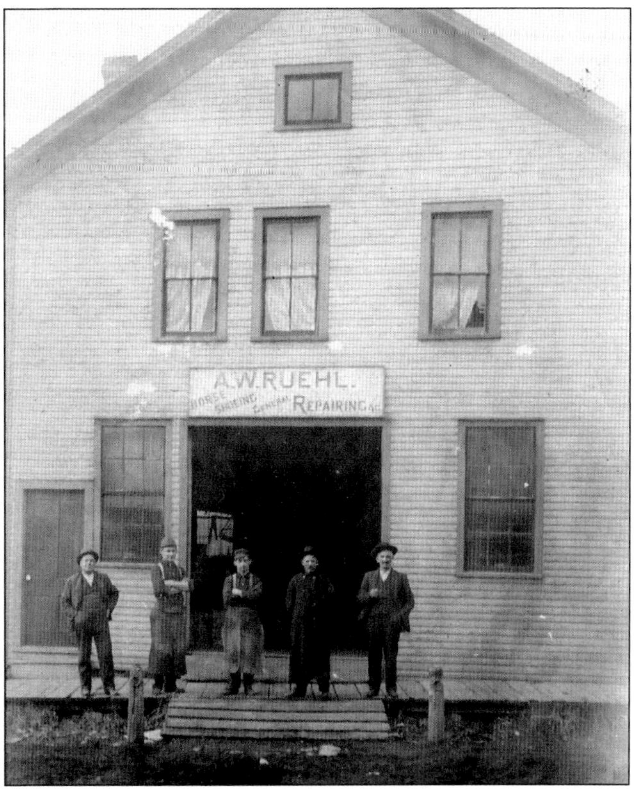

A. W. RUEHL. Horse-shoeing and general repairs were done at the shop that was kept quite busy at the beginning of the 20th century. Shown are, from left to right, August Ruehl, Joe Schmick, Emil Albert, August Werblow, and an unidentified man. This site later became Kruel's Dairy. (Courtesy Paul Kruel.)

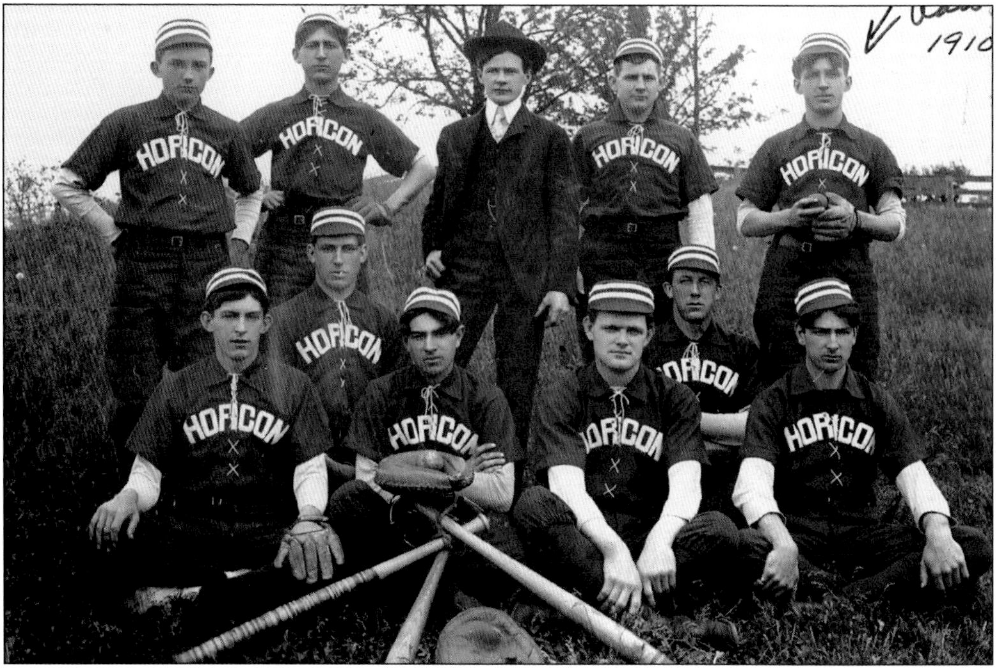

City Baseball Team. Before becoming a champion of the restoration movement on Horicon Marsh, a young Louis "Curley" Radke played baseball on the city team. Radke is pictured in the upper right corner of this 1910 photograph. (Courtesy Horicon Historical Society.)

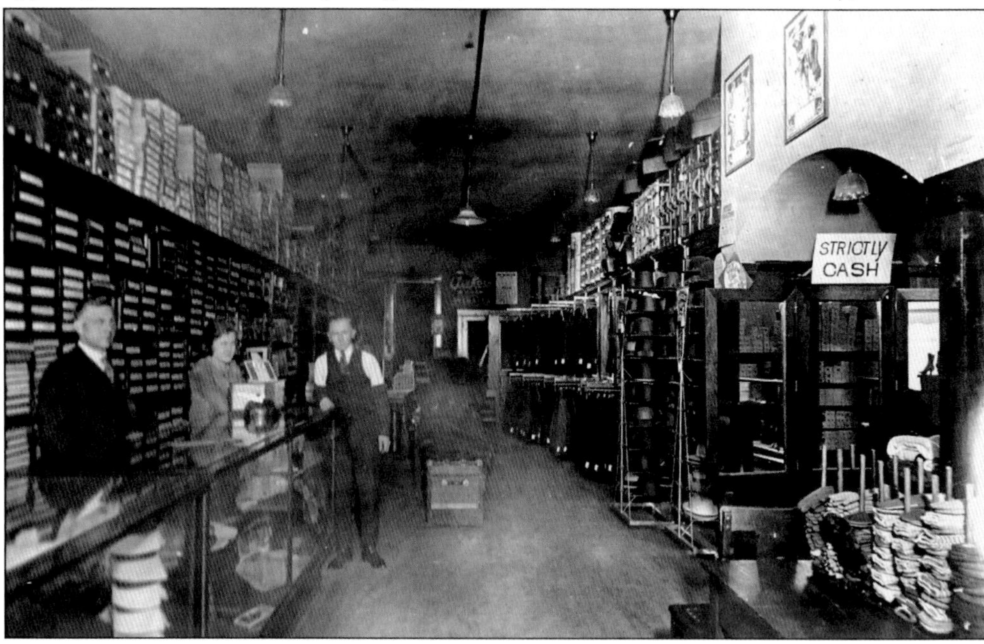

Schneider and Ulrich, 1919. Waiting on a customer are, from left to right, Ervin and Francis Ulrich and patron Wally Oberdiek. This photograph shows the clothing portion of the business, while the shoe section was located on the other side of the store. Ernst Schneider and Ervin Ulrich served the town for many years before separating to become Schneider's Shoe Store and Ulrich's Clothing Store. (Courtesy George and Margaret Schneider.)

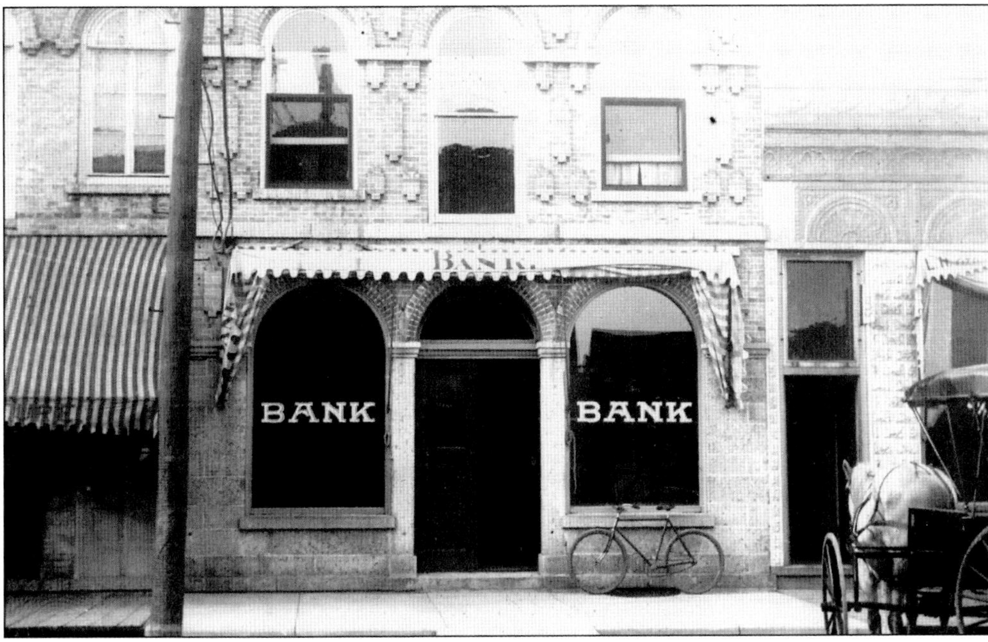

Horicon State Bank. The bank, which operated at this location from 1896 to 1914, opened its doors for business on September 6, 1896, with a paid-in capital of $15,000. The first officers were president Daniel Van Brunt, vice president; John Little, cashier; C. A. Hart, assistant cashier; Charles Hawks; and director Arthur Wilcox. This original bank building was later occupied by the Horicon Furniture Company. (Courtesy Fred Schwertfeger.)

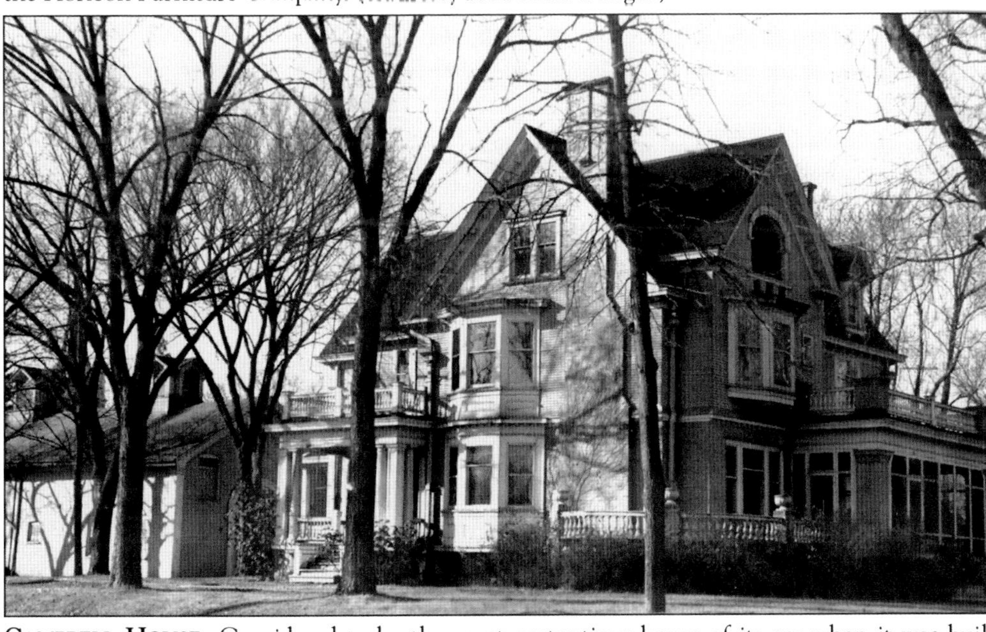

Campbell House. Considered to be the most pretentious house of its era when it was built for Ida Van Brunt and her husband, Stephen Campbell, the home went through many owners before becoming the current Honeybee Inn Bed and Breakfast run by Fred and Barbara Ruka. Staying at this beautifully restored century-old home is a joy not to be passed up when visiting the city. (Courtesy Paul Kruel.)

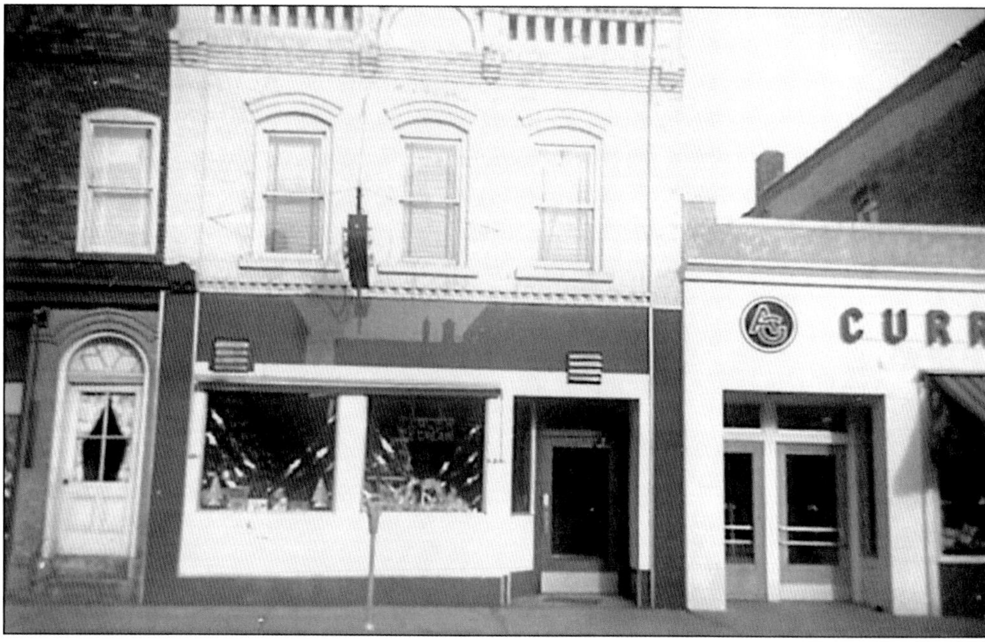

MANOLIS' POOL HALL. A Greek immigrant, Tom Manolis, or "Tom the Greek," was a man of Horicon legend. In 1919, he opened a pool and billiards recreation hall on East Lake Street. Later adding a luncheon counter, it was run by his daughters Athena and Dorthea after the death of his wife, Dimitra, in 1979. The building was a mainstay in town until it was razed for John Deere Horicon Works parking in 2007. (Courtesy Horicon Reporter.)

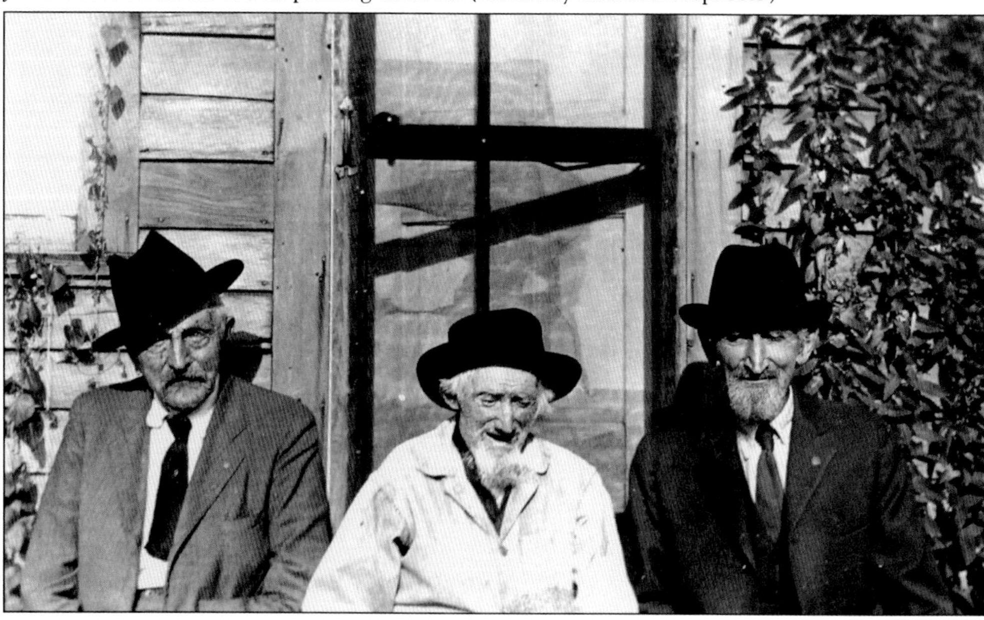

THE 29TH WISCONSIN VOLUNTEER INFANTRY. These three revered men were the last surviving members of the Grand Army of the Republic at the time the photograph was taken. From left to right are Julius Beyer (age 95), Charles Discher (age 84), and Eli J. Tyler (age 84). Tyler was in Company K, and the other two men were in the locally raised Company C. (Courtesy Horicon Historical Society.)

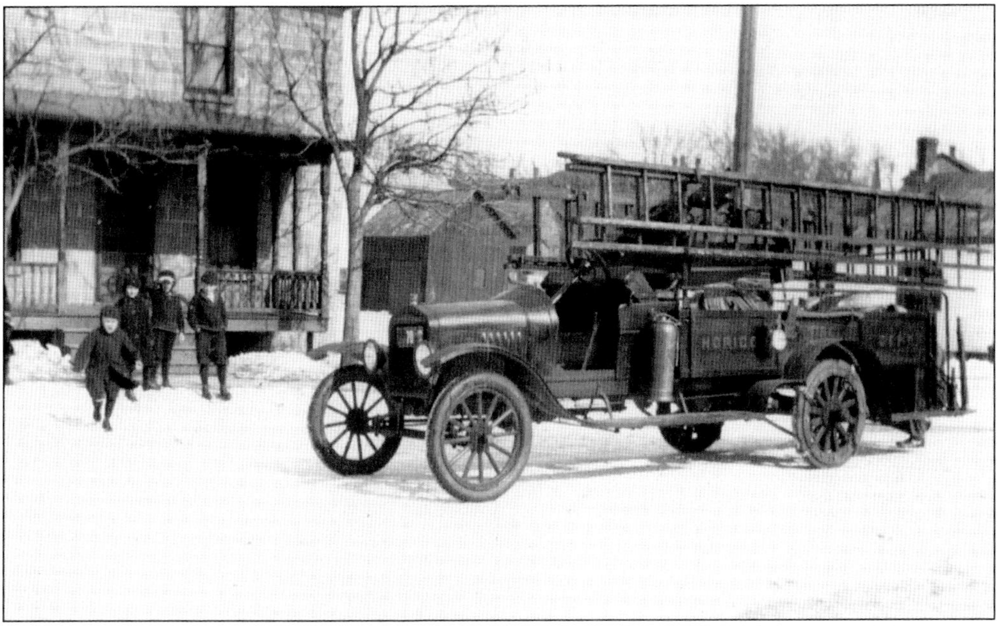

HORICON FIRE DEPARTMENT. While a fire department was established prior to 1893, it took until that year to organize the group and purchase a fire engine. The first engine owned was the Silsby Steamer, which was sold in 1912. Until 1946, the department was entirely voluntary until the city council set up a small fee to be paid to firefighters responding to the alarm. (Courtesy Paul Kruel.)

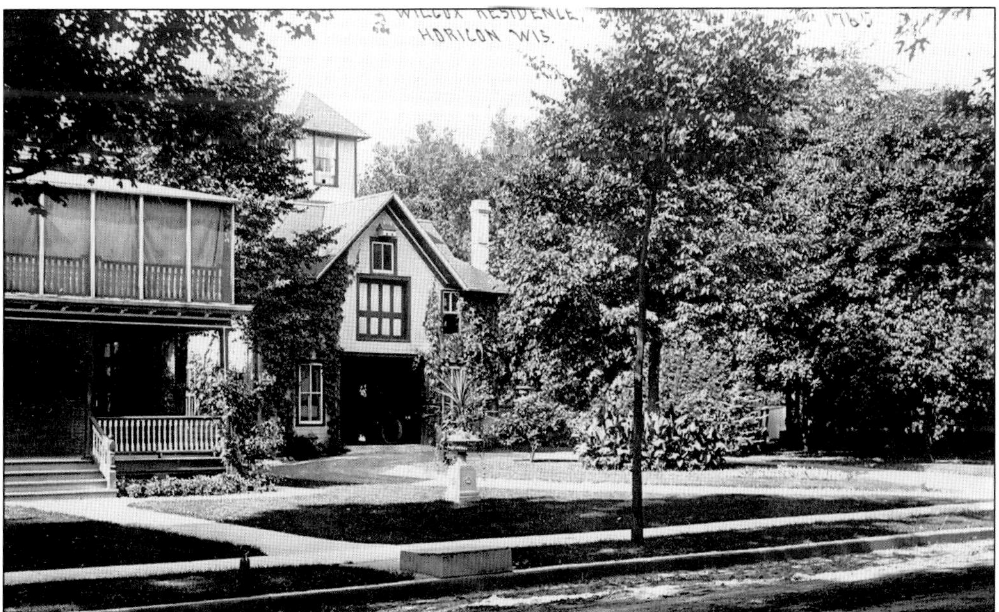

WILCOX RESIDENCE, 1920S. Built by Arthur Wilcox and his wife, Hattie Belle Van Brunt Wilcox, the property commanded the entire block. A teahouse and a carriage house, which later became the garage, were also on the North Cedar Street lot. In 1886, ownership changed to the Sullivan family, but a fire in 1988 destroyed the home. The Sullivans rebuilt and maintain the property today. (Courtesy Mary Sullivan.)

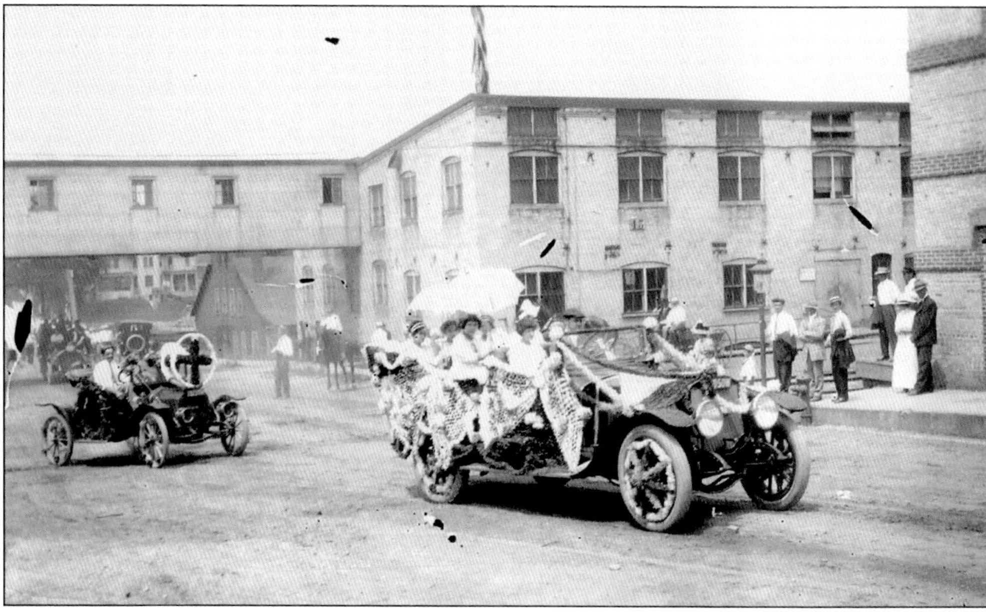

FOURTH OF JULY, 1920S. The Fourth of July was always celebrated in grand style in the city as residents decorated everything, including their cars, for the annual parade. In this undated photograph, cars drive up Lake Street in front of the John Deere Horicon Works building. Although the parade no longer remains a holiday tradition, John Deere Horicon Works still carries on. (Courtesy Mary Sullivan.)

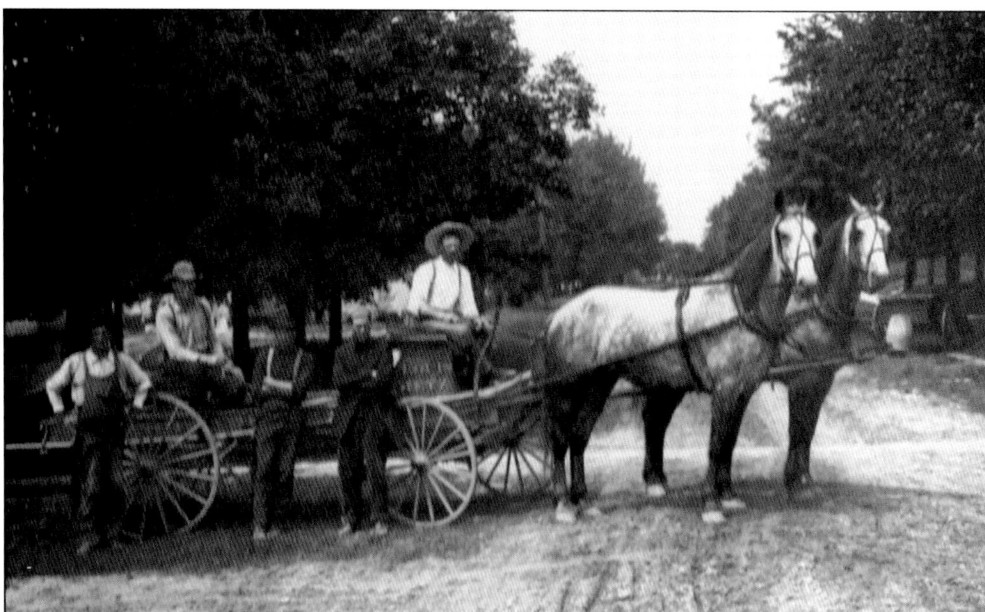

DIETZ HARDWARE. Louis Dietz opened his store in 1882, and he later taught Herman Wilke the trade. In 1904, Wilke took over the business and worked, along with his son Sydney, in the hardware and services industry. Eventually the building located at the northwest corner of East Lake and Vine Streets became home to the First National Bank. (Courtesy Horicon Historical Society.)

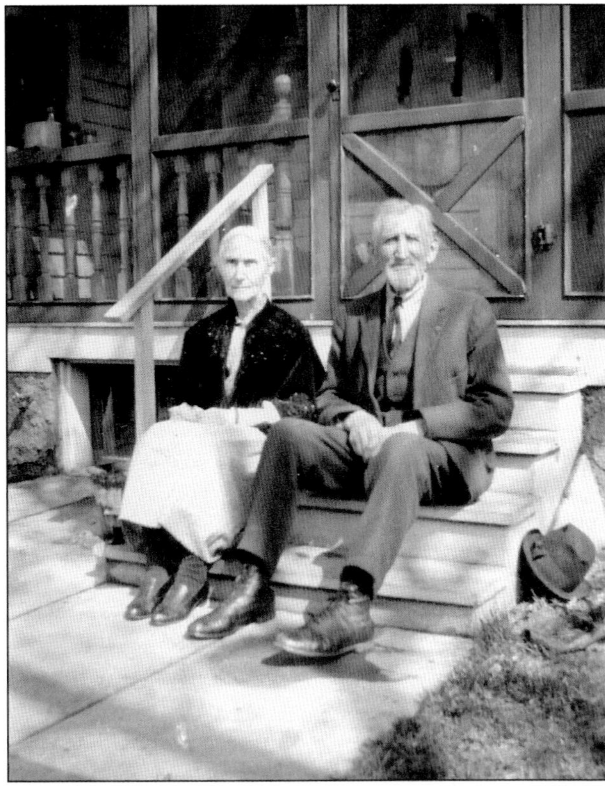

The Dischers, 1923. Charles Discher and his wife were well known in the community as Charles had served in the Civil War. Years later, City Park was renamed in his honor and has been known as Discher Park ever since. The renaming of the park was a fitting tribute to the man who, in 1901, took on the task of planting 100 trees in City Park. (Courtesy Horicon Historical Society.)

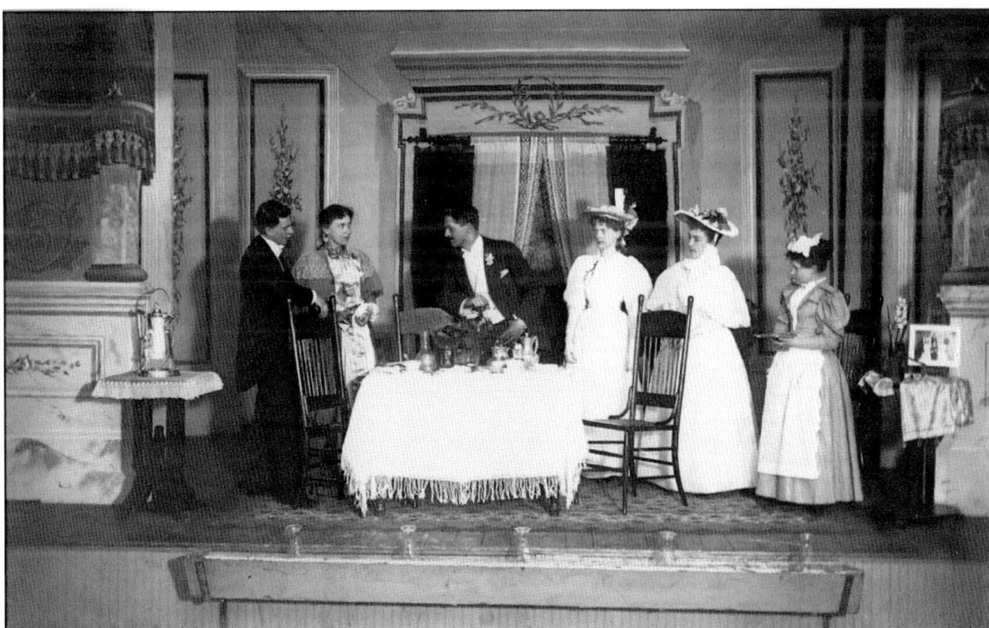

Plays and Theater. Interestingly, the entire community would participate in organizing and acting in the theatrical productions that took place on the second floor of the old city hall building. The owners of the largest companies in town would work by day and act by night in these classic stage productions. (Courtesy Horicon Historical Society.)

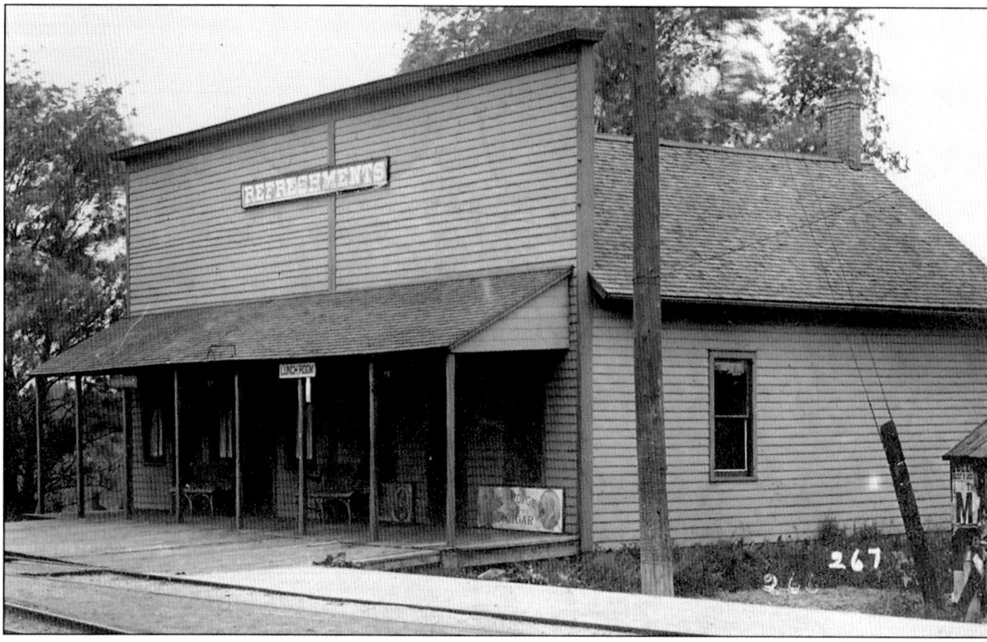

DEPOT RESTAURANT. Originally an eating house run by Betsy Trumball, this business was managed for 25 years near the dawn of the 20th century by Milo Pluck. With the changes in transportation, the facility stopped taking lodgers but remained a restaurant and tavern. It was still around in the late 1940s but no longer exists today. (Courtesy Paul Kruel.)

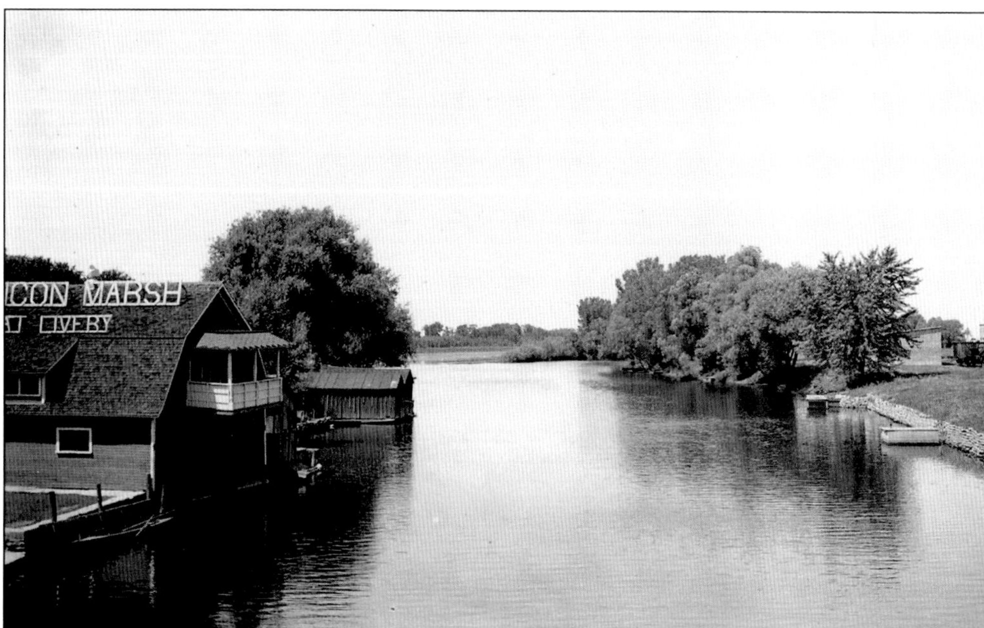

MARSH LIVERY. Earl Snyder began researching the construction of plastic boats and ran the boat livery on the Rock River after selling his bottling factory in 1932. His son Reed returned home after World War II and worked with his father on both of the endeavors. The livery was located on the property of the present-day Rock River Tap. (Courtesy John Karsten family.)

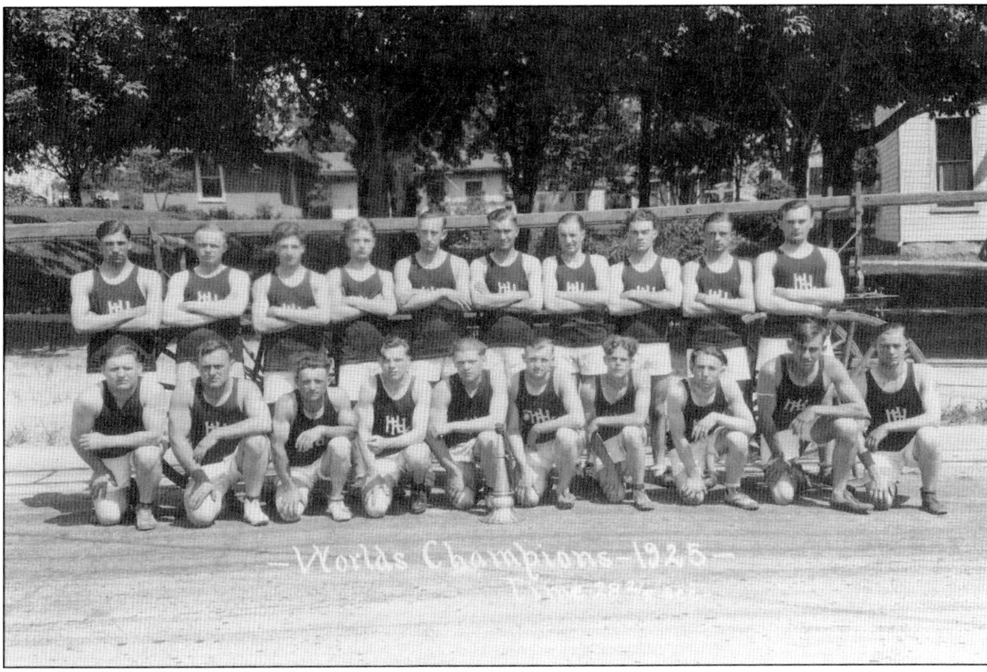

WORLD RECORD, 1925. Horicon's Hook and Ladder Company set a new world speed relay record in Watertown at 28.40 seconds. Before achieving this feat, the department also competed in the first Dodge County Fireman's Tournament held at Theresa in 1898 and in the state tournament in Waupun, held at that time. (Courtesy Horicon Historical Society.)

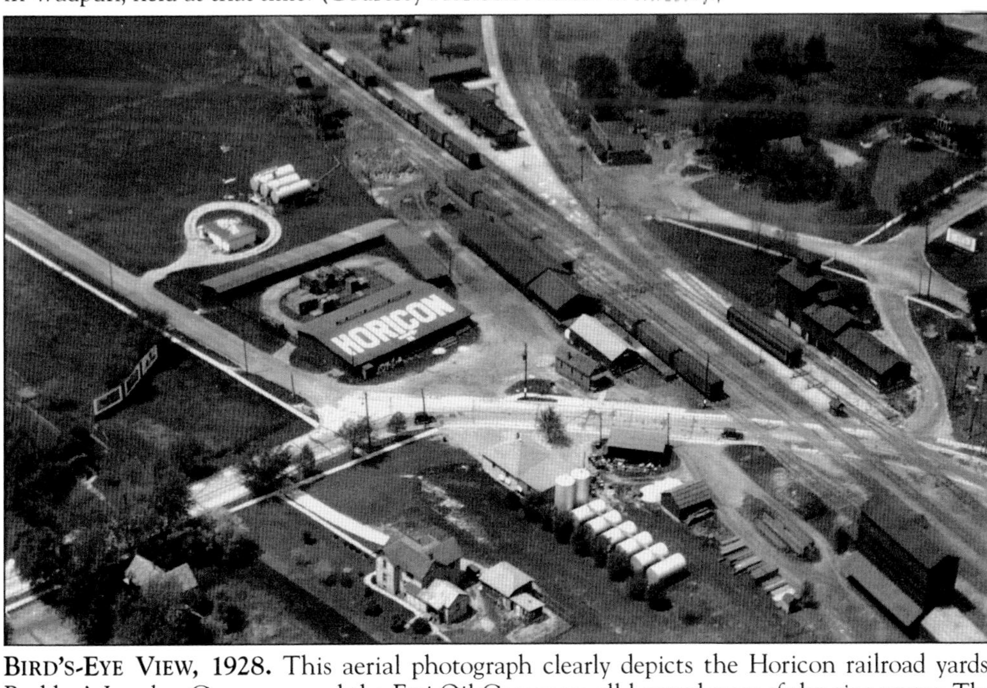

BIRD'S-EYE VIEW, 1928. This aerial photograph clearly depicts the Horicon railroad yards, Bodden's Lumber Company, and the Frei Oil Company, all located west of the city center. The railroad made transportation of goods to neighboring towns and other large cities a prosperous venture for the businesses of Horicon. (Courtesy Paul Kruel.)

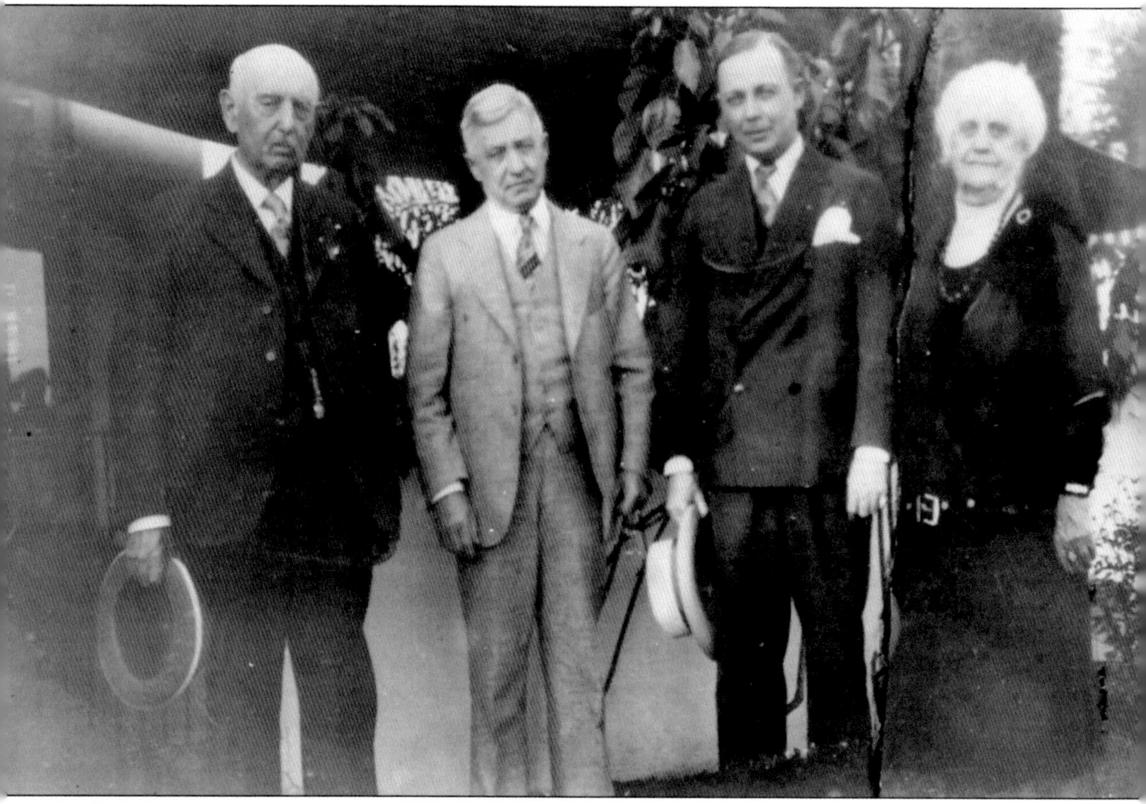

Prominent Community Members, 1928. Willard Van Brunt, along with Arthur W. Wilcox and his son Howard Wilcox, pose with Willard's half-sister Ida Van Brunt Campbell. Willard's history can be read in chapter 2. Arthur was an original director of Horicon State Bank, was married to Hattie Van Brunt, and worked at Van Brunt Manufacturing. After Willard retired, he moved to California to live with Ida. In 1926, he commissioned Wilmington Boat Works to build him the best sport-fisher yacht that money could buy at a staggering cost of $120,000. Named the *Ida May* after his sister, dignitaries, U.S. presidents, and Hollywood celebrities enjoyed fishing with Willard. He died in 1935 after suffering injuries from a fall on the *Ida May*. Purchased in 1935 by comedian Stan Laurel, it was renamed *Ruth L.* after his wife. Later owned by Jonah Jones and renamed *Nada III*, the yacht was commandeered during World War II and patrolled for enemy submarines off the coast of California. It has been lovingly restored and is once again the *Ida May*. (Courtesy Paul Kruel.)

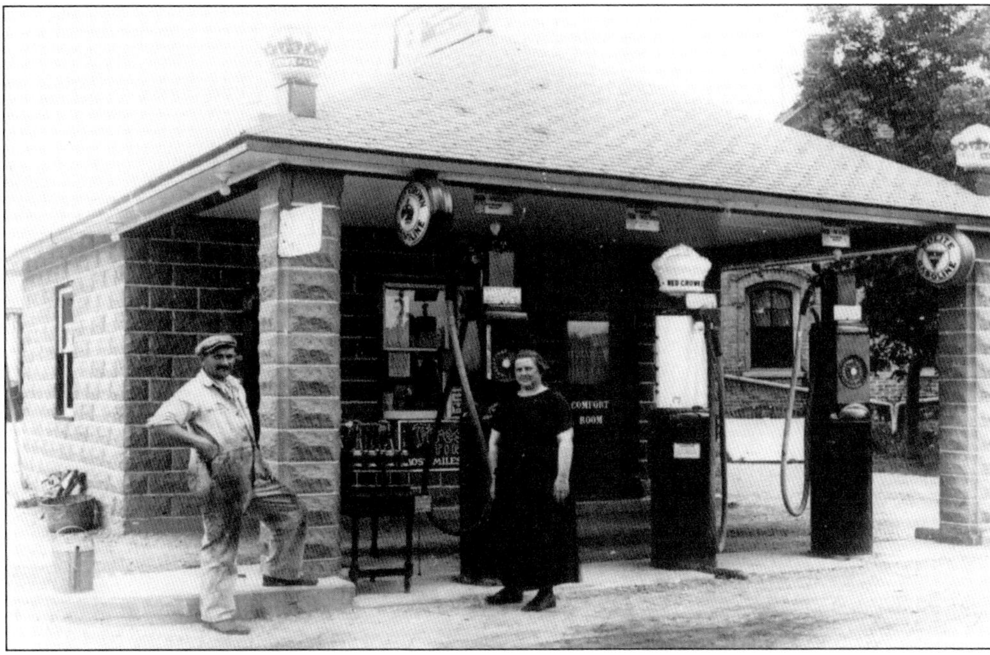

WEBER'S GAS STATION, 1930S. Conveniently located at the corner of Washington and Main Streets, Weber's filling station was a fixture in the community for many years. In 1951, Sam Thompkins purchased the station, which was then known as Sammy's, and his son-in-law Wayne Samplawski worked for him. Samplawski then bought the shop from Thompkins in 1965 and still owns the property today. (Courtesy Keith Pahl.)

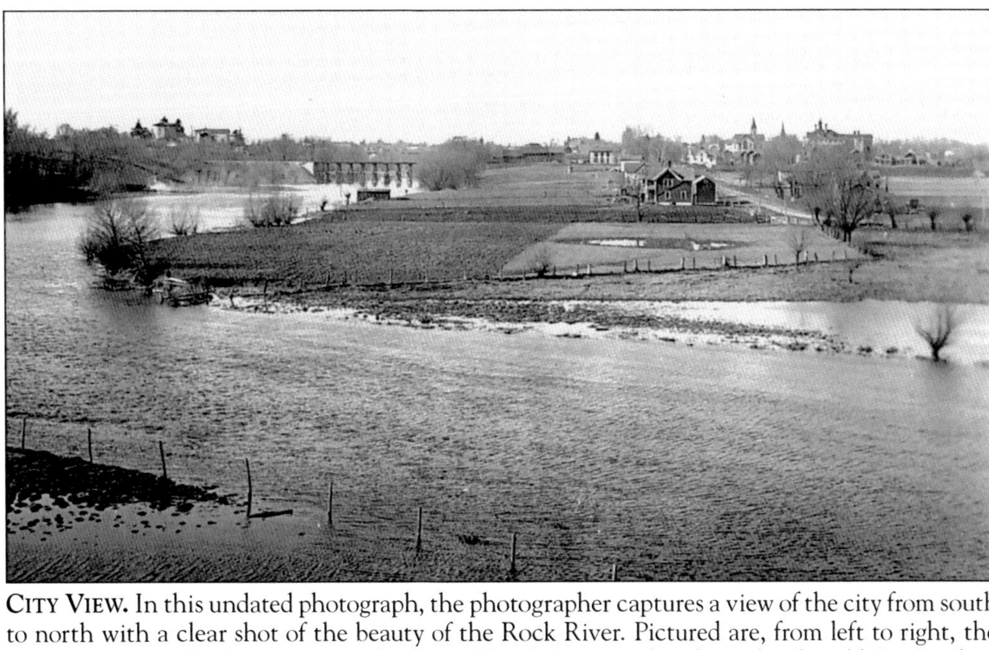

CITY VIEW. In this undated photograph, the photographer captures a view of the city from south to north with a clear shot of the beauty of the Rock River. Pictured are, from left to right, the Octagon House (built around 1855), the Hubbard Street railroad trestle, the old St. Stephen Lutheran Church (now home to MarshView Ministries Christian Reformed Church), and Academy Hall. (Courtesy Frank Owens.)

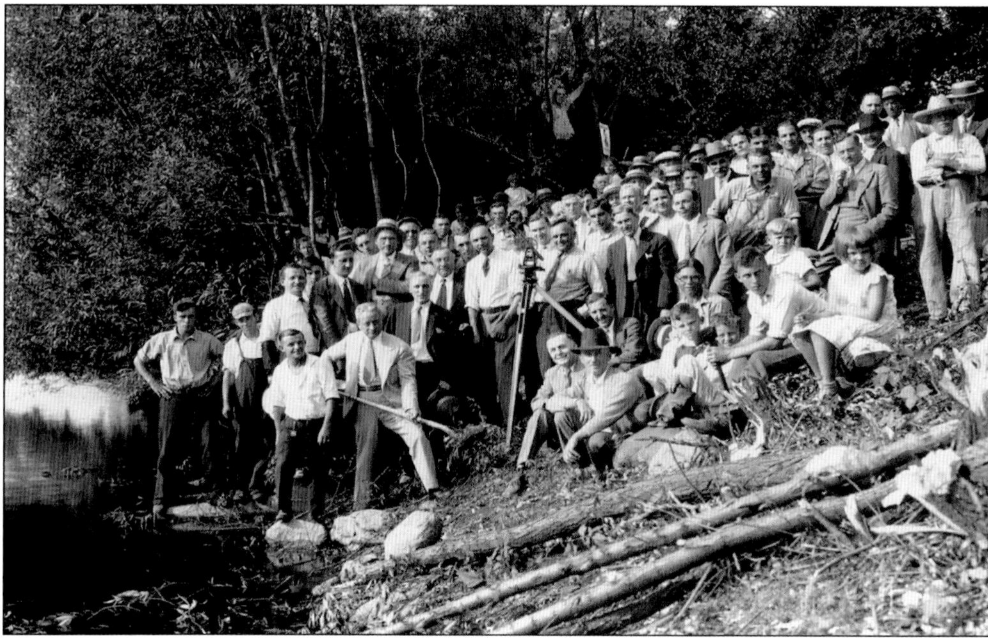

GROUNDBREAKING FOR DAM, 1930. The state legislature passed the Horicon Marsh Wildlife Refuge Bill in 1927 and authorized expenditures for purchasing land from surrounding landowners and the building of a dam. On August 12, 1930, a crowd gathered to watch the first shovel of dirt get turned in the ceremonial show of work to commence on the dam. (Courtesy Wisconsin Department of Natural Resources.)

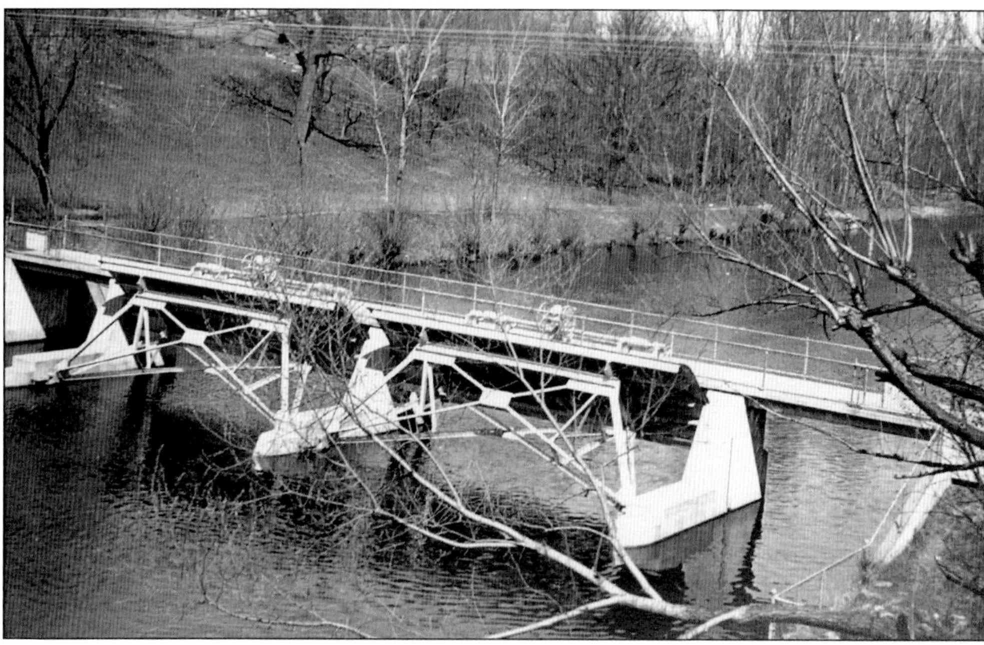

NEW DAM, 1930. On Sunday, August 25, 1935, the official dedication of the conservation dam was held after it was built on the Rock River in 1930. Once the dam gates were closed in October 1934, the peat fires ravishing Horicon Marsh were extinguished as water levels rose. This valuable dam is still in operation south of the city center today. (Courtesy Charlotte Burrow.)

Two

MANUFACTURING BY VAN BRUNT, JOHN DEERE, AND GARDNER

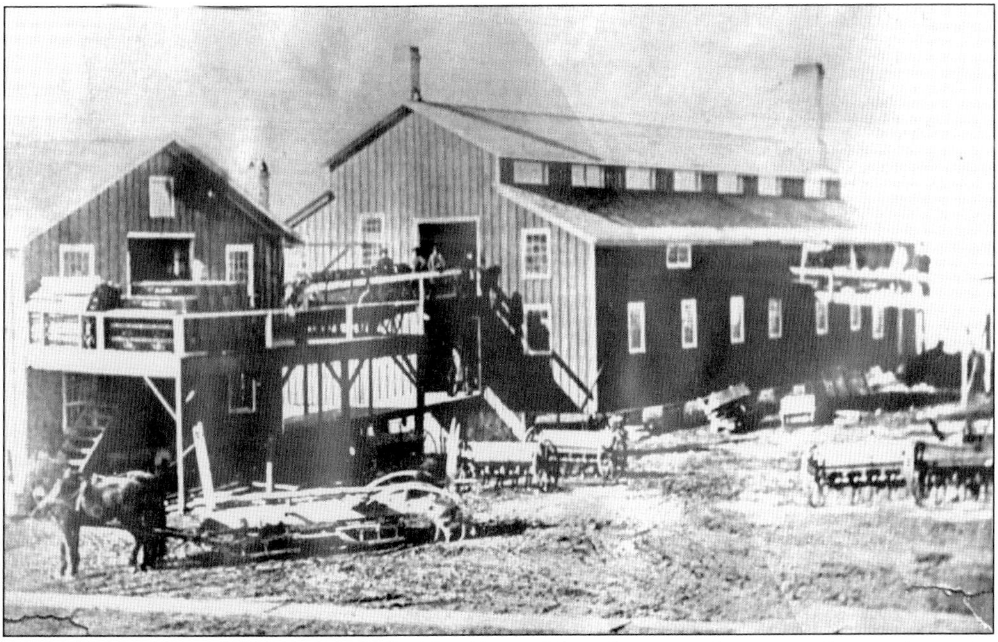

SEEDER PLANT, 1861–1864. In 1861, Van Brunt Manufacturing began producing the grain seeder to assist farmers with planting their crops. Before the invention hit the market, pigeons would ravage the seeds in the grain fields. This new machine scattered seeds through tubes from a grain box with wooden bars that had shovels following behind to cover the seed with soil. (Courtesy Paul Kruel.)

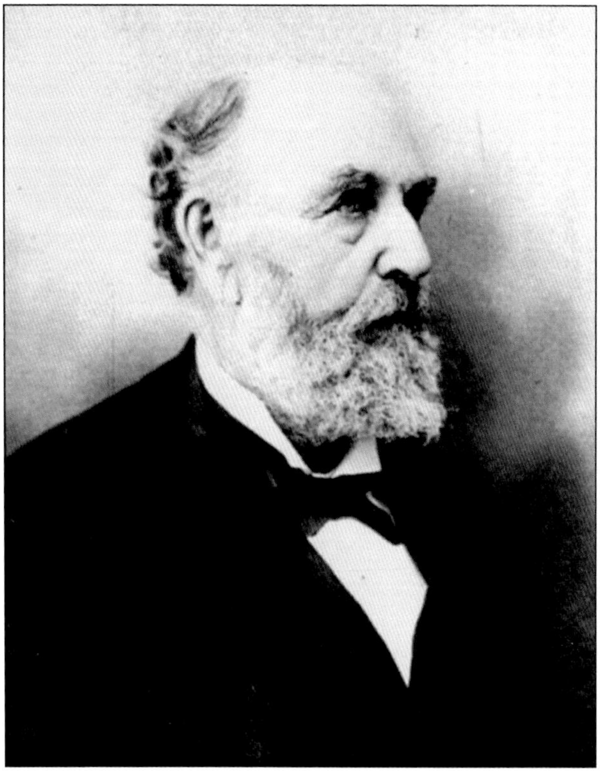

DANIEL C. AND GEORGE VAN BRUNT. Daniel C. Van Brunt (left) is well remembered throughout Horicon for bringing the world the grain seeding machine, a revolutionary planting device used to plant seed deep enough into the ground to prevent the wild pigeons from eating the crop. Along with his brother George, who in 1860 used a turnip to carve the first model of the force-feed device, they created what was to become an empire in the farming industry. George worked alongside Daniel until he left the company in 1866. Over the years, the company continued to thrive and grow, becoming the world's leading grain drill factory. In 1911, Van Brunt Manufacturing Company merged with Deere and Company and remains today as the John Deere Horicon Works. (Courtesy Buzz Vanderhei.)

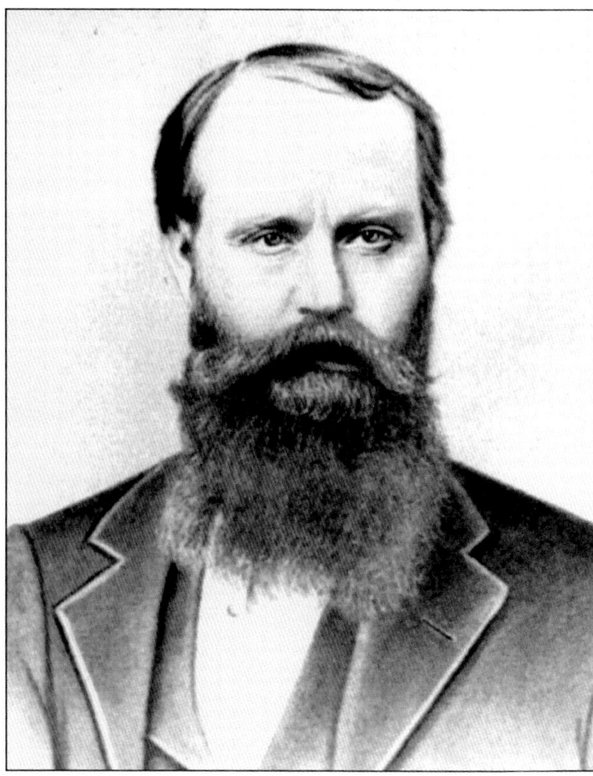

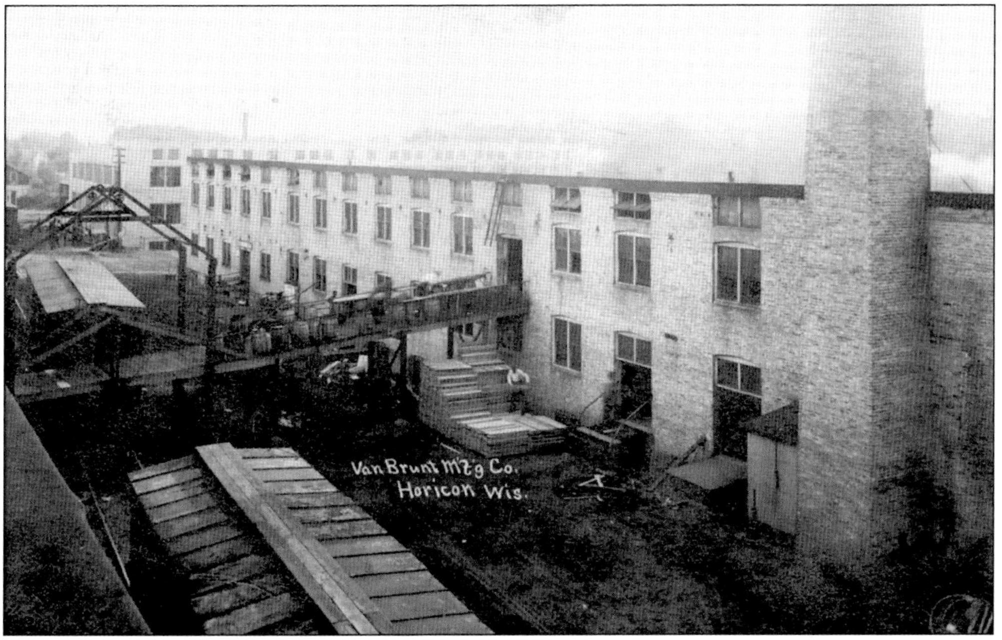

VAN BRUNT FOUNDRY. In 1863, when Hiram Barber purchased S. B. Kellog's share of the company, a new foundry was built. In 1864, part of today's factory was added, and in 1865, several shops were built to accommodate the company's expansion. In 1883, Judge Barber bought out Daniel and ran the business for three years before reselling to Daniel, W. C. Wood, and R. S. Barber. (Courtesy Horicon Historical Society.)

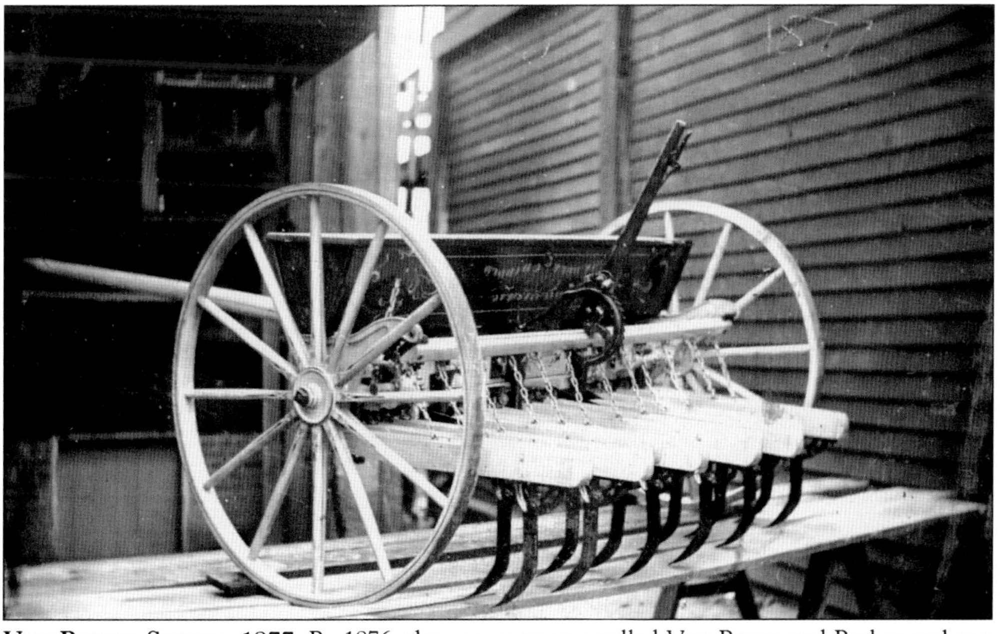

VAN BRUNT SEEDER, 1877. By 1876, the company was called Van Brunt and Barber and was owned by Daniel and R. S. Barber. In 1882, ownership changed again, and the company was known as Van Brunt and Wilkins Manufacturing Company, with Henry Wilkins having an interest in the business. (Courtesy Horicon Historical Society.)

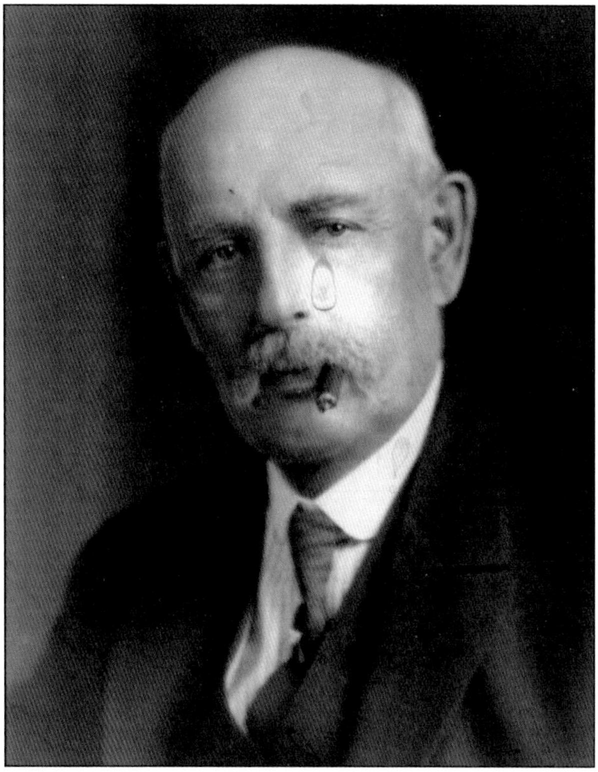

WILLARD VAN BRUNT. Daniel C. Van Brunt's eldest son worked his way up through the company, having started as an apprentice in his father's factory. He was made shop superintendent at the age of 21. He, like his father and uncle George, was interested in the future and making products that would benefit the farmer. (Courtesy Horicon Historical Society.)

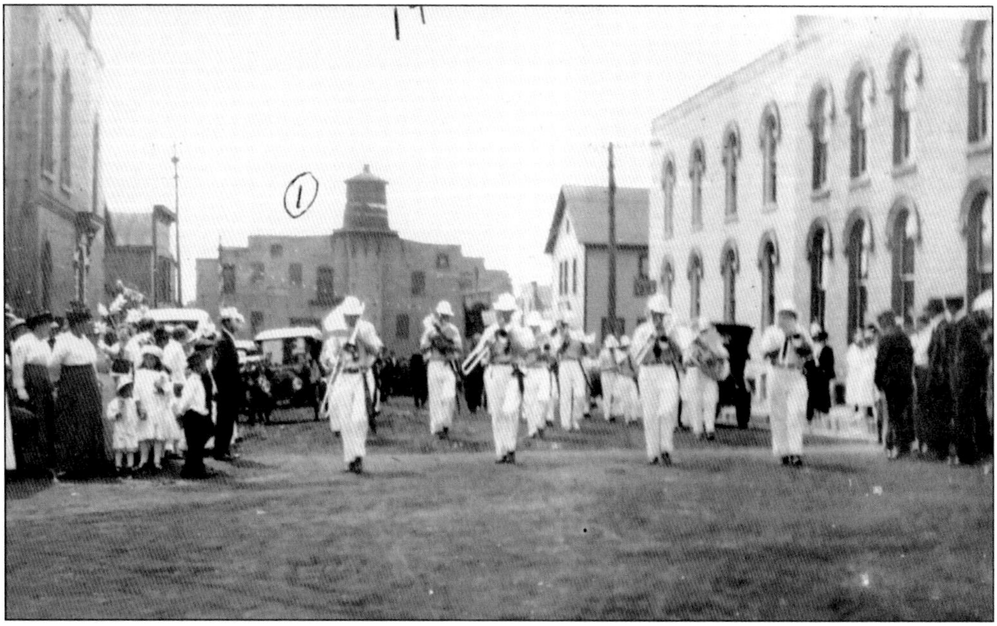

OLD STONE SHOP, 1907. In 1872, Willard and Spencer Davis formed Van Brunt and Davis and sold grain drills in their new venture. The company also made hay forks, hay mowers, and a revolving milk safe. They called the design of their first grain drill "the New Van Brunt." When Willard's father rejoined the competition in 1873, they changed the name to the "Monitor." (Courtesy Paul Kruel.)

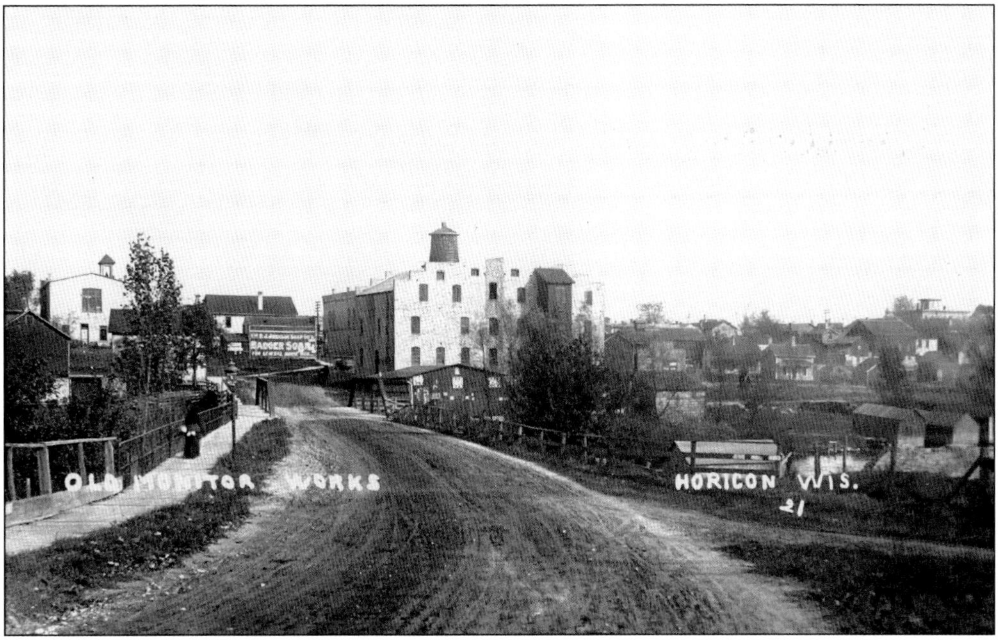

MONITOR WORKS, 1908. In 1893, Willard sold his interest to Davis, who moved the company to St. Louis Park near Minneapolis. The company was later sold to Minneapolis-Moline Plow Company, and the equipment took that company's name. Willard moved to California after the sale of his share but returned to Horicon in the late 1890s to once again work on his inventions. (Courtesy Horicon Historical Society.)

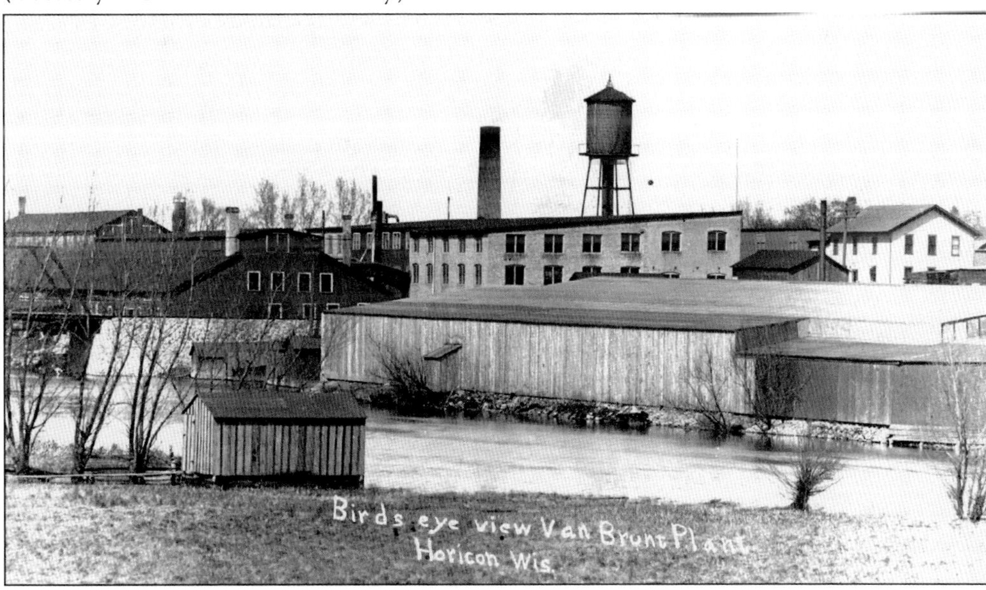

VAN BRUNT PLANT, 1908. Upon Daniel C. Van Brunt's death in 1901, son Willard ran the plant. During the next 10 years, Willard worked with Theodore Erdman, the company's chief pattern maker, and obtained several patents. In 1900, Willard introduced the revolutionary single-disc drill, and shortly thereafter, a double-disc grain drill was designed. Both improved the uniformity and accuracy of planting, and the basic principles are still used today. (Courtesy Horicon Historical Society.)

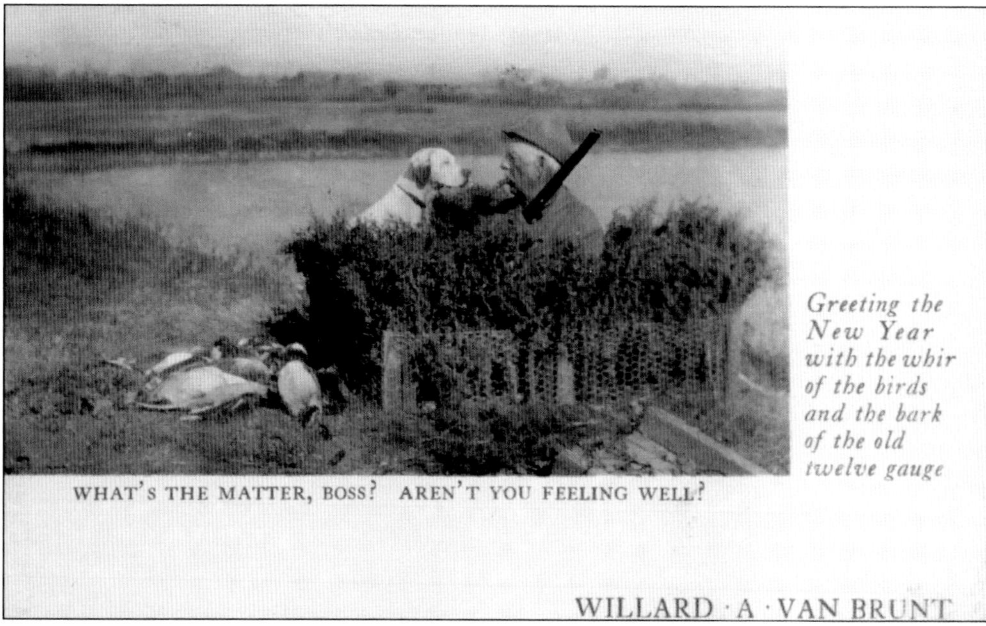

WILLARD'S HOLIDAYS. A favorite pastime in the area has always been hunting and fishing. Here Willard Van Brunt shows both his humorous side and the pleasure that he took in hunting when he had a postcard designed for sending a personal holiday greeting. (Courtesy Horicon Historical Society.)

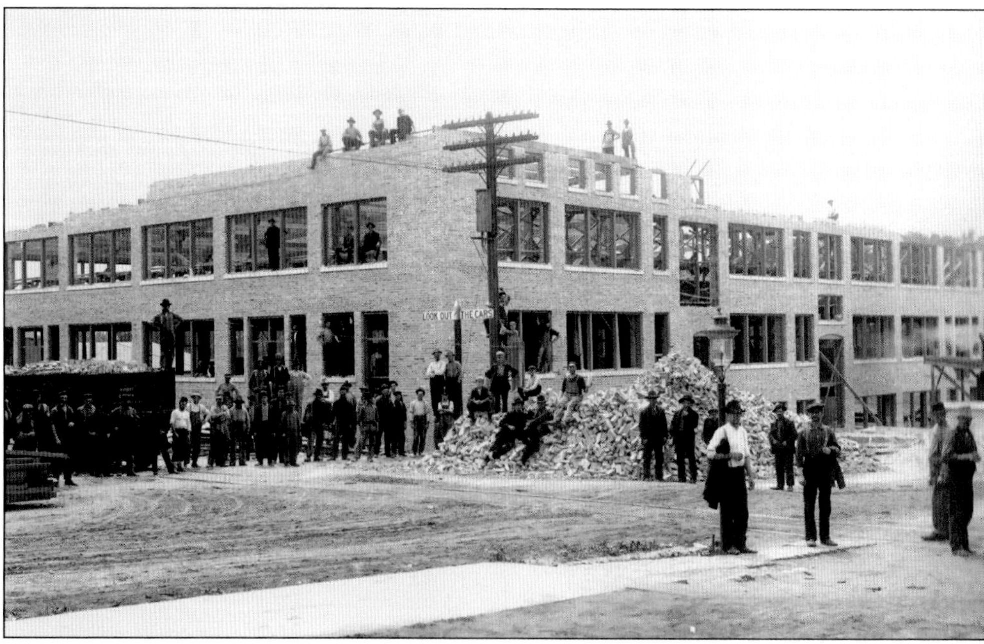

JOHN DEERE EXPANDS, 1910. During Willard's years in charge, the company prospered and was ready for growth. A major fire in 1905 caused extensive damage, and in 1910, work began on building C, used for assembly and production. An iron bridge above the street connected the new manufacturing building with the old. A tunnel was built below Lake Street as a secondary access to connect the buildings. (Courtesy Horicon Historical Society.)

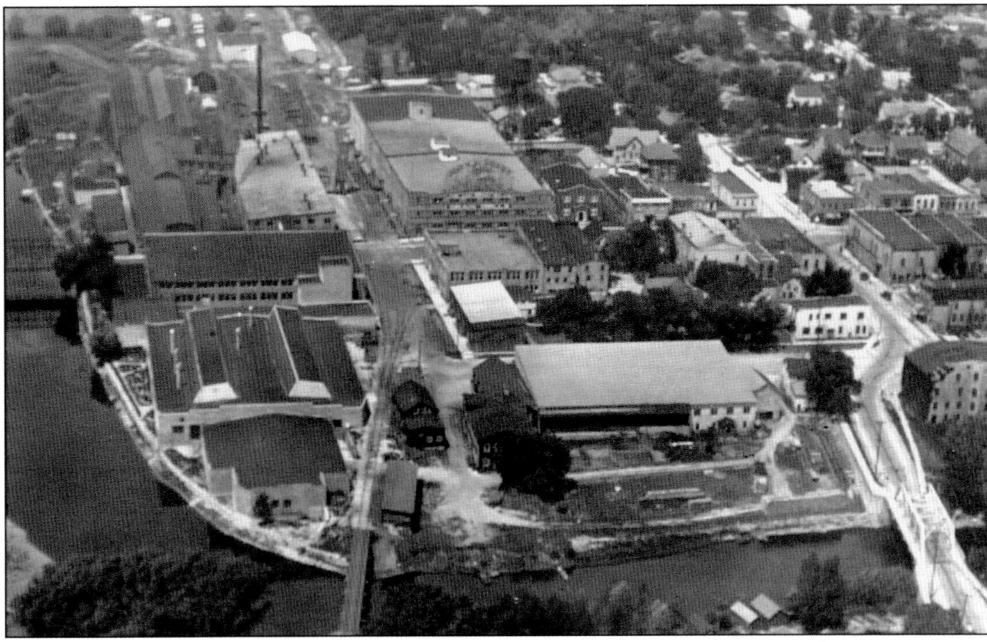

BIRD'S-EYE VIEW, 1928. Van Brunt shut down for many months but reopened in May 1922. By the mid-1920s, orders were coming in from foreign countries and grain drills were manufactured for Argentina and Russia. A shipment of drills was also sent to Gen. Alvaro Obregon, the former president of Mexico. (Courtesy Paul Kruel.)

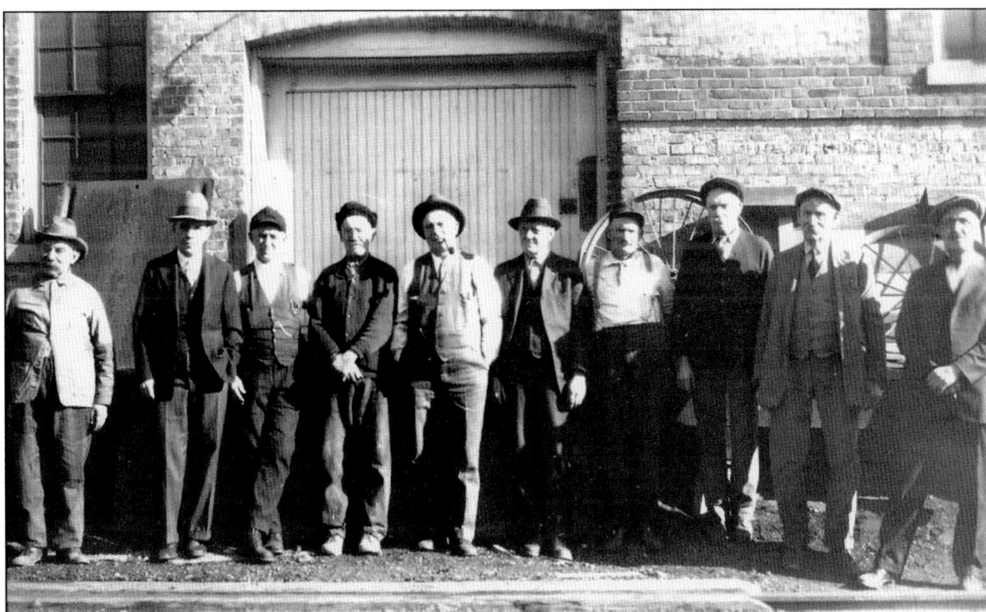

VAN BRUNT PLANT, 1931. On February 4, 1931, these workers commemorated their many years of service. Pictured are, from left to right, with their years of service noted in parentheses, Fred Schielke (47), John Schaeffer (20), August Classen (40), Fred Berggren (32), E. W. Simon (40), Louis Last (40), Marion Falkinham (25), Charles Schulz (47) Dave Yorgey (61), and Theodore J. Erdman (31). (Courtesy Horicon Historical Society.)

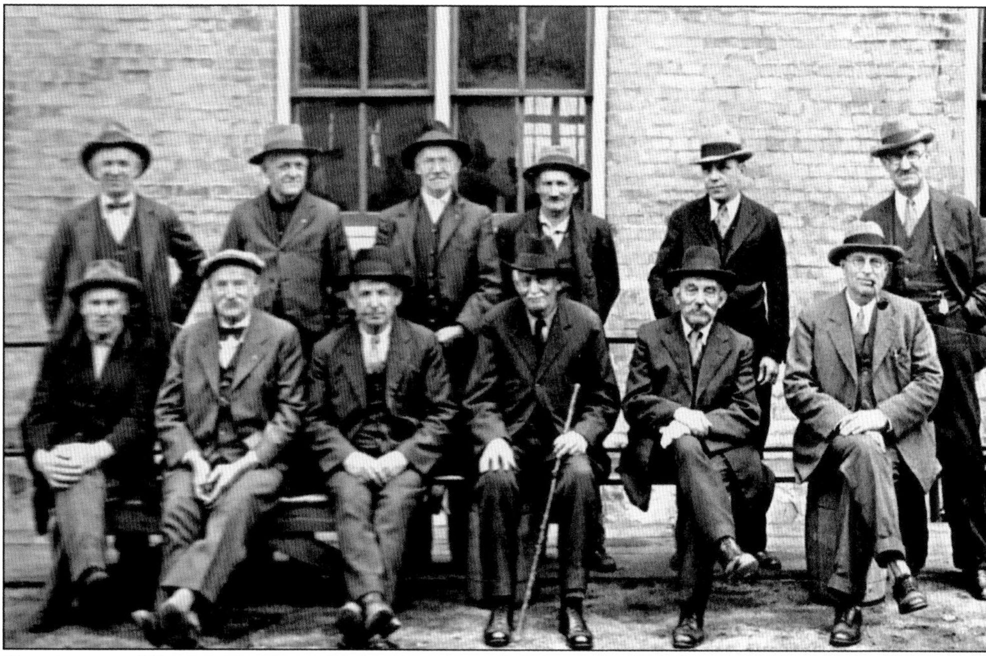

VAN BRUNT WORKERS, 1932. In this anniversary photograph, each man is listed with his years of service noted in parentheses. They are, from left to right, (first row, sitting) Carl Schultz (48), Dave Yorgey (61), Edward Knop (30), George Propst (52), Fred Schielke (47), and Emil Simon (41); (second row) August Classen (41), Louis Last (41), Fred Berggren (33), Marion Falkinham (26), John Schaeffer (21), and Theodore J. Erdman (33). (Courtesy Horicon Historical Society.)

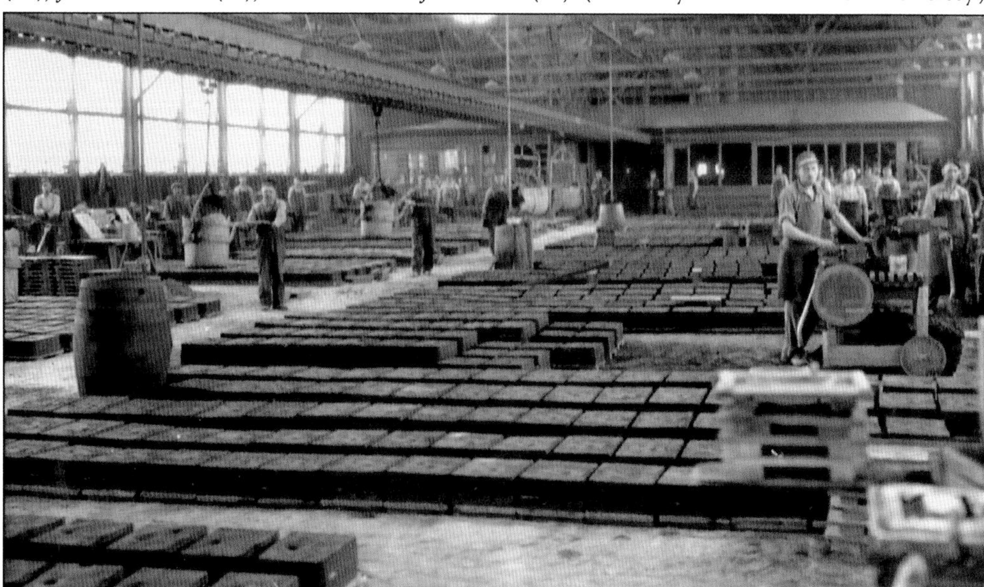

VAN BRUNT FOUNDRY, 1940. For the first 100 years, the factory came equipped with its own foundry. Some modernization occurred over the years with the addition of overhead pouring ladles and plates, rather than wooden patterns, and the foundry was disbanded in 1963 to allow centralization of operations in Iowa. Robert Gensmer is the man in the foreground holding the bull ladle. (Courtesy Horicon Historical Society.)

WORLD WAR II EFFORTS. During the war, Van Brunt Manufacturing Company, now owned by Deere and Company, utilized some of its equipment to build cargo carriers. Some $212 million worth of equipment was produced for the war and navy departments, including tank transmissions, ammunition, trailers, and aircraft parts. Frames such as this one were used in the manufacturing of these products. (Courtesy Horicon Historical Society.)

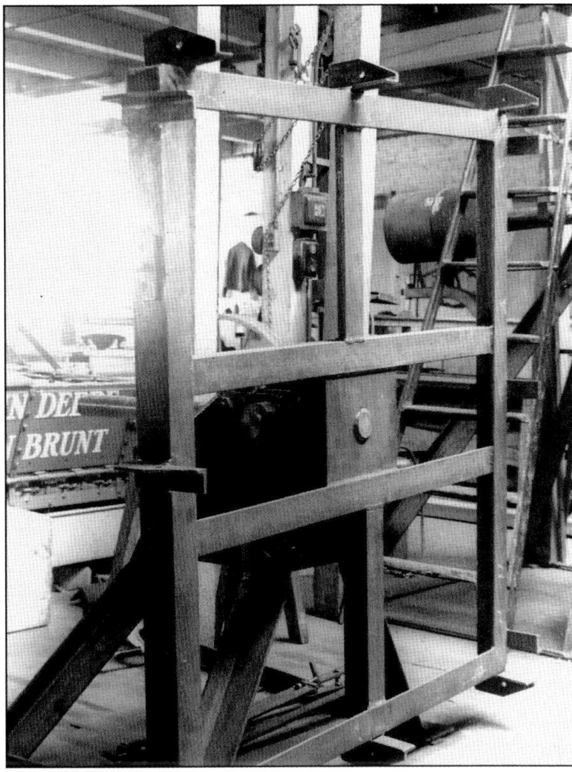

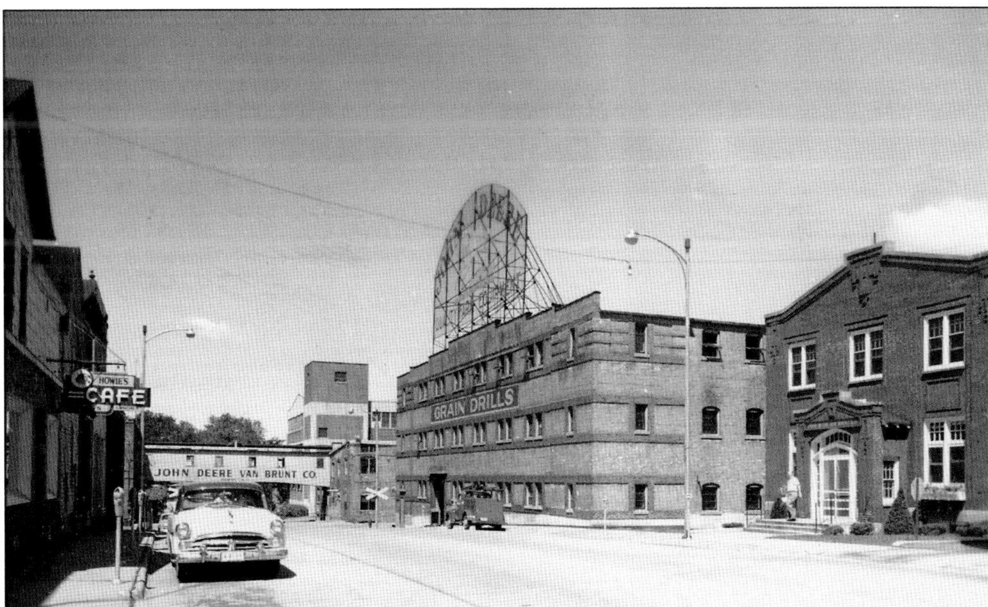

LAKE STREET SHOP, 1950S. In November 1947, the company again changed names, becoming John Deere Van Brunt Company. When a new grassland drill was introduced in 1953, the Van Brunt name no longer appeared on the hopper. Red Van Brunt wooden boxes were also changed to John Deere green and yellow steel grain boxes. By 1964, all equipment bore only the name John Deere. (Courtesy Bob Blankenheim.)

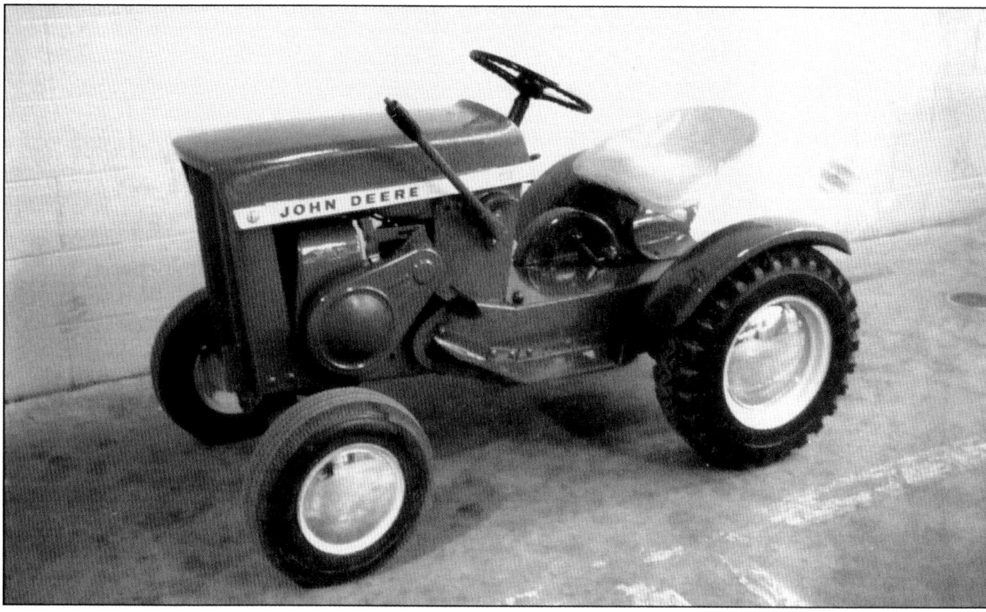

LAWN AND GARDEN TRACTOR, 1963. By 1958, the company name had changed again to the John Deere Horicon Works. In 1963, the first lawn and garden tractor came off the line. Shown is the first model 110 with an exclusive feature of a safety interlock system that allowed the tractor to only start when in neutral with the power take-off (PTO) disengaged. (Courtesy R. G. Sharkey.)

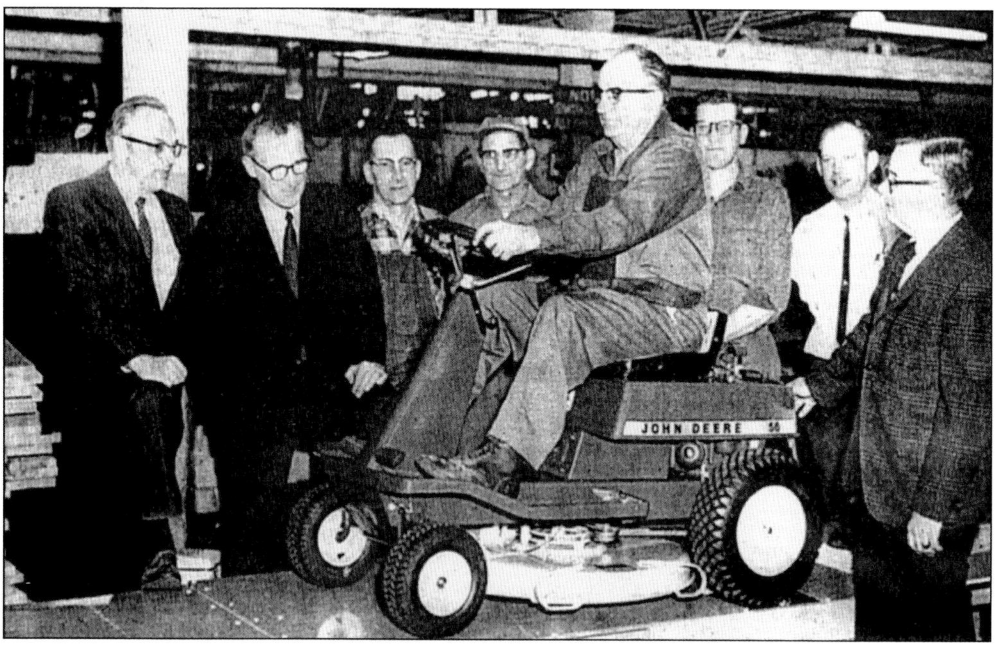

RIDING MOWER, 1969. With the coming of the lawn and garden tractor came the closing of the foundry to make room for production lines. Pictured watching the first riding mower come off the assembly line are, from left to right, general supervisor Warren Hofman, manufacturing superintendant Siegfried Stellberg, Eddie Flouro, Wilbert Rediske, Archie Robertson, Bob Miescke, Roy Mellenthien, and general manager John Moore. (Courtesy R. G. Sharkey.)

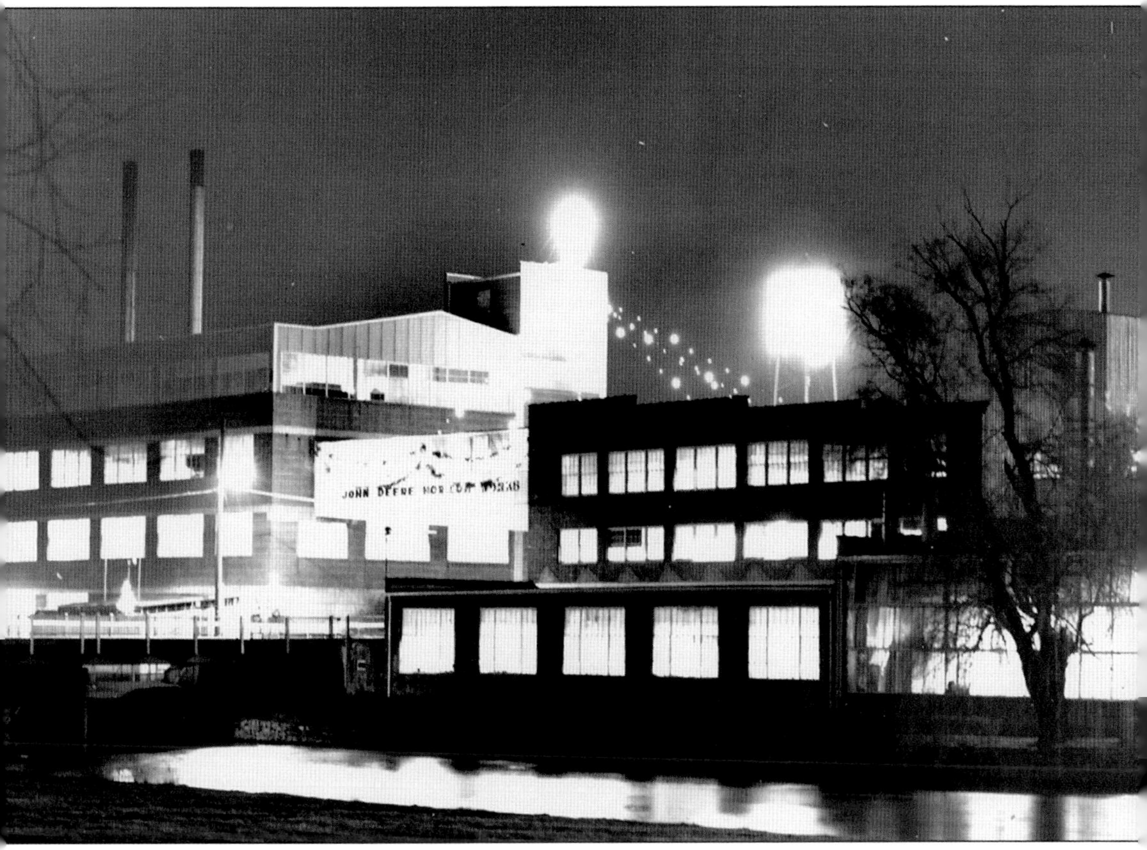

JOHN DEERE HORICON WORKS, 1960S. Tractor prototypes were built at the factory and sent to the Rio Grande Valley for testing in the winter of 1963. In 1965, the model 110 tractor received an Industrial Design Exhibition Award at the Industrial Trade Fair and Congress sponsored by the Los Angeles Chamber of Commerce. With the growth of the lawn and garden tractors came the end to the foundry at the Horicon facility. On May 1, 1984, the factory produced its one-millionth tractor, just 21 years after it entered the business. As of 1986, 125 years after the inception of the company, 34 buildings had been constructed on the present-day site of John Deere Horicon Works. Today the company continues to be the city's largest employer. It also partners with the city as it tests mowing equipment during the summer months in Horicon parks and area fields. (Courtesy Horicon Reporter.)

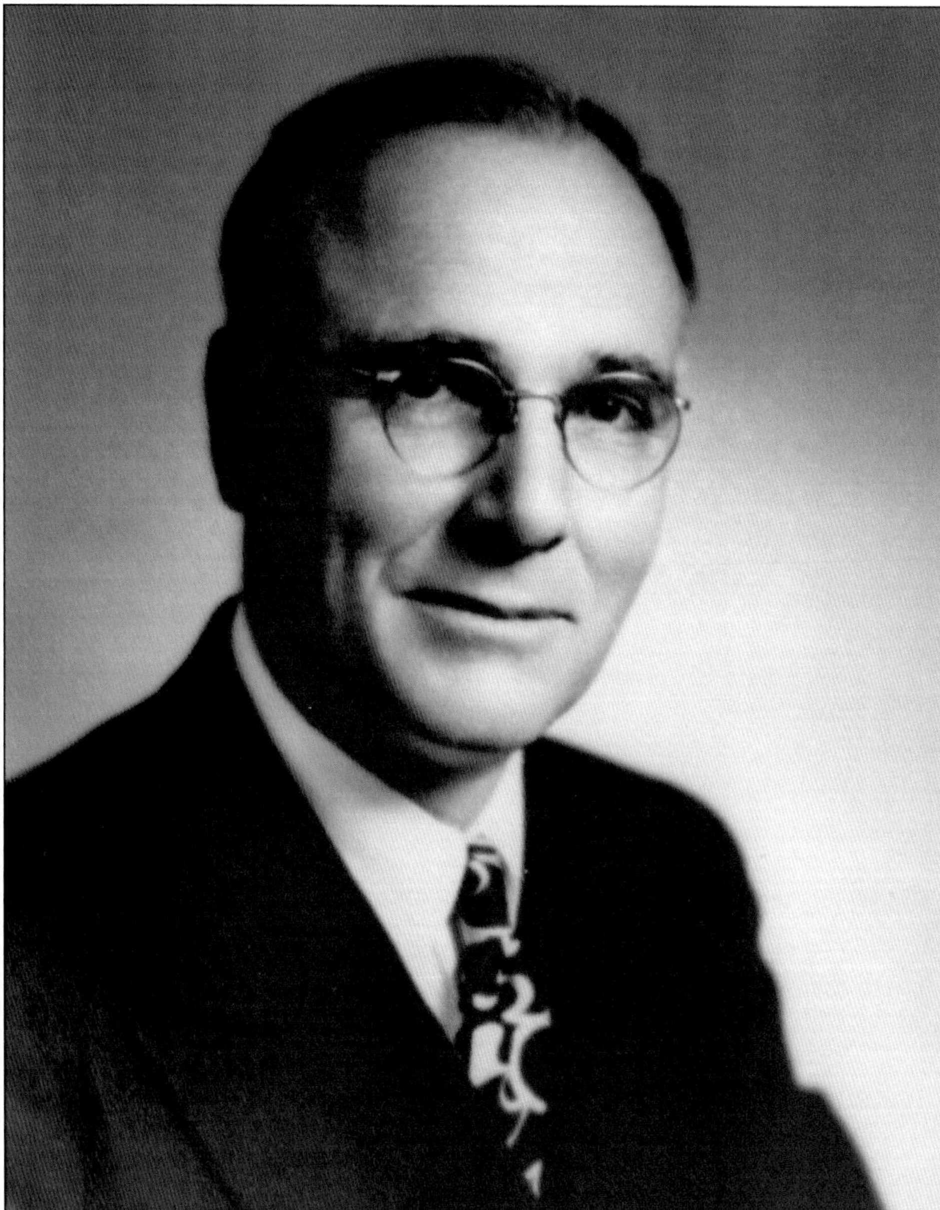

Clarence J. Gardner. After serving as an officer during World War I in the Russian phase of operations, Clarence Gardner worked in the Van Brunt Manufacturing Company as a traffic manager. In 1928, Gardner purchased the IDEAL Barn Equipment Company, and Gardner Manufacturing was incorporated on November 1. Equipment and other machinery were installed for the building and finishing of sheet metal articles. Gardner began selling excess fabrication capacity to perform contract fabrication work for local companies. In 1937, Gardner purchased the rights to what was to become the "bug zapper." For the next 40 years, it had three product divisions—barn equipment, sheet metal fabrication, and insect electrocutor. The company continues manufacturing today with grandson Mark Sullivan being the only remaining family member in the business, working as quality manager. Unfortunately, a fire in 1988 destroyed the family's archives and photographs of the company. (Courtesy Mary Sullivan.)

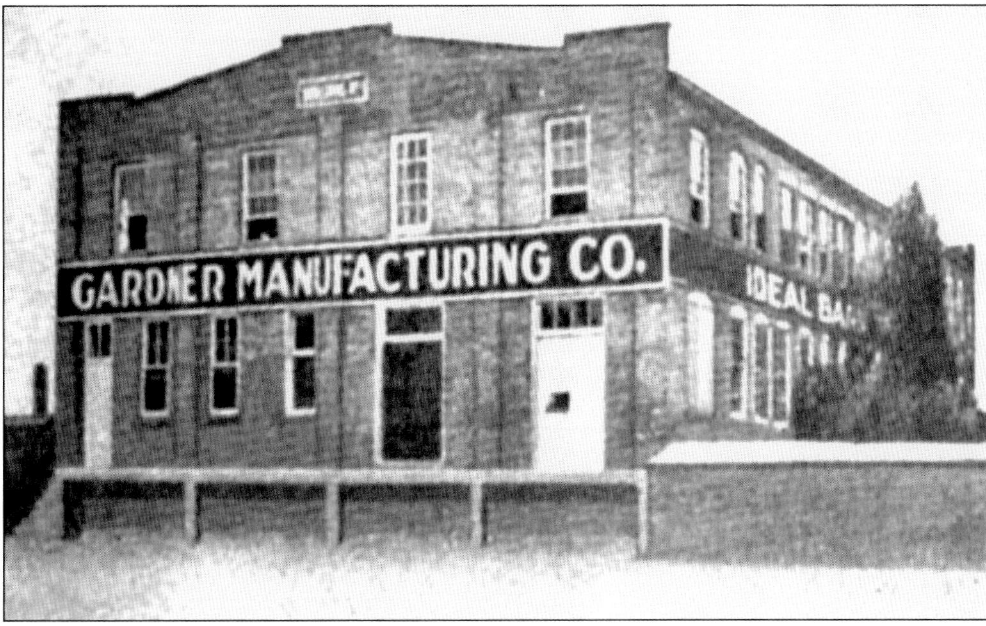

GARDNER BUILDING NO. 1. Building No. 1 was acquired, along with other assets, by Clarence J. Gardner when he purchased the IDEAL Barn Equipment Company in 1928. During World War II, the company produced electrical switches and control boxes for navy ships and army truck cabs. Later expansion included building No. 2 before its move to the current location in Horicon Industrial Park. (Courtesy History of Horicon.)

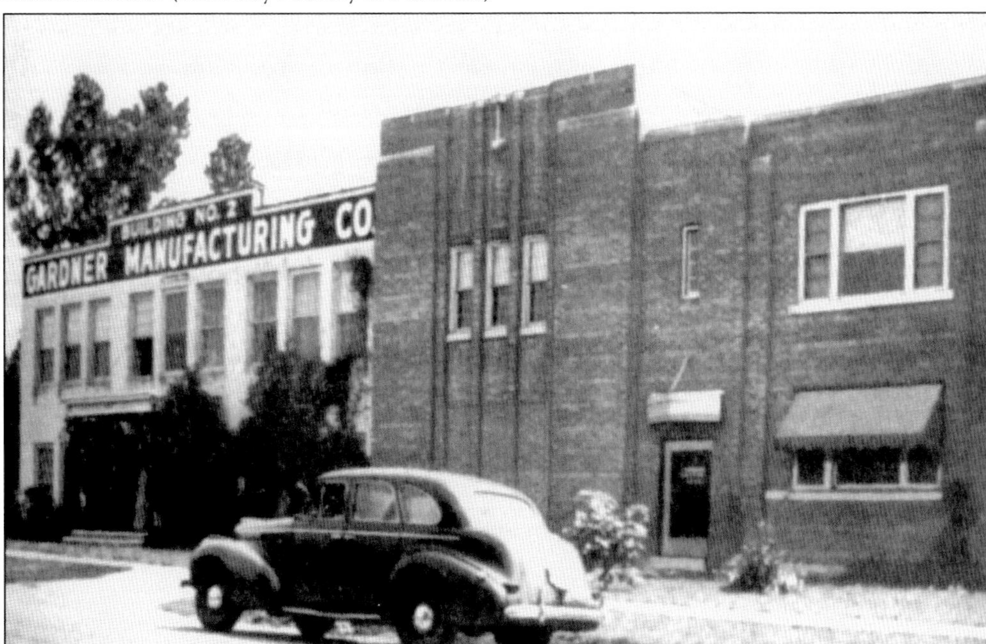

GARDNER BUILDING NO. 2. Located on Kansas Street, the expansion was required to fulfill the orders for sheet metal fabrication as well as their other product lines. Today the company has 108 employees at its new facility in Horicon Industrial Park with plans to expand in 2008. (Courtesy History of Horicon.)

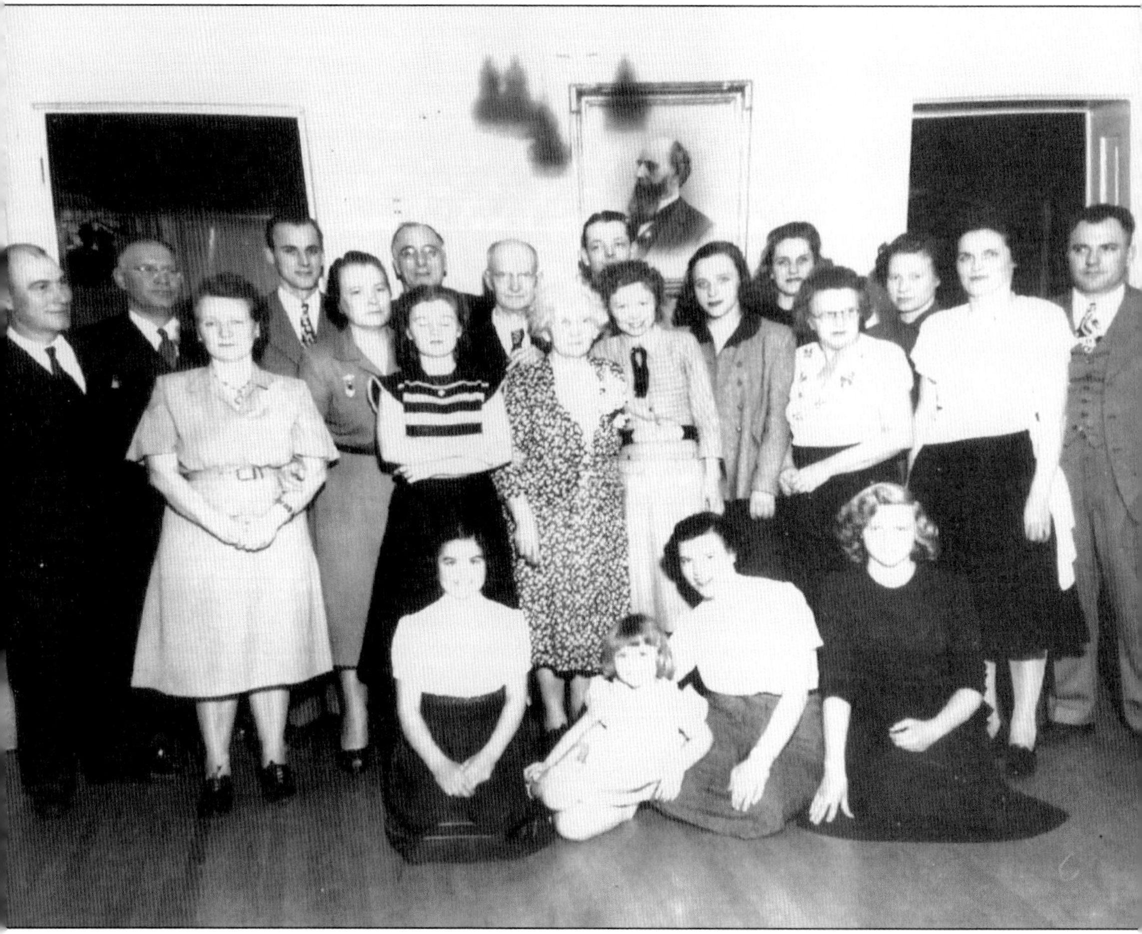

GARDNER FAMILY GATHERING. The Bodden, Gardner, and Sullivan families have been intertwined in the community for more than 100 years. Bodden Lumber Company and Gardner Manufacturing employed many townspeople, and although Bodden Lumber Company is no longer in business, Gardner Manufacturing continues to expand its commerce. Seen here are, from left to right, (first row, seated) Bobbie Gardner, Mary Gardner, Ellen Gardner Lyman, and Ann Gardner Nickodem; (second row) Priscilla Gardner MacDonough, Leone Gardner Hanratty, Leone MacDonough Franzen, Teresa Huettner Gardner, Larrie Gardner, Jessie Gardner, Mildred Bodden Gardner, and Mildred Gardner; (third row) John Gardner, Ed Gardner, John C. Gardner, Clarence John Gardner, John Gardner, Art Sullivan, Mary Gardner Sullivan, Chris Gardner, and Bob Gardner. (Courtesy Jane Sullivan.)

Three

A Town Grows

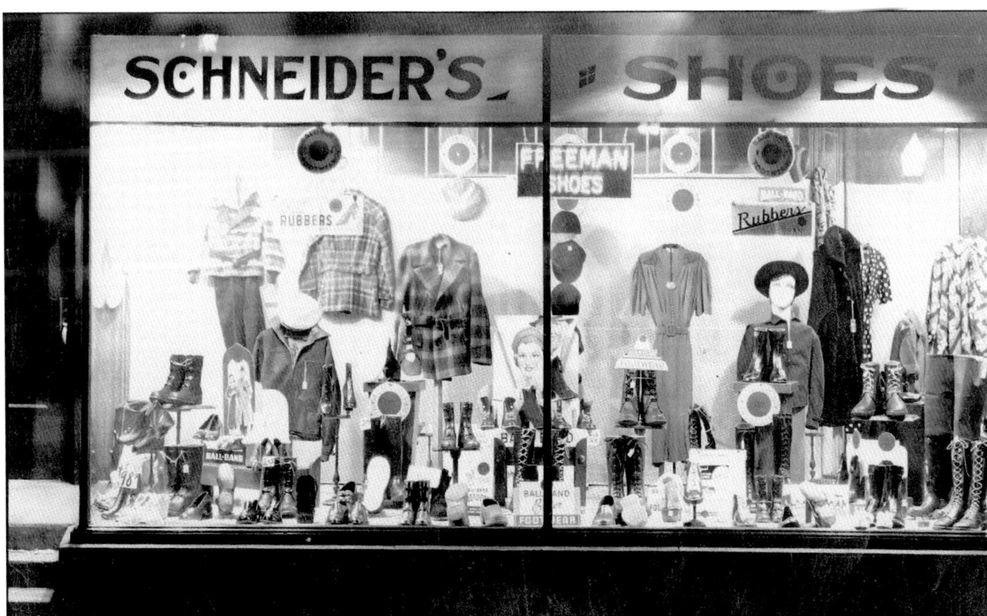

SCHNEIDERS, 1939. Beginning business in the early 1900s, Ernst Schneider and Ervin Ulrich sold men's clothing and shoes at 308 East Lake Street. Ernst's son, George, returned home from service in the navy during World War II, and together they operated a general merchandise store in the Odd Fellow building. (Courtesy George and Margaret Schneider.)

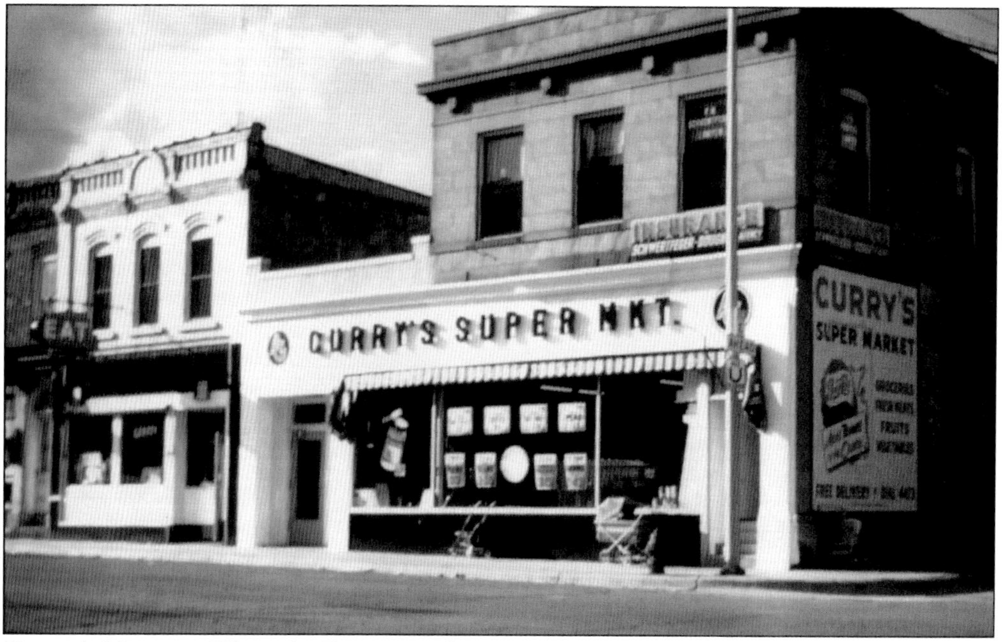

CURRY'S MARKET. When the Depression hit Horicon, First National Bank closed its doors in 1932. Kroger moved from its downtown location to the former home of the bank at what is the present-day northwest corner of East Lake and Vine Streets. After being in business since 1928, Kroger sold out to Irving Curry, who changed the name to Curry's Market. Curry, along with his wife, Emma, and sons Robert and Budford, expanded a few years later when they bought out the one-story appliance shop run by Jake Kolb and Bob Splinter, shown above. The name then changed to Curry's Super Market. Shown below, in the store, from left to right, are Budford Curry, Esther Zarndt, Emma Curry, and Irving Curry II. (Courtesy Christa Curry.)

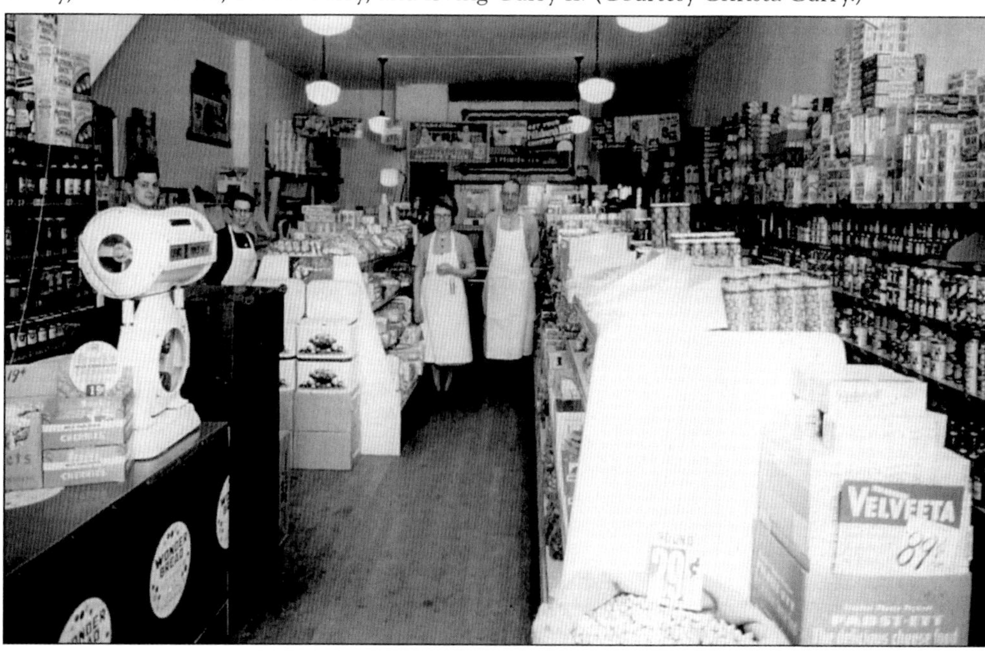

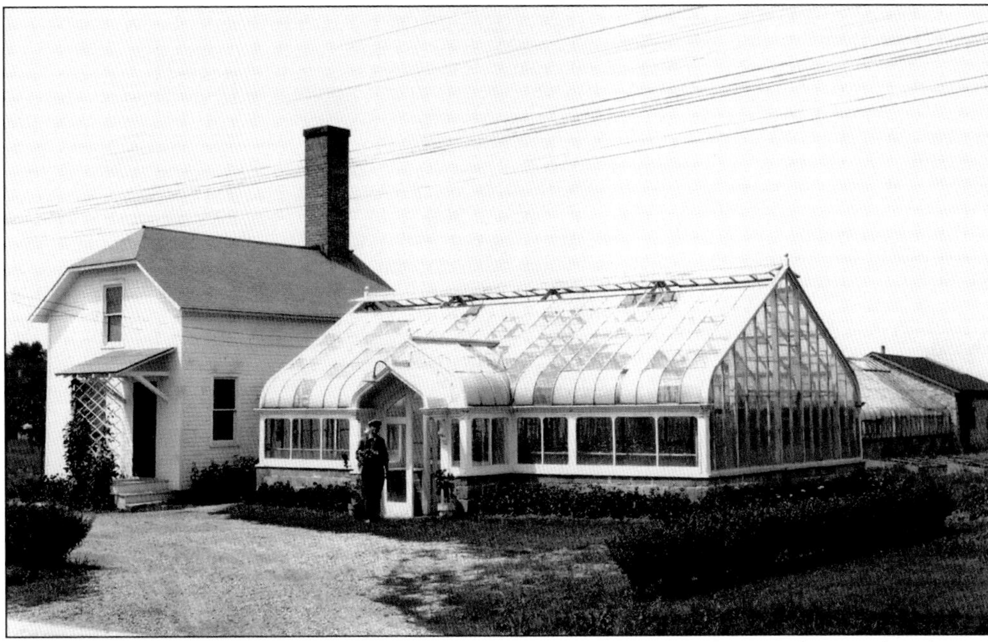

KIESOW FLORAL, 1930S. Henry Kiesow began working in the greenhouse of Howard Wilcox in 1914. Returning from France after World War I, he and his brothers Rudolph and Walter bought the greenhouse in 1923, located in the 200 block of Washington Street. They were the local distributors of many beautiful plants. (Courtesy Horicon Historical Society.)

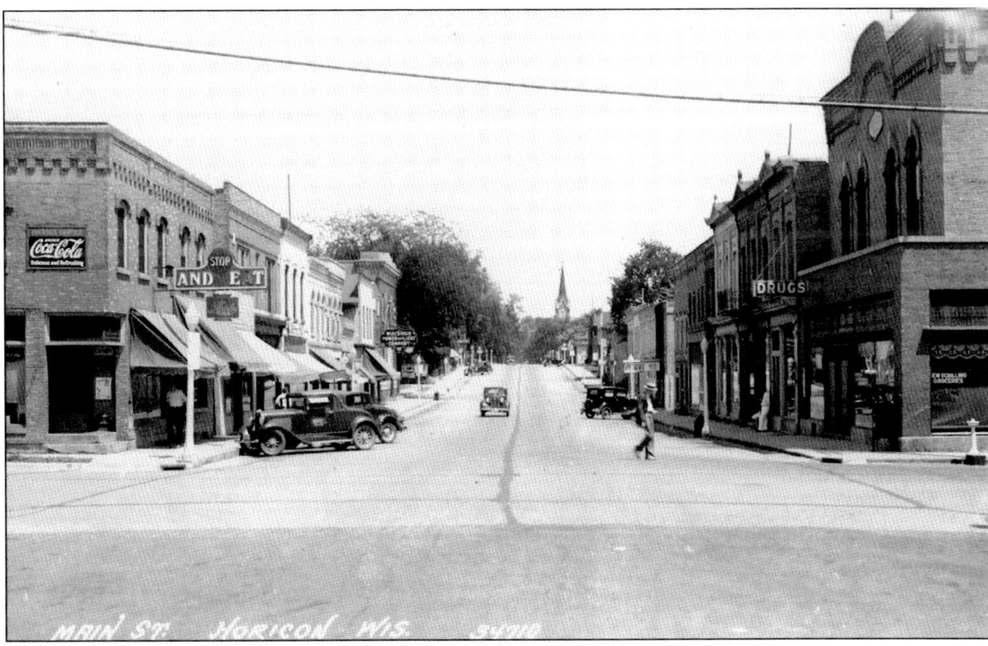

MAIN STREET, 1930S. Looking east, businesses pictured on the left side of the street include Frank Bossman's restaurant on the corner with his tavern next door. Across the street on the first floor of the Odd Fellows building was Schneider's, a general merchandise store, with Bossman's Drug Store located to its right. (Courtesy Horicon Historical Society.)

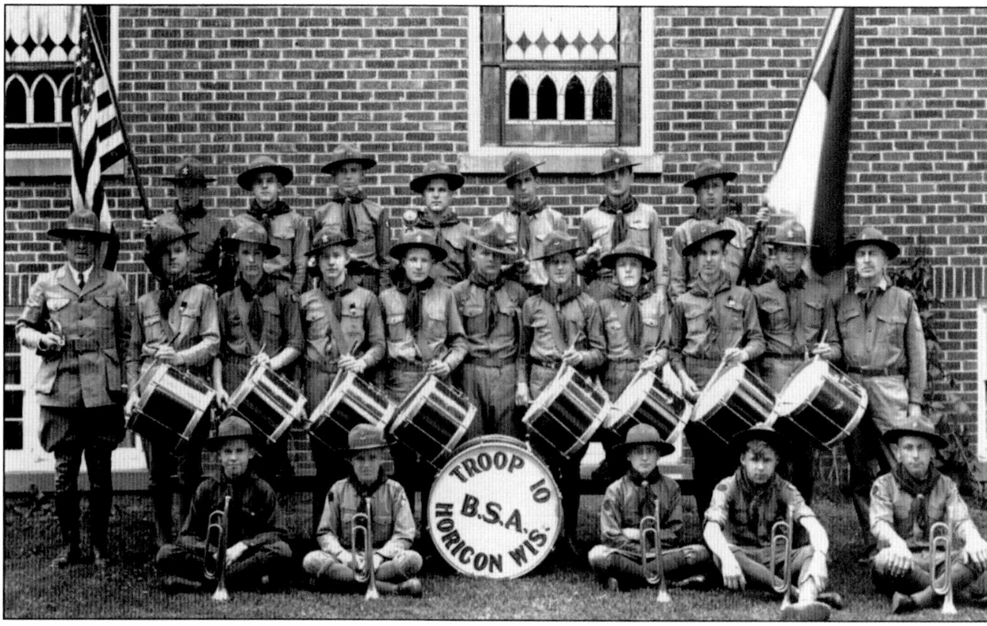

BOY SCOUT TROOP 10, 1932. Seen here are, left to right, (first row) Franklin Freinwald, John Naffin, Robert Neill, Blair Erdman, and Martin Krueger; (second row) drum corps leader Larry Hanson, Wendel Port, ? Erdman, Fred Ulrich, Elton Casper, Clifford Helbing, Bruce Newbauer, Raymond Gadow, Lester Erdman, Ray Smith, and scoutmaster Pastor Haupt; (third row) James Higbee, Glen Ulrich, Raymond Freinwald, Bernard Traeger, Louis Plageman, Stanley Lyons, and Vinnie Vynovick. (Courtesy Horicon Historical Society.)

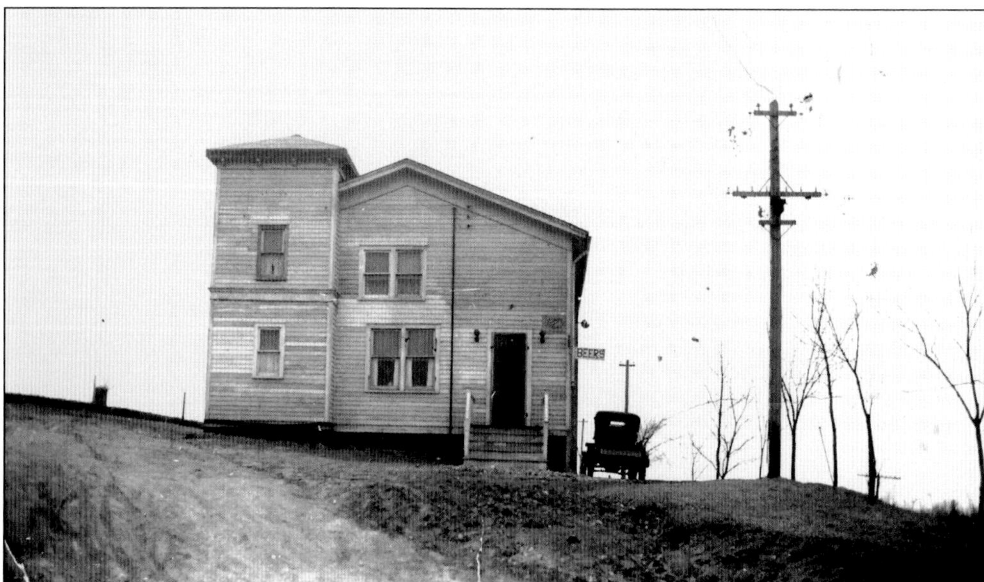

EAGLE HILL TAVERN, 1933. After spending its first years as a Presbyterian church on South Cedar Street, the building was moved to the top of Eagle Hill Road for use as a tavern. It was known for years as the "Old Clubhouse," and proprietors Bobby Burrow and her husband, Lee "Pappy" Burrow, welcomed visitors. After Pappy's death, Bobby continued to run the tavern, and in 1983, she celebrated 50 years in business. (Courtesy Charlotte Burrow.)

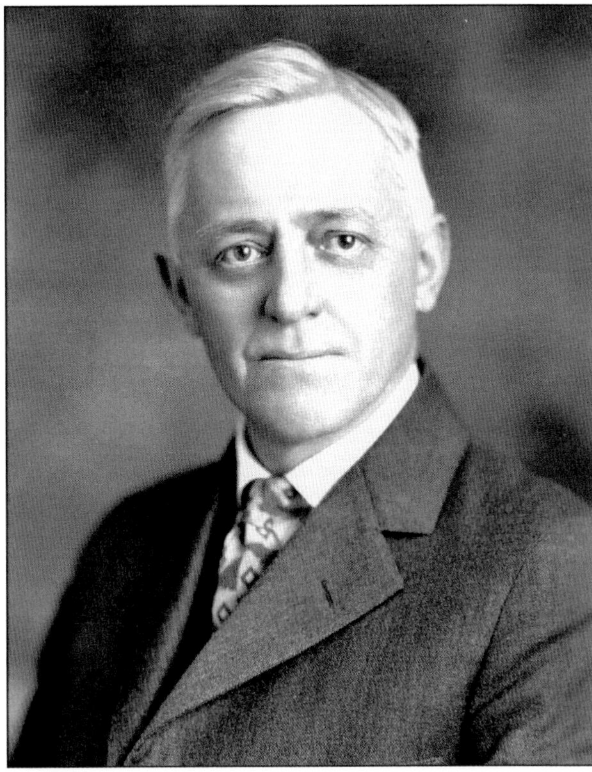

Louis Last Sr. It is not known if he wrote this poem himself or if he just liked its sentiment, but it is nonetheless found written on the back of this photograph and signed by Louis Last: "I've been with you for many years, I am with you heart and soul, No matter what the task may be, Stop not, until you've reached your goal." (Courtesy Horicon Historical Society.)

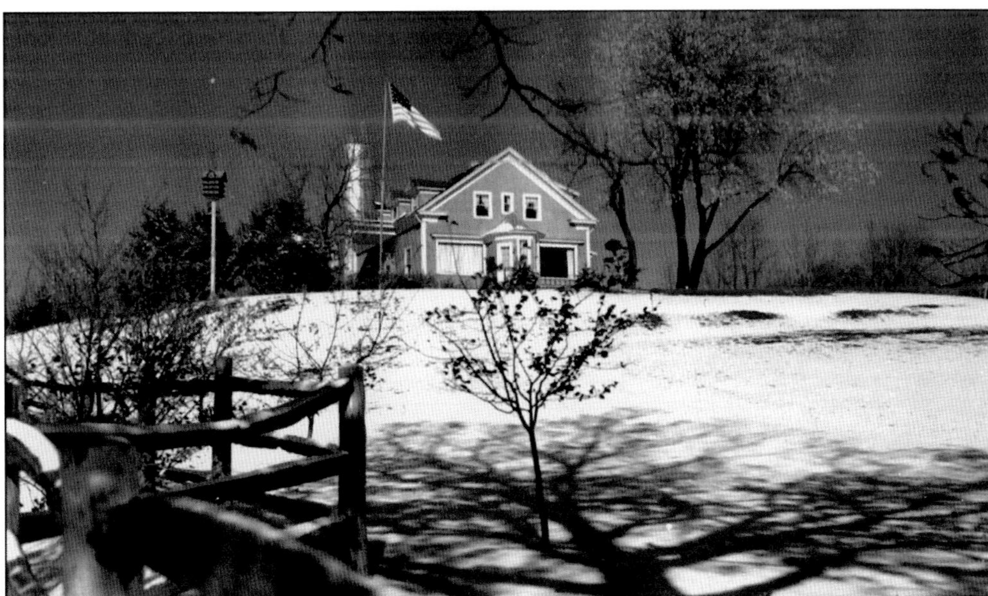

Doc Karsten's Home. Dr. Fred Karsten purchased the building originally known as the Old Country Club and turned it into a home to raise his family. The family lived there for many years, enjoying the view from the top of the hill, before moving to the Campbell home on Walnut Street. Today the home continues to prominently overlook the city as a private residence. (Courtesy John Karsten family.)

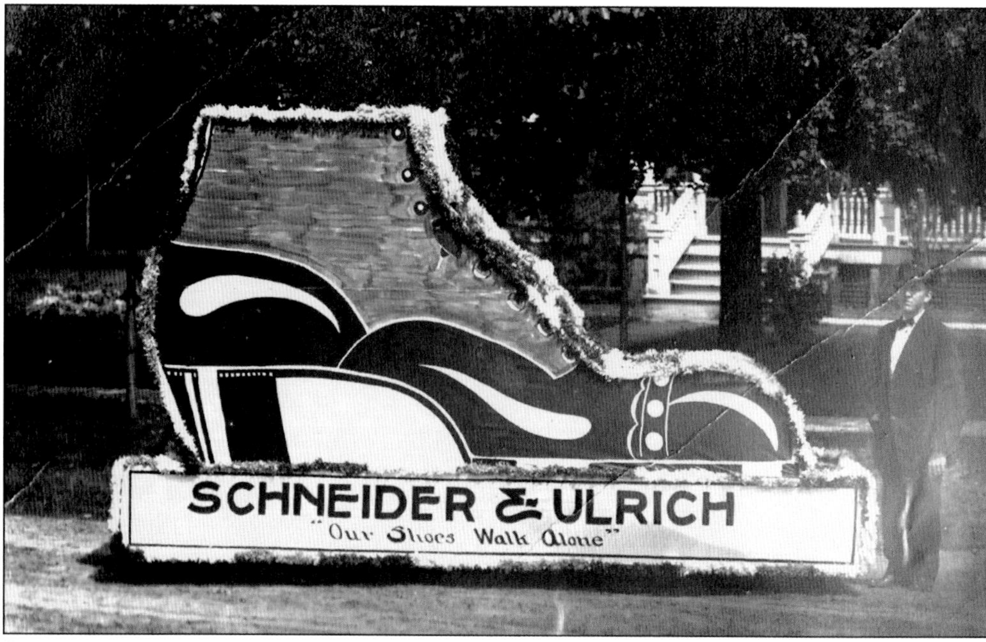

SCHNEIDER AND ULRICH. Parades in the city included floats of different sizes and shapes and usually promoted the business that paid for the construction of the float. This wonderful woman's shoe float proudly advertised the business in town where many a child had his first foot measurement. (Courtesy George and Margaret Schneider.)

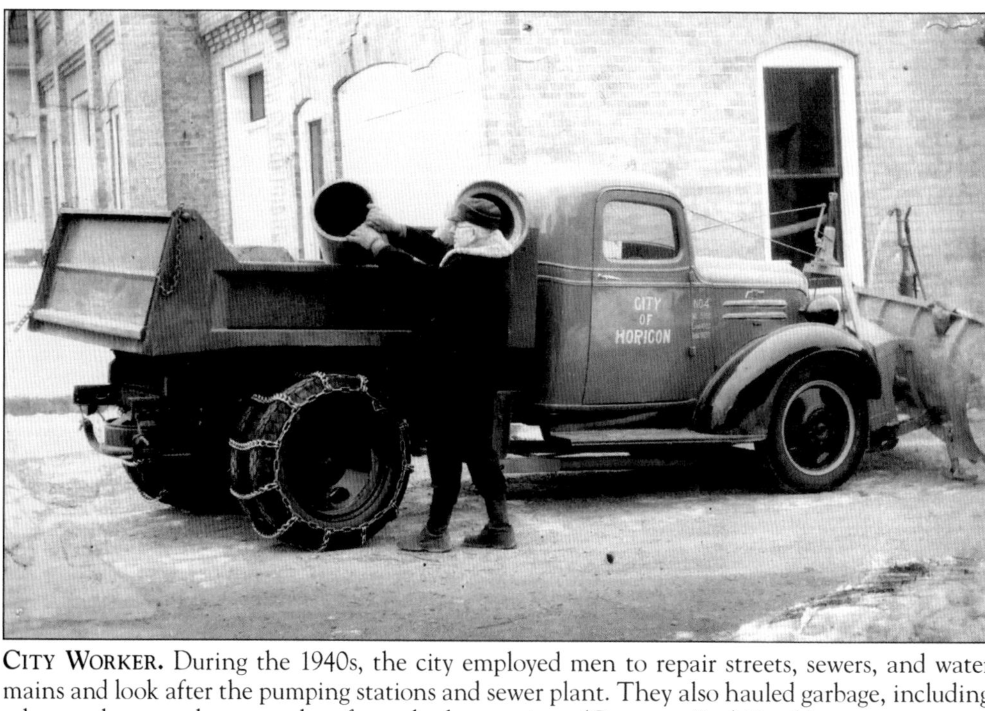

CITY WORKER. During the 1940s, the city employed men to repair streets, sewers, and water mains and look after the pumping stations and sewer plant. They also hauled garbage, including ashes, and removed snow and performed other services. (Courtesy Paul Kruel.)

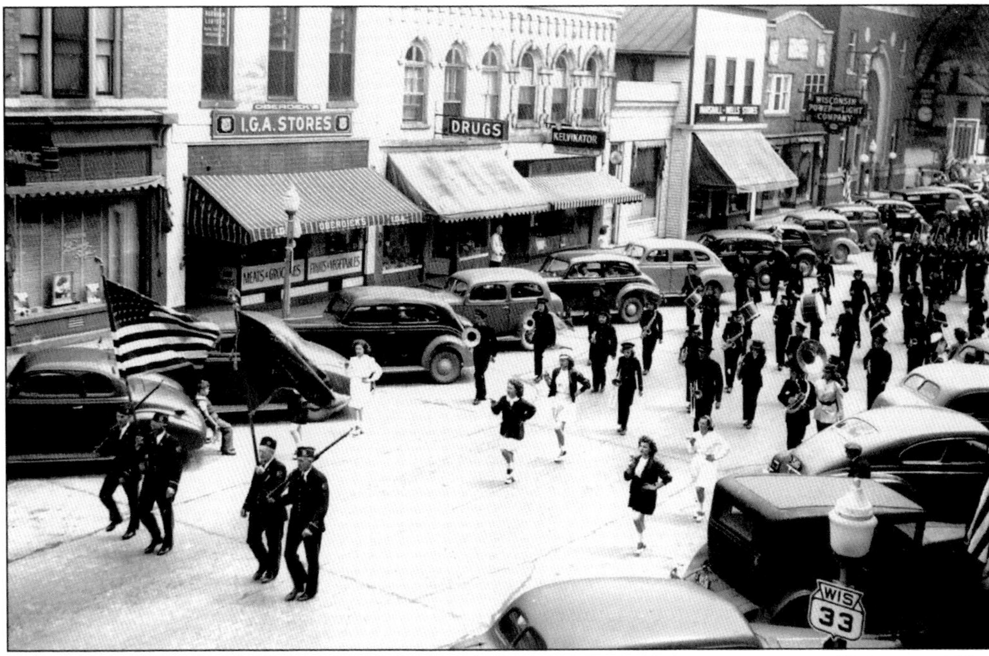

MEMORIAL DAY PARADE, 1940. The town has always been very patriotic, and Memorial Day brought out the best in the people. Leading the parade is the color guard. From left to right are World War I veterans Waldemar Marquart carrying a rifle, Paul Schilling carrying the American Flag, Ernst Schneider carrying the legion flag, and Emil Wegner carrying a rifle. (Courtesy Horicon Historical Society.)

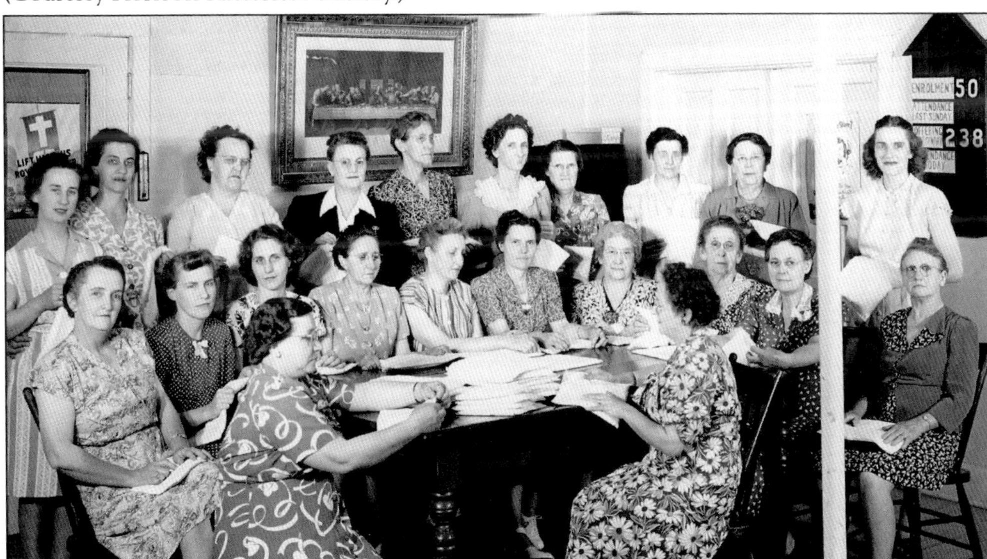

WORLD WAR II FOLDING BANDAGES, 1940S. Red Cross workers headed by Elvira Kohlman are, from left to right, (first row) Esther Genzmer and Louise Feustel; (second row) Sylvia Yorgey, ? Confare, Wyona Eddie, Clara Ulrich, Marcella Krueger, Hilda Willie, Martha Georgii, Lillie Krueger, Alma Miescke, and Minnie Salzman; (third row) Ardis Bernges, Mildred Wendland, Leona Kruel, Elvira Kohlman, Ida Heller, Lillian Zuebtke, Elsie Coyer, Alice Ulrich, Anna Bodden, and Mary Sullivan. (Courtesy Horicon Historical Society.)

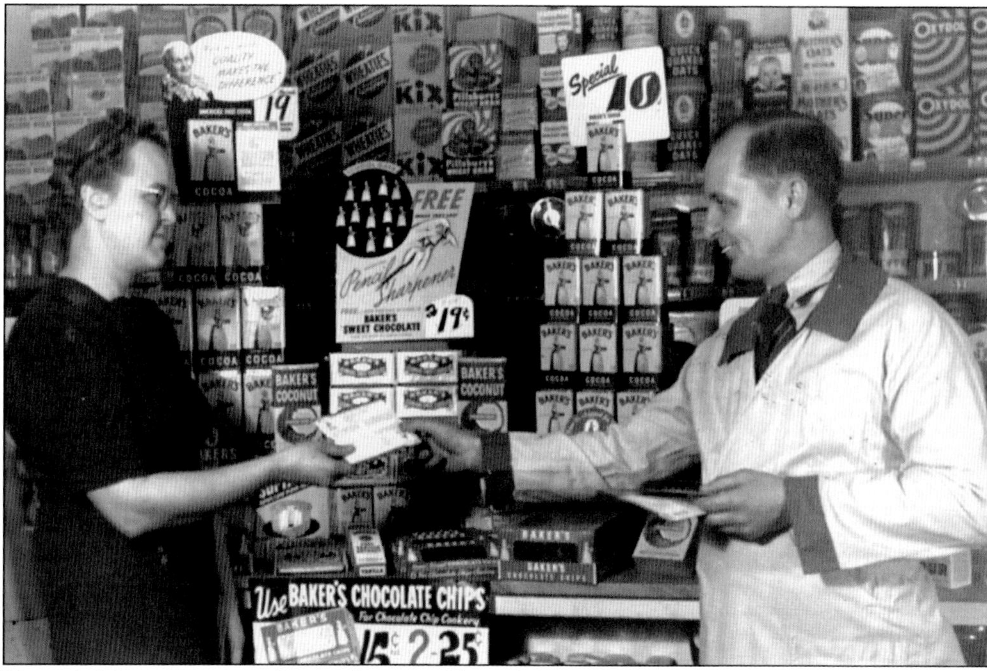

KRUEL'S MARKET, 1942. Originally owned by Adolph Kruel Sr. and run as a meat market from 1896 until 1922, the store was sold to Paul Derber, who owned it until 1930. He then sold the business to Adolph Kruel Jr. and his wife, Leona. It then became a combination grocery and meat market boasting "Dealer in Fresh and Salt Meats, Fish and Sausages—Highest Price Paid for Hides." After owning the store for more than 13 years, it was time for Adolph, or Addie, as he was known, to give it a well-deserved face-lift. The store is shown below after its remodel. Although the tree pictured at left in this photograph has since been removed, the building continues to stand on the southwest corner of East Lake and Elm Streets and is home to Old Time Food Store. (Courtesy Paul Kruel.)

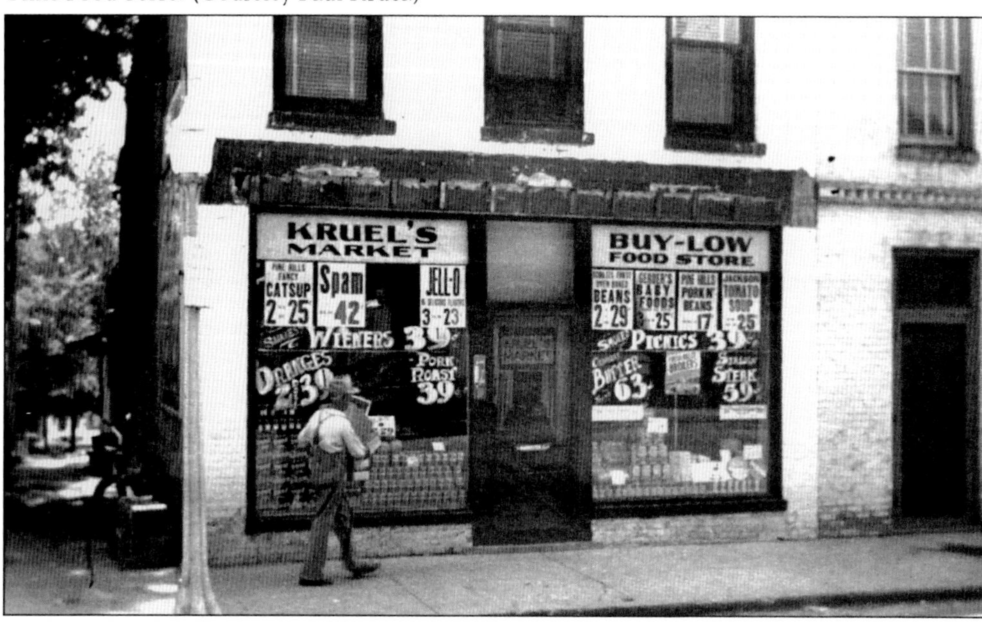

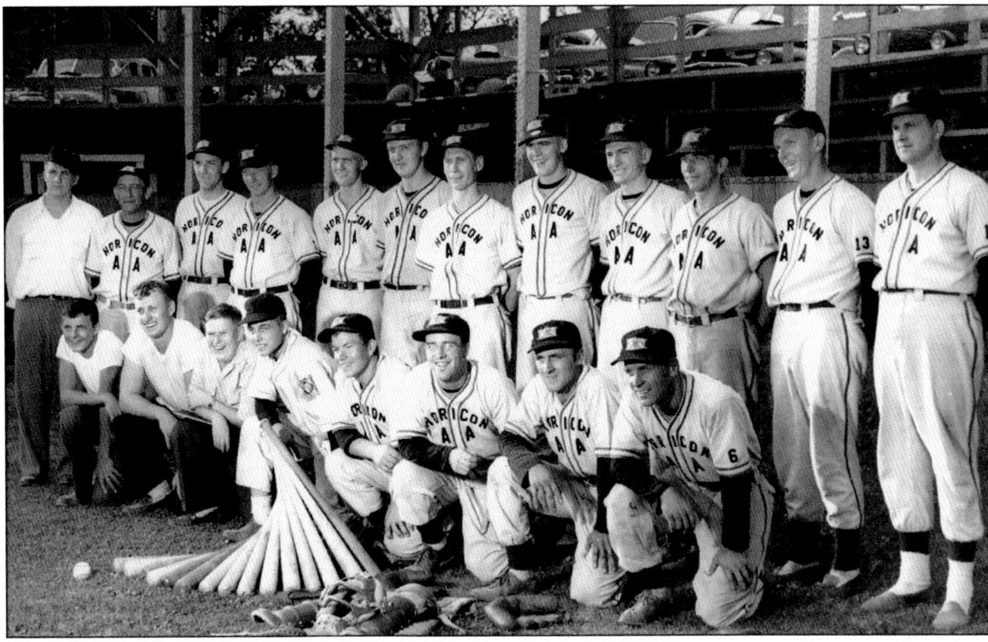

CITY BASEBALL TEAM, LATE 1940S. Sports can be a big affair in a small town. Seen here are, from left to right, (first row) Carl Steffen, Lloyd Wagener, Russell Goll, Keith Schwartz, Reinhard Kiesow, Merlin Frank, Elroy Johnson, and Orville Kiesow; (second row) John Weber, Bud Johnson, George Schneider, Emil Greshay, Orville Kamrath, Bud Bischoff, Ray Schilling, Elroy Kamrath, Don Plageman, Boyd Rohde, Emil Bischoff, and Joe Beall. (Courtesy Horicon Historical Society.)

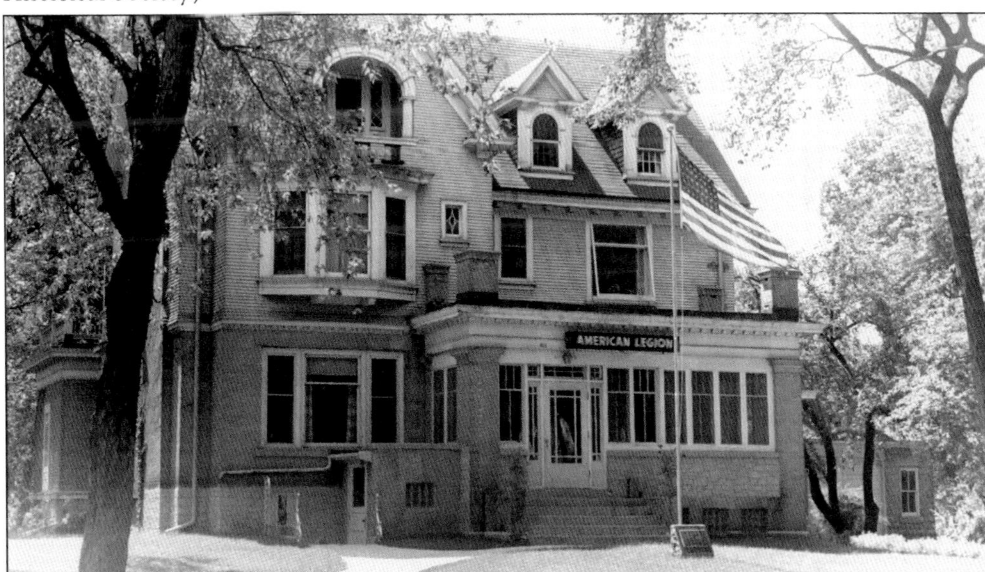

AMERICAN LEGION POST. Originally known as the Campbell house, then the C. B. Cotton property, the home was offered to the Legion post and was used as such from 1945 until 1963. Due to high upkeep, the Legion opened a beer bar in the basement, which was the subject of much controversy. Dr. Fred Karsten bought the property in 1963 and converted it to family use. (Courtesy John Karsten family.)

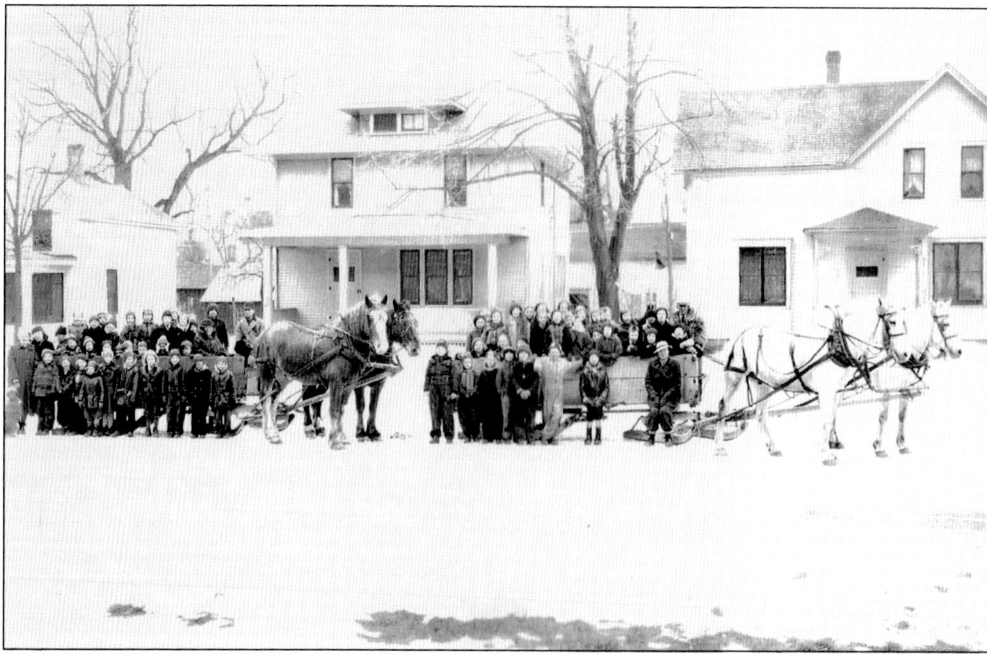

CHRISTMAS OUTING. George Schneider recalls that Russell Wilcox had daughters in school, and for a special treat for the schoolchildren, he had horse-drawn sleighs take the students from school and ride about the city streets. Although the year in which this photograph was taken is unknown, it harkens back to a time when the simple things in life were enjoyed by one and all. (Courtesy George and Margaret Schneider.)

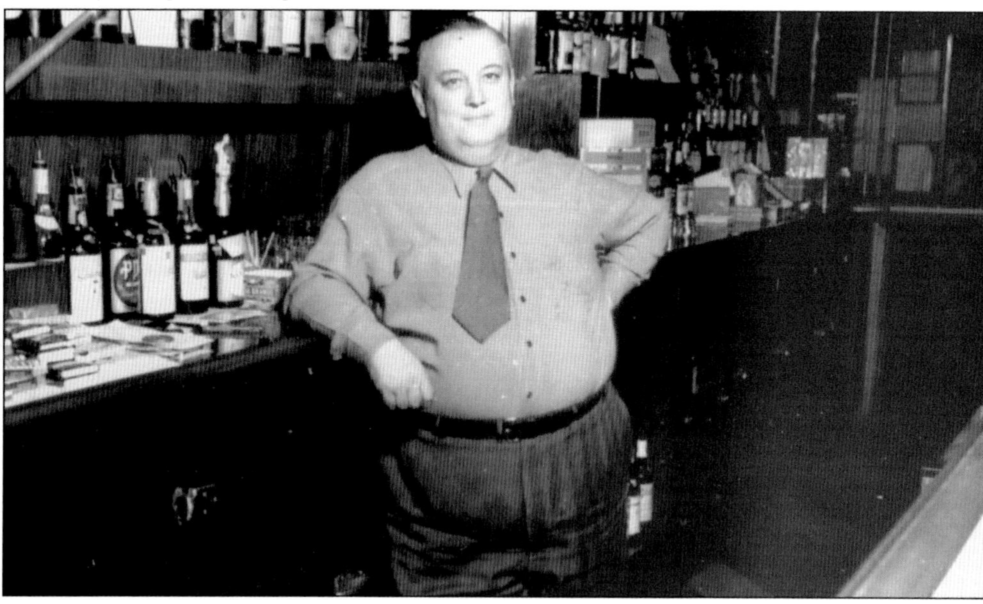

CARL "FAT" KASTEN, 1945. Beginning his operations in 1930, Kasten was an active member of the city's chamber of commerce. It is fitting that the building that housed Fat's Tavern now houses the Horicon Chamber of Commerce and the Rehse Insurance Agency. Kasten, an avid fiddle player, was known to frequent Eagle Hill Tavern and play for the guests. (Courtesy Rehse Insurance Agency.)

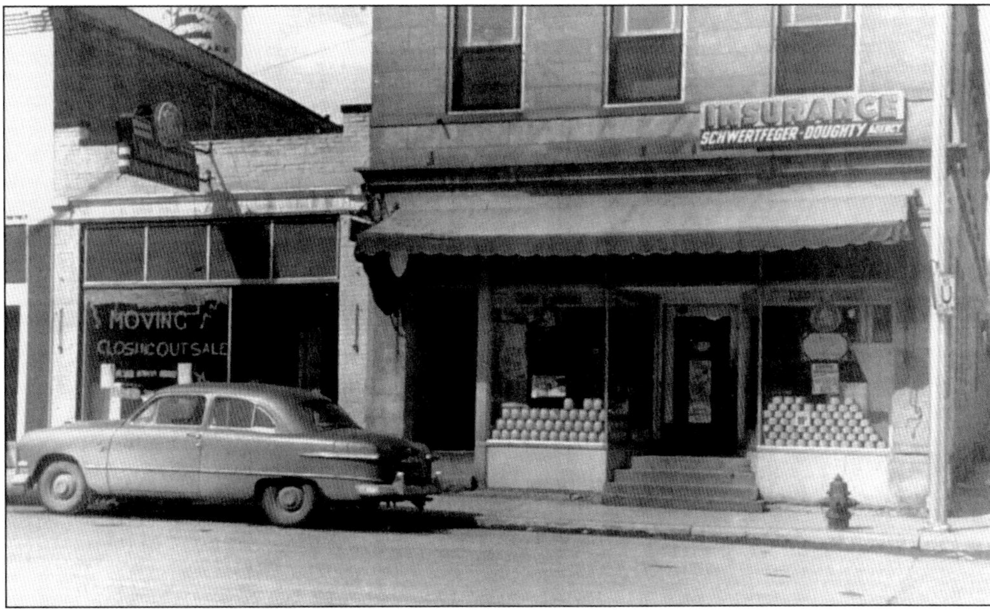

SCHWERTFEGER-DOUGHTY INSURANCE. Attorney Fred Schwertfeger returned from service in World War II and along with his sister Esther Doughty-Luckhardt opened the Schwertfeger-Doughty Insurance Company on Lake Street. Later Doughty-Luckhardt would be elected to the Wisconsin State Assembly, serving from 1963 to 1983. She continues to reside in Horicon. Curry's Market was located on the first floor of the same building. (Courtesy Christa Curry.)

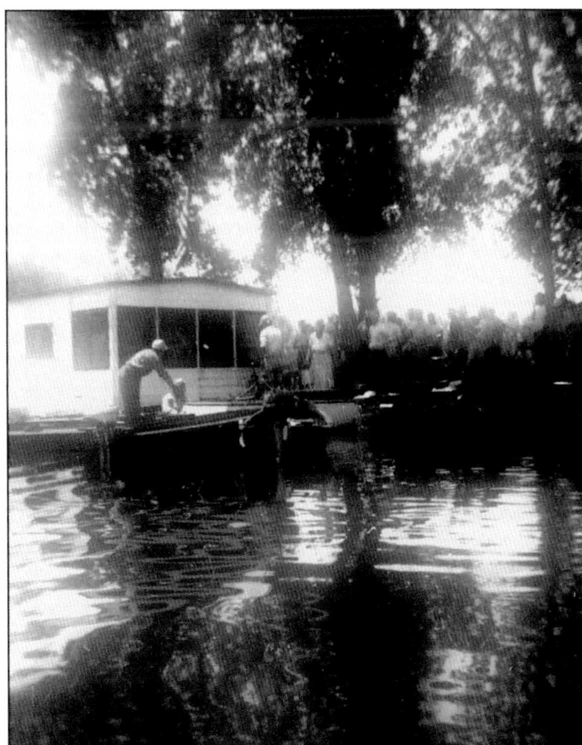

VETERANS' FISH FRY, 1940S. Known by all to take care of the veterans in the area, Horicon tavern keepers Bobby and Lee Burrow would take men out for a day of fishing on their boat. At the end of the day, Bobby would cook the fish and feed the veterans a full meal, always letting them know their efforts serving their country were well appreciated. (Courtesy Charlotte Burrow.)

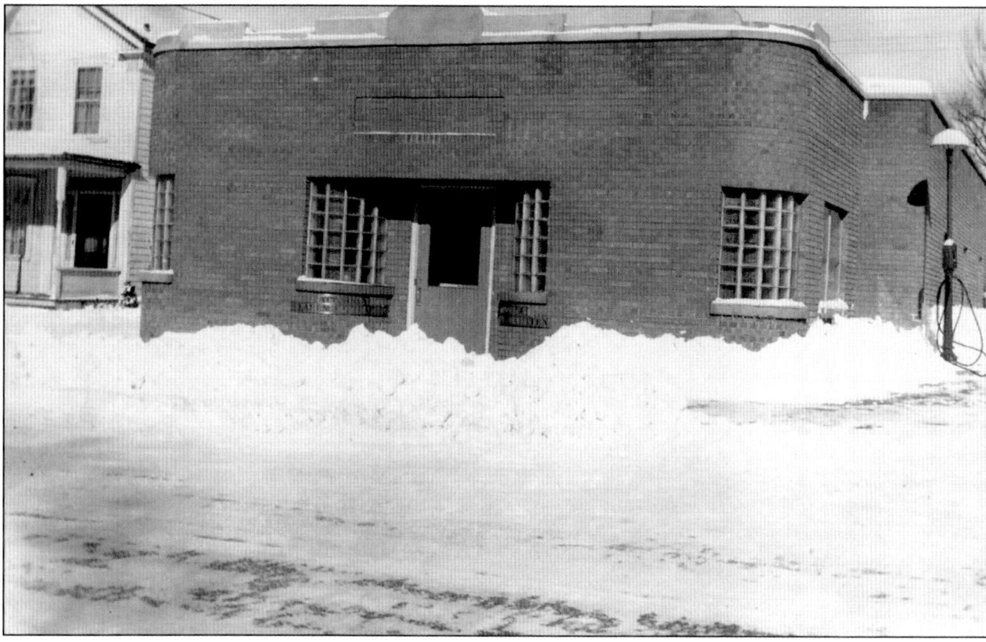

KARSTEN AND TRAEGER, 1948. Needing a more spacious facility at which to see his patients, Dr. John Karsten paired up with attorney Clarence Traeger and built this art moderne building located at 514 East Lake Street. Karsten's office was on one half of the building, and Traeger's was on the other. The building remains today and is easy to locate due to its unique architecture. (Courtesy John Karsten family.)

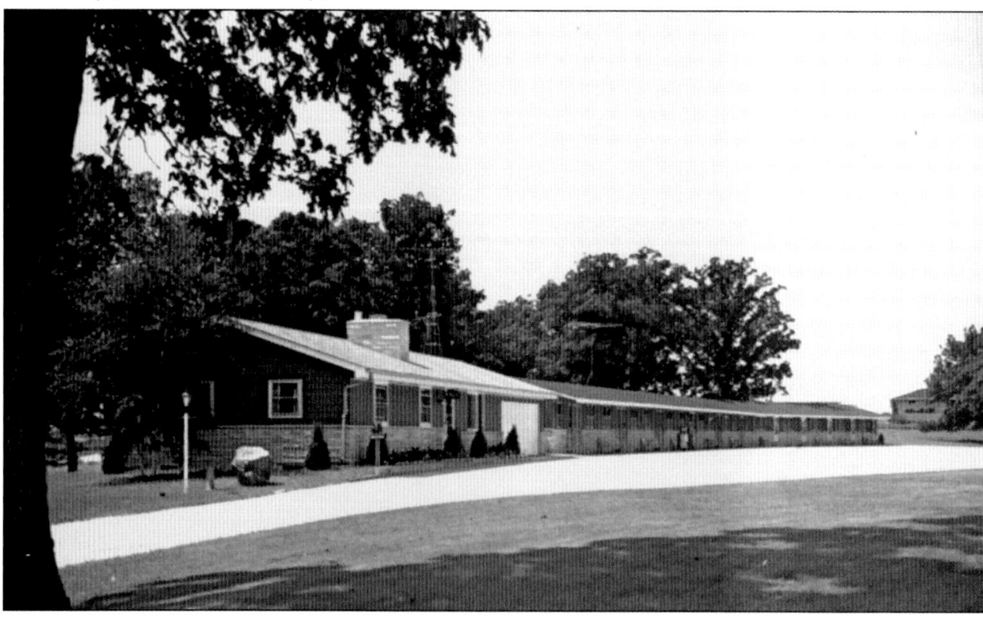

ROYAL OAKS MOTEL, 1950S. Upon entering Horicon from the east, visitors know they have reached the city when they see the Royal Oaks Motel off Highway 33. Built in 1954, the motel has been catering to visitors ever since. Current owners Robert and Joan Cira have been managing the motel since 1986, when they purchased it from her parents, Ruth and Richard Weber. (Courtesy Horicon Historical Society.)

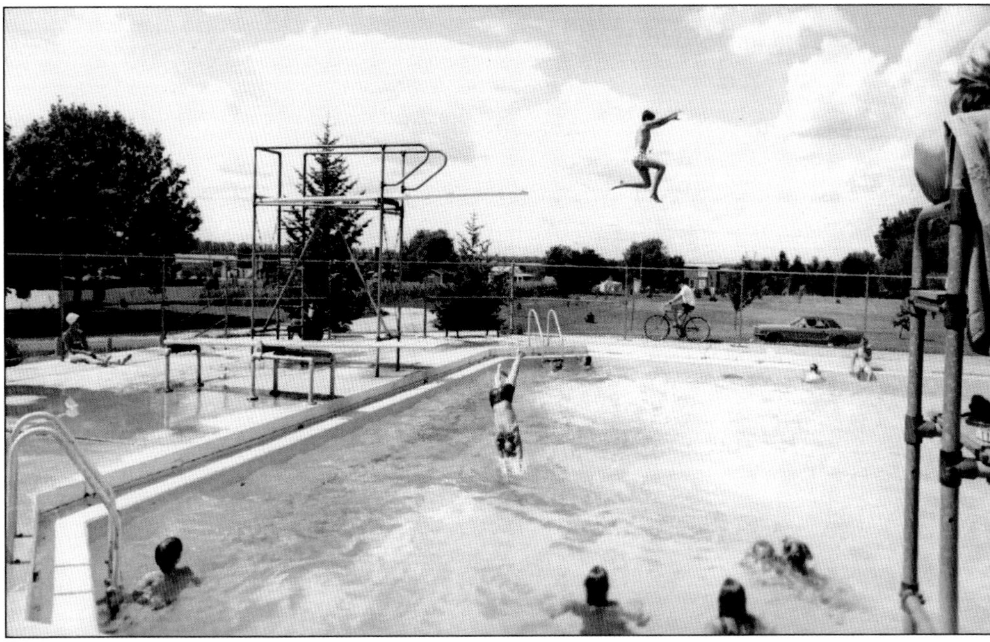

SWIMMING POOL. Discher Park was home to the swimming pool in the 1950s and has since been replaced with the larger and improved Aquatic Center at 800 North Finch Street. Generations of children have enjoyed the water from Memorial Day to Labor Day each year, taking lessons and showing off their skills. Special events throughout the summer months provide a fantastic setting for fun family gatherings. (Courtesy Horicon Reporter.)

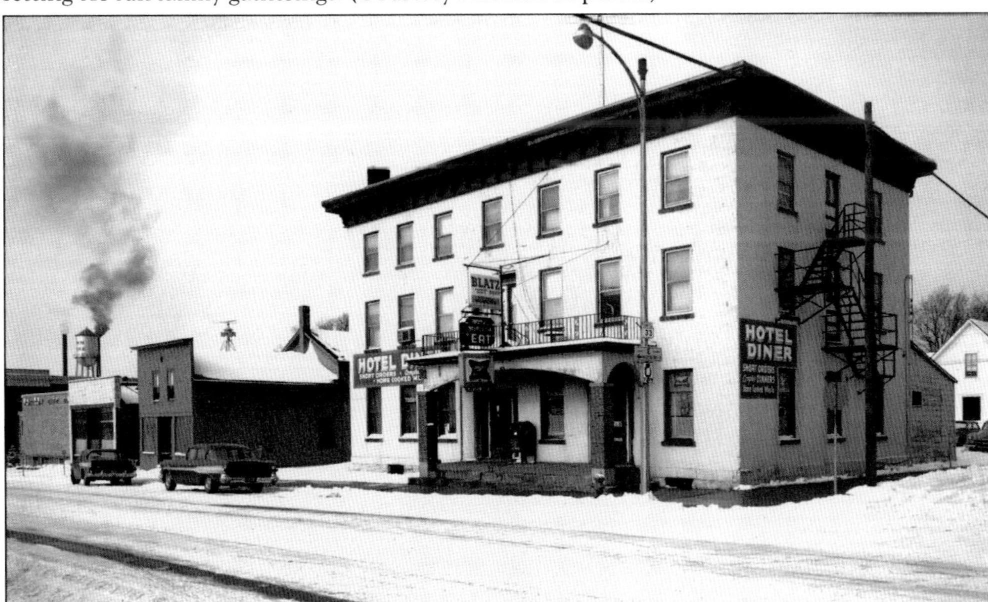

HORICON HOTEL, 1950S. Built in 1855 by Peter Winter, the hotel changed many times over its years in the city. Situated on East Lake Street and South Elm Street, Anna Weymier's good home cooking was known by visitors and residents alike. After Weymier's departure in 1946, William Messner added a lunch counter and new kitchen equipment. The building was razed with the federal building now occupying that parcel. (Courtesy Horicon Historical Society.)

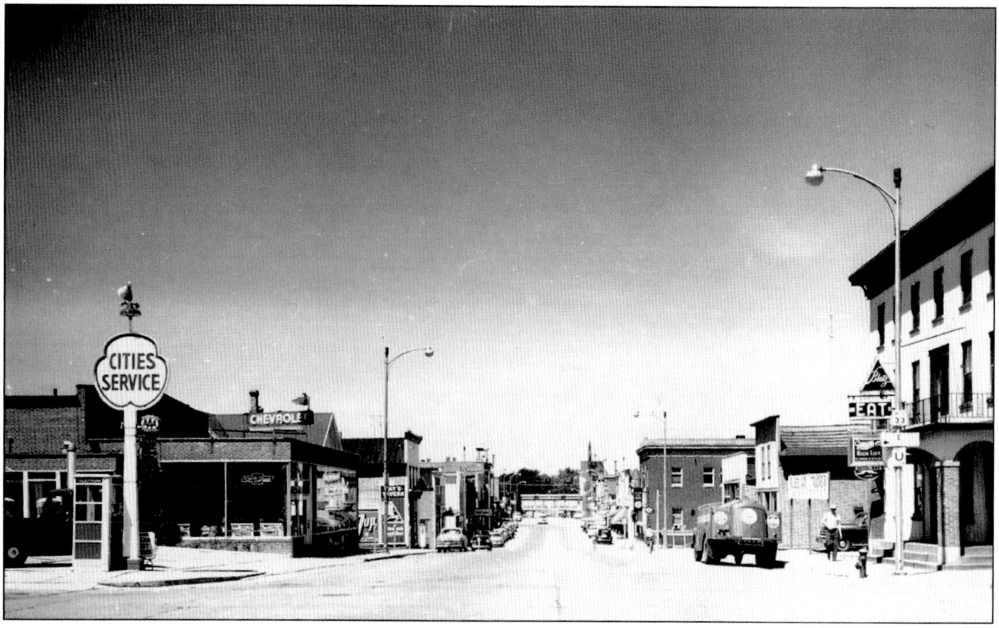

CITIES SERVICE AND CHEVROLET DEALER. Located at 417 East Lake Street across from the Horicon Hotel, car sales and repair were available at Cities. Fat's Tavern was within walking distance and John Deere-Van Brunt Company is visible in the background. The corner is now home to Mother's Day Family Restaurant. (Courtesy Horicon Historical Society.)

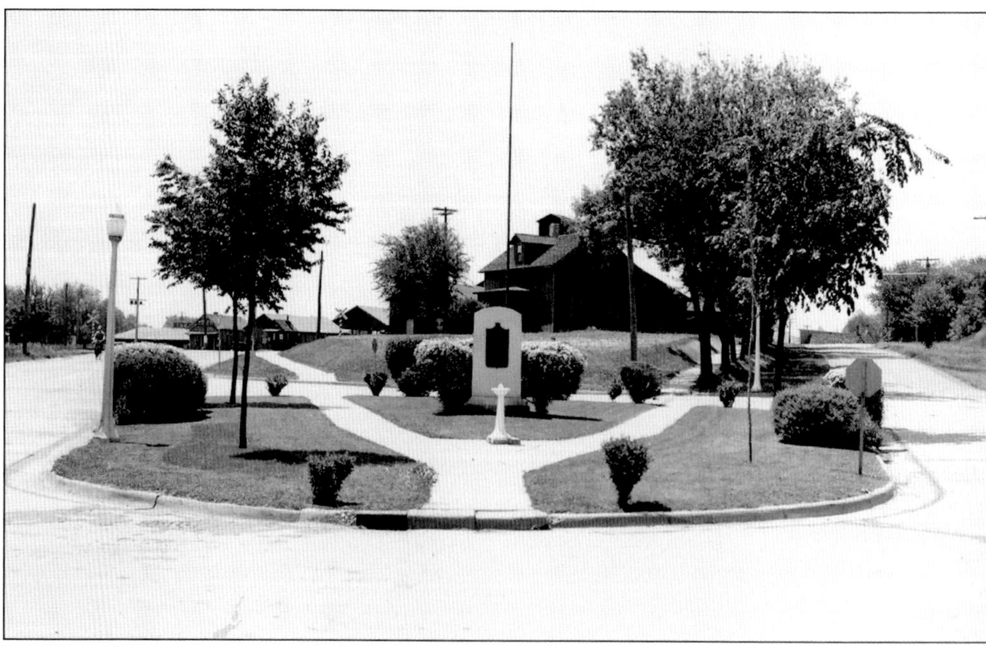

VETERANS' MEMORIAL. Located at the intersection of Barstow and Kansas Streets, Horicon's Veterans' Memorial honors the hometown heroes who lost their lives fighting for freedom. Sadly for this small town, 24 names are engraved in stone, spanning World War I, World War II, Korea, Vietnam, and Desert Storm. (Courtesy Horicon Historical Society.)

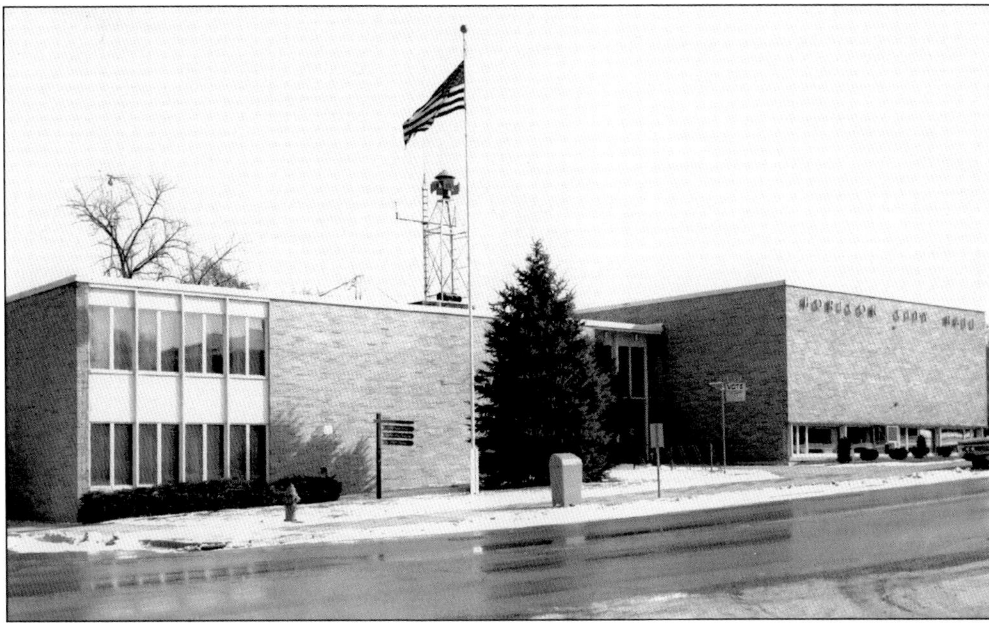

CITY HALL, 1957. Horicon's first city hall was located west of the present East Lake and Vine Streets intersection on the south side of the road. Construction began in 1892 with William Firehammer of Horicon being awarded the $15,760 contract. When the new city hall was constructed, it housed the fire, EMS (emergency medical services), and police services on the first floor, where the Horicon Public Library is located today. (Courtesy Horicon Historical Society.)

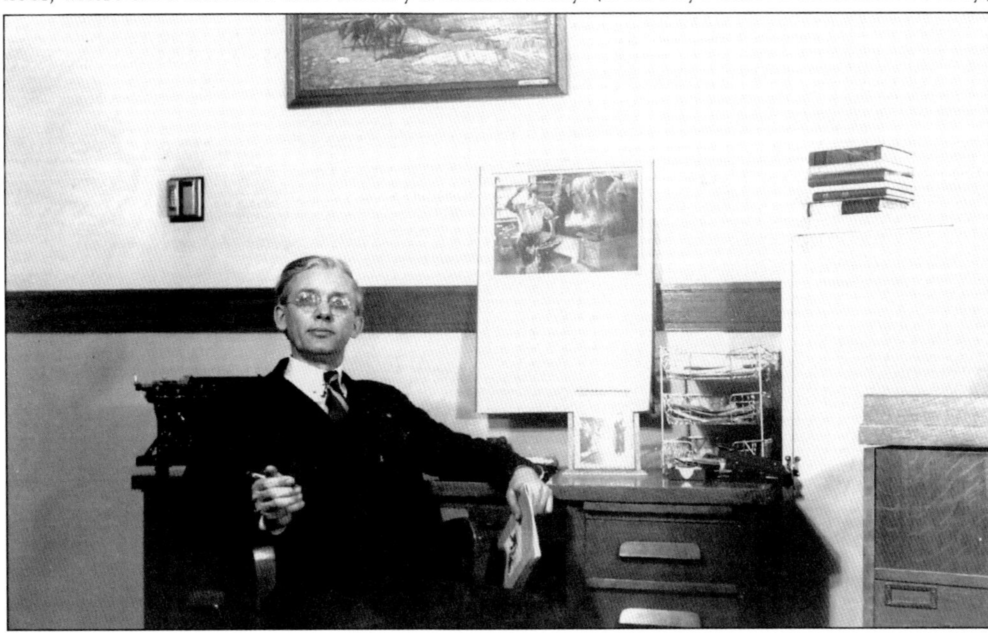

WALTER BUSSEWITZ. The popular school superintendent was head of the Horicon School District for many years. Always community minded, Walter Bussewitz was very active in the Horicon Rotary Club, serving as district governor for numerous years. He also coauthored the invaluable *History of Horicon* with schoolteacher Allie Freeman in 1948 and ran as a Democratic candidate for the Wisconsin State Senate's 13th District in 1954. (Courtesy Horicon Historical Society.)

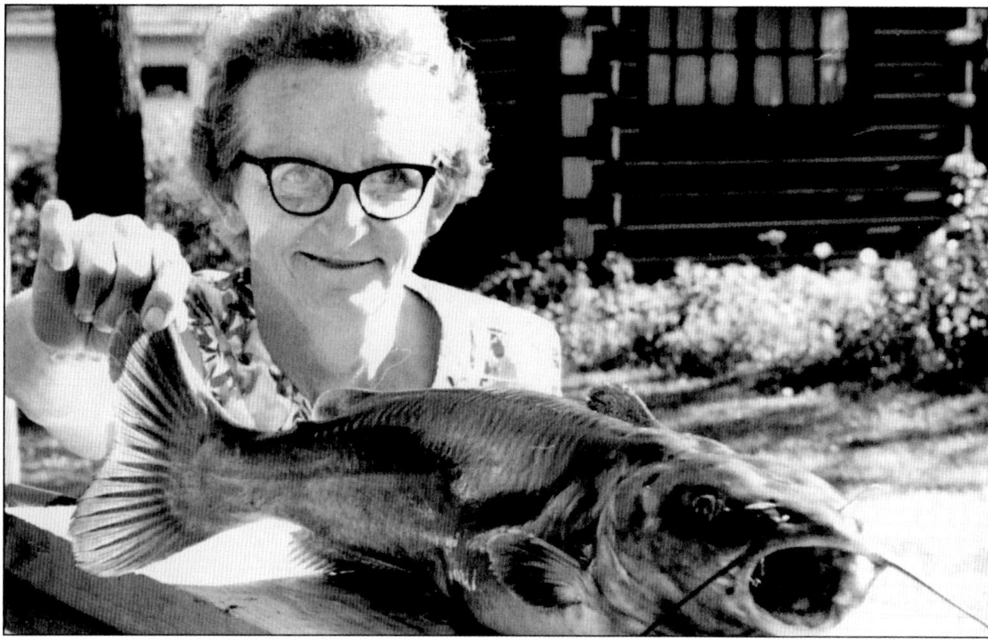

FISHING, LATE 1950S. Catfish could be found in abundance in the Rock River and made for a great family meal. Alice Henkel, wife of Lawrence, proudly shows off the six-pound catfish that she caught using only a cane pole and a worm. (Courtesy Horicon Reporter.)

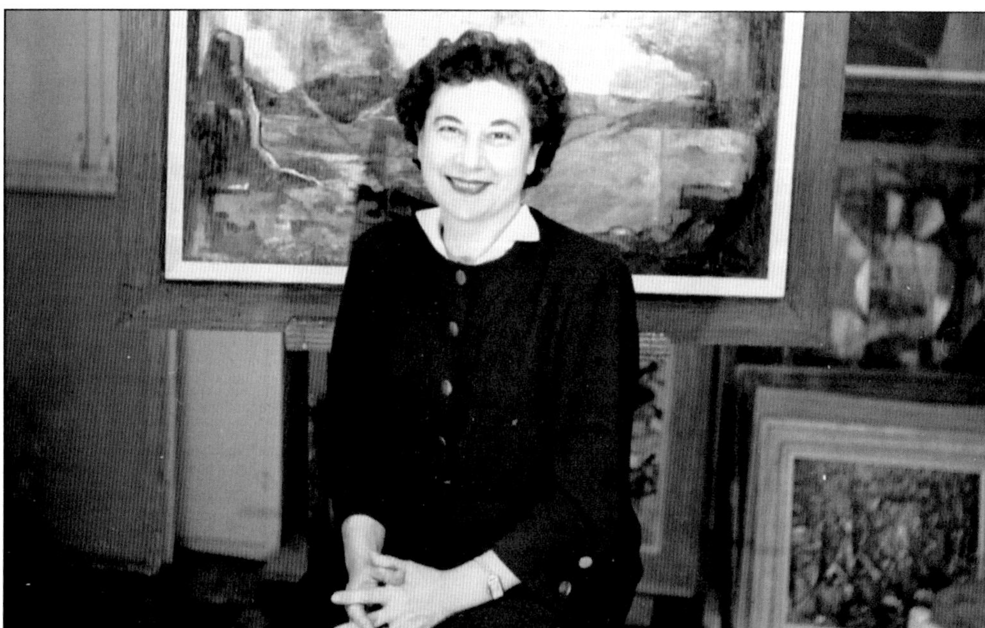

MIMI DUBOIS BOLTON, 1950S. Paul and Anna Hoffman's adopted daughter, named Frieda Hoffman at birth, became well known. She wrote the book *So I Became an Artist: An Autobiography of Mimi Dubois Bolton, Painter, Author, Poet.* She is sitting in front of her painting *Summer Landscape*. The Horicon Historical Society happily received a table donated by Mimi Bolton that was made by her father, Paul. (Courtesy Horicon Historical Society.)

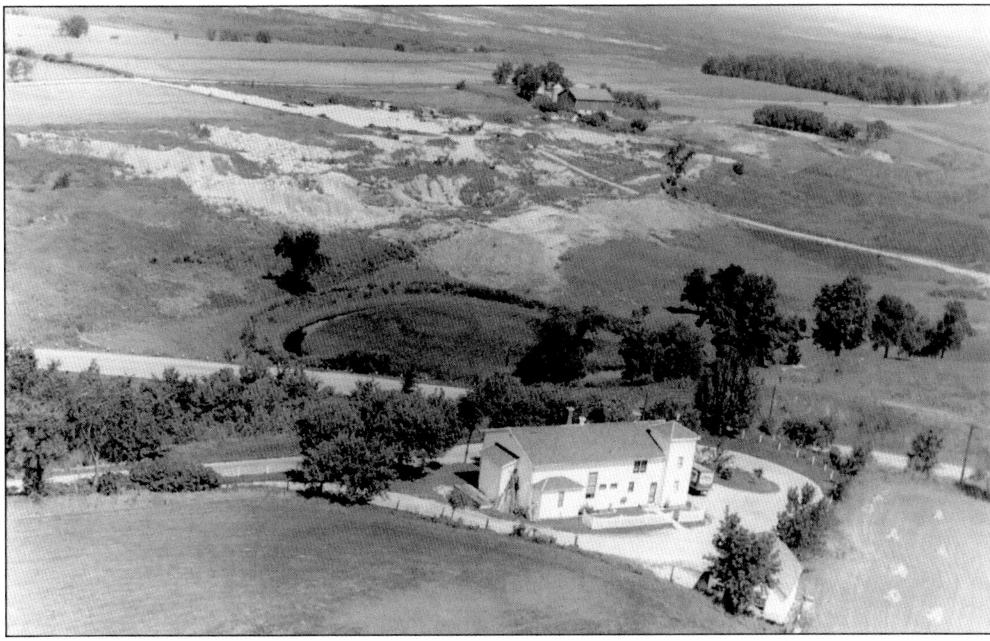

EAGLE HILL, 1950S. When Bobby and Lee Burrow opened their tavern, there was no running water. For three years, they carried water uphill from a nearby farm and melted snow in the winter to do the washing. To remedy the problem, in 1936, Lee dug a 900-foot trench by hand down the hill to the water main to bring water up to the tavern. (Courtesy Charlotte Burrow.)

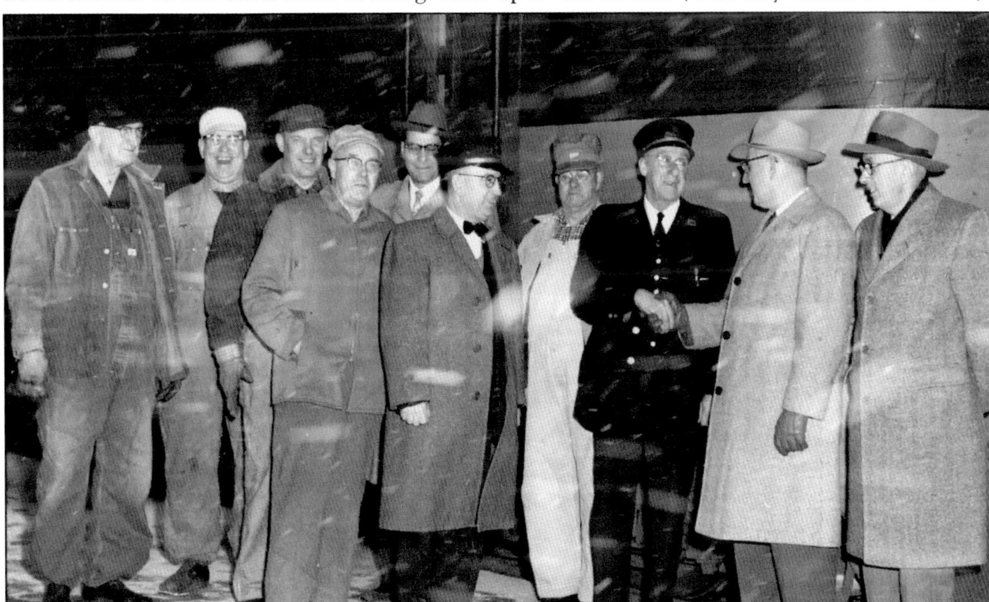

CENTURY OF RAILROAD, 1955. Celebrating 100 years of service to Horicon, the Chicago, Milwaukee, St. Paul, and Pacific Railroad observed the event at the depot. Present are, from left to right, engineer Paul Denis, fireman M. Cawley, depot agent Clair Brunner, baggage man A. A. Pinske, district trainmaster Paul Bridenstine, conductor Ray Foley, brakeman Don Powell, morning passenger train conductor A. G. Ingles, Mayor Ben Tietz, and city clerk Merlin Bernges. (Courtesy Patrick Brunner.)

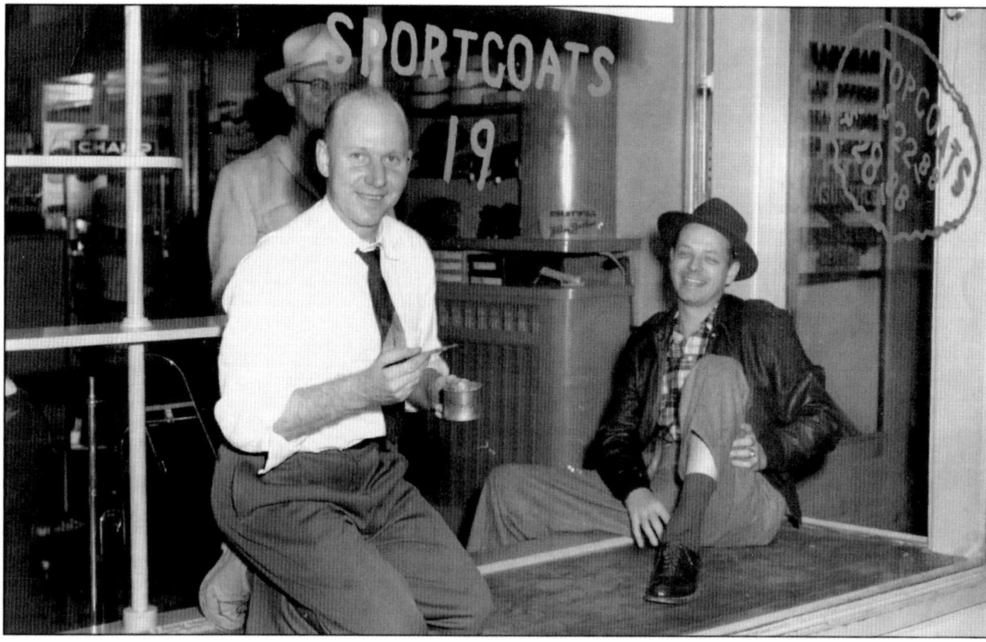

ULRICH'S CLOTHING STORE, 1956. Fred Ulrich, on left, chats amicably with Art Sullivan (seated) while painting his advertising on the front of the store. Fred's father, Ervin Ulrich, had run a clothing store in town for 28 years before he passed away with Fred continuing the family tradition. Today Michelle Wanie's American Family Insurance Agency is housed in the building. (Courtesy Mary Sullivan.)

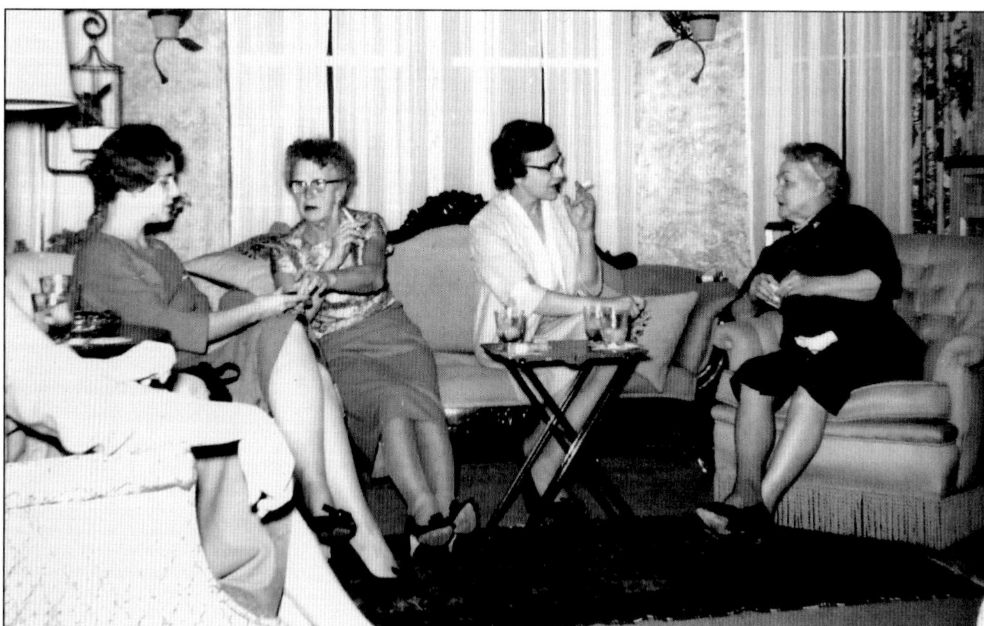

CHRISTMAS, 1958. Enjoying an evening during the holiday season are members of the well-known Gardner family. Pictured are, from left to right, an unidentified woman; Mildred Gardner, wife of Clarence Gardner and owner of Gardner Manufacturing; Jessie Gardner, daughter of Mildred and Clarence; and Daisy Sullivan, mother of Arthur Sullivan. (Courtesy Mary Sullivan.)

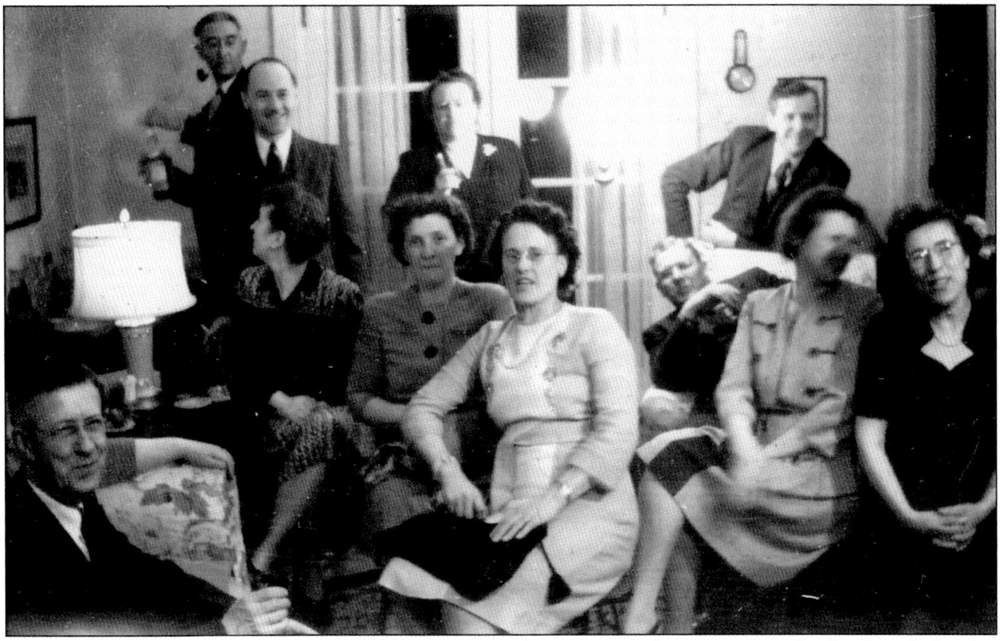

SOCIAL GATHERING. Many town residents would gather in the evenings for food and drinks, while others would sit for a round of Sheepshead, a local card game. Seated are, from left to right, Sidney Wilke, Lois Bird, Hazel Radcliffe, Leona Wilke, Elmer Howe, Zelda Mitchell, and Emma Curry. Standing are, from left to right, Lynn Osborne, Gibbie Bird, Dot Jones, and Gomer Jones. (Courtesy Horicon Historical Society.)

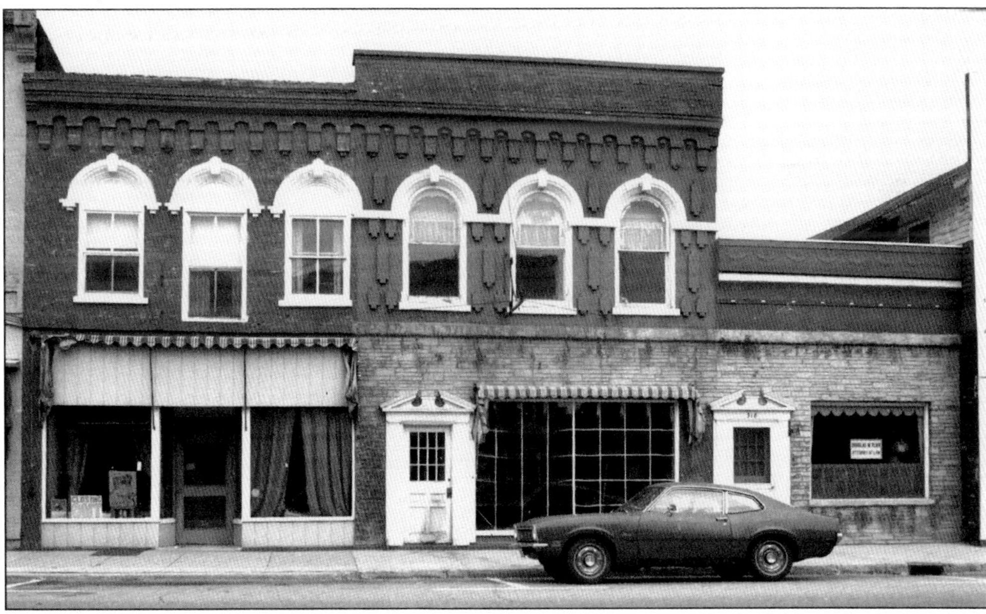

LAKE STREET SHOPS. Located west of today's Horicon Bank, all the buildings in this undated photograph have been razed. Pictured at the left is the building that housed a tin shop before a drugstore took up residence. Next door, the Wisconsin Telephone Company was the second-floor tenant while a furniture store was located at street level. The one-story building's final incarnation was as Roy Maas's photography studio. (Courtesy Fred Schwertfeger.)

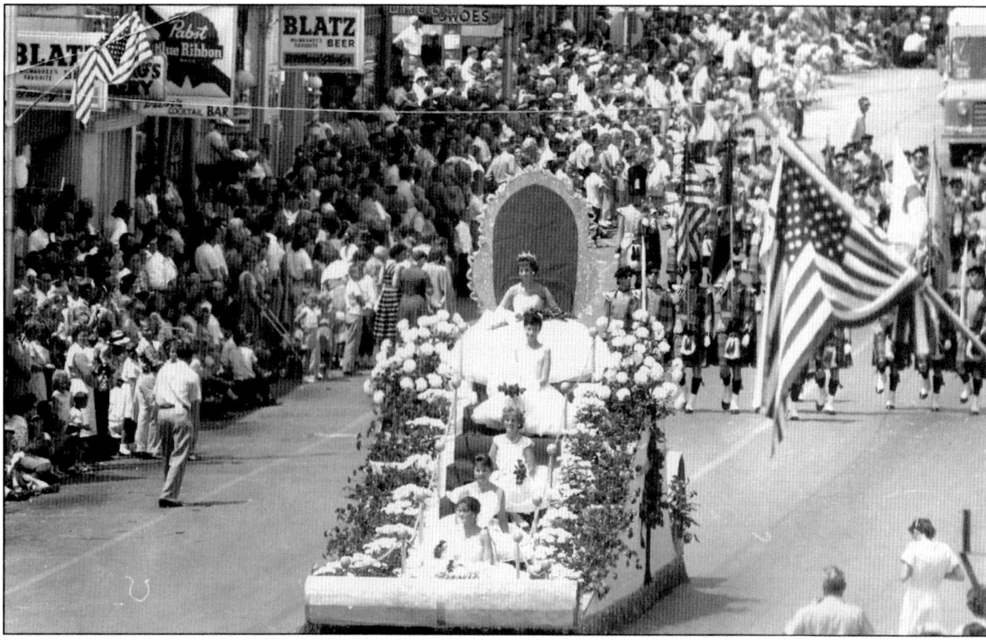

MARSH DAYS PARADE, 1960. Each year a new queen and her court were chosen among the many entries to grace the float of honor. Pictured are "Queen" Sandy Schultz and her court. Although the last Marsh Days Parade made its way down East Lake Street in July 2006, the traditional queen contest carries on today as part of Horicon's Rock'n River Jam festival every June. (Courtesy Horicon Reporter.)

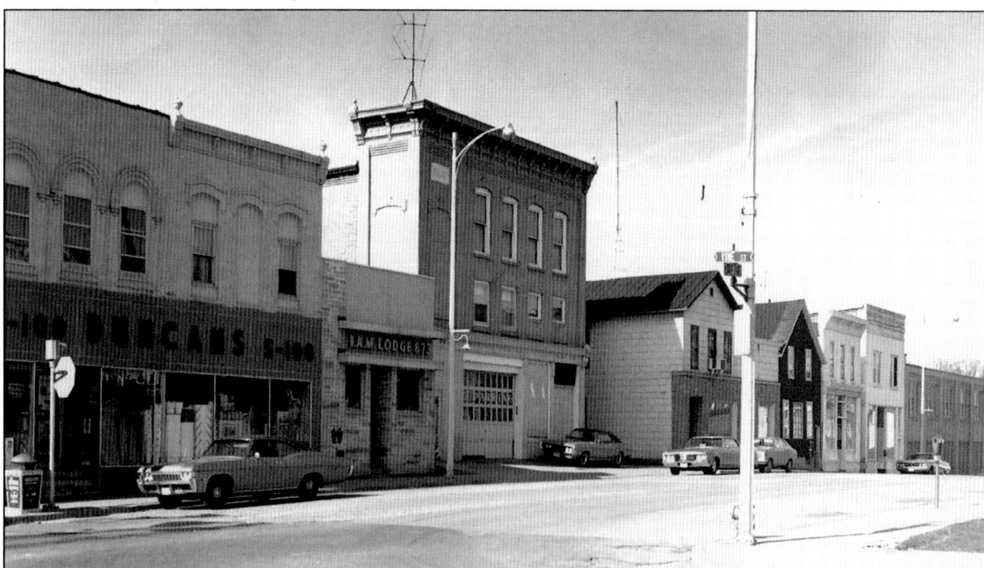

DUNCAN'S STORE, 1960S. Located at the corner of Vine and Lake Streets, Duncan's was known as the five-and-dime store. To the right is the International Association of Machinists (IAM) Lodge 873. Tom Manolis, known as "Tom the Greek," owned the restaurant with a pool and billiards room across from Duncan's. The Wagners owned the bowling alley next to Manolis's. All have been razed for John Deere Horicon Works parking lots. (Courtesy Horicon Historical Society.)

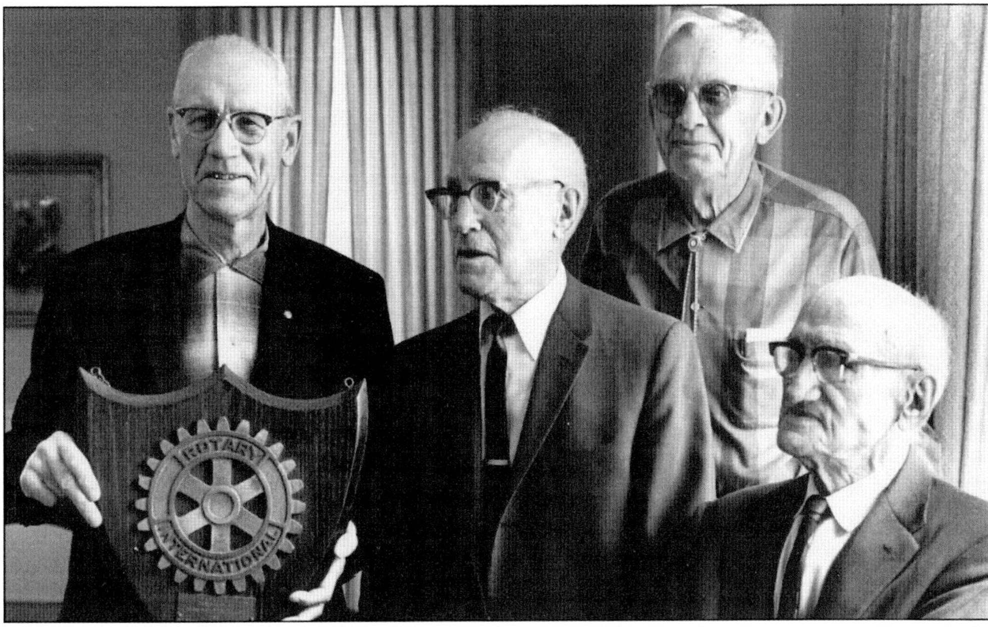

ROTARY CLUB HONORS, 1962. Frank and Henry, the Bodden brothers, were pillars of the community. Receiving honors from two charter members are, from left to right, Chris F. Brandt, former Mayville and Horicon Power and Light manager; Henry; W. R. Bussewitz; and Frank. Henry worked in the accounting department of John Deere Horicon Works, and Frank retired in 1957 as a lumber and fuel dealer in Horicon. (Courtesy Horicon Reporter.)

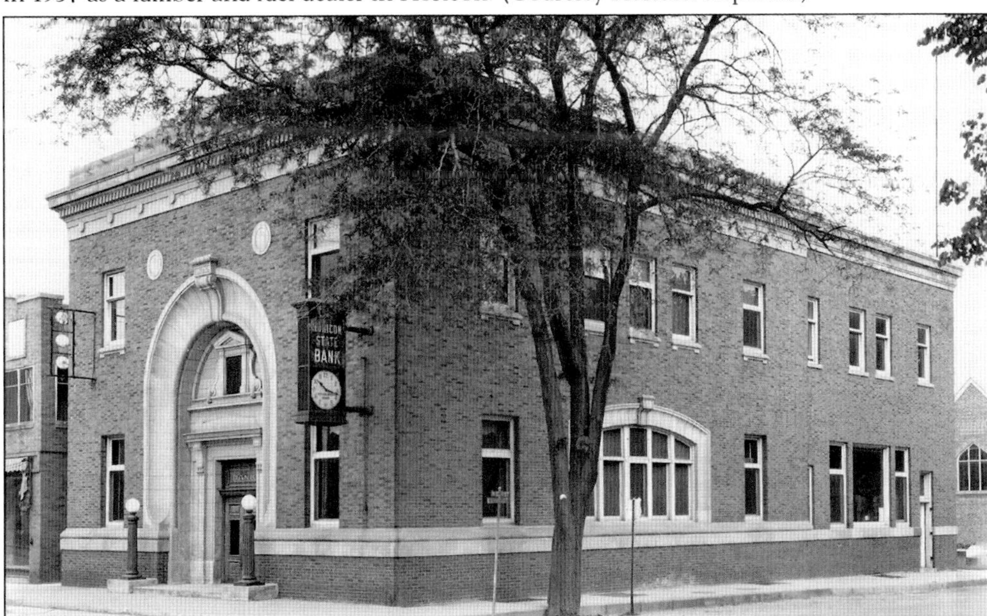

HORICON STATE BANK. Horicon State Bank was established in 1896, one year before the Village of Horicon received a city charter and officially became the City of Horicon. In 1914, the bank moved from its original location to its current home at 326 East Lake Street. This Beaux-Arts style building was designed by the notable Milwaukee architectural firm Buemming and Guth. (Courtesy Fred Schwertfeger.)

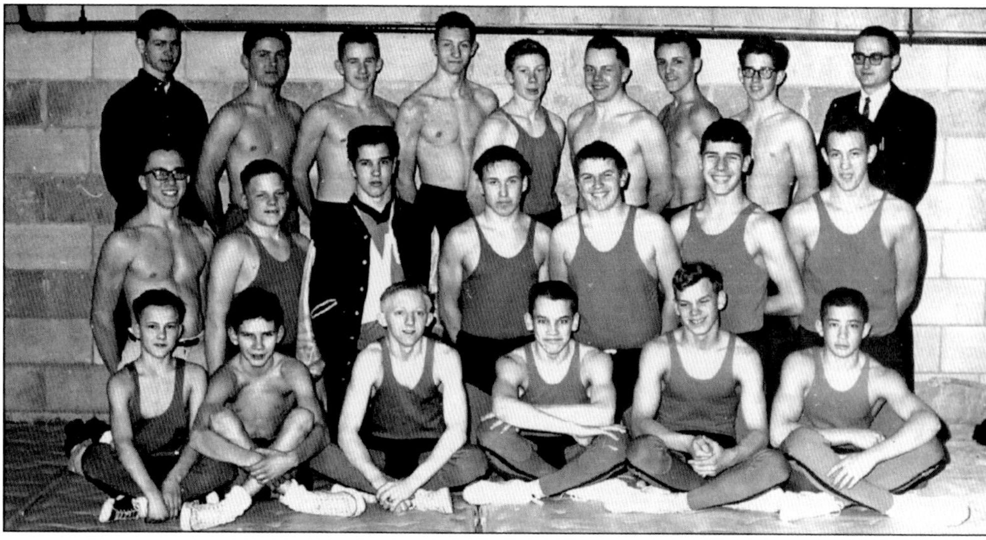

WRESTLING, 1962–1963. Coach Jerome (Jerry) Traughber was both a science teacher and a wrestling coach. Seen here are, from left to right, (first row) Ken Flouro, Ken LaGrange, Russell Wolfgram, Richard Gensmer, John Schroeder, and George Macheel; (second row) Stan Nickel, Gary Hurelle, Andy Schultze, Patrick Brunner, Ed Guptill, Ed Pahl, and Art Gysbers; (third row) Russell Schroeder, Rinehold Wendt, Don Snyder, Harvey Gysbers, Rich Louden, Randall Schroeder, Wayne Hawkins, Dennis Froehlich, and coach Jerome Traughber. (Courtesy Patrick Brunner.)

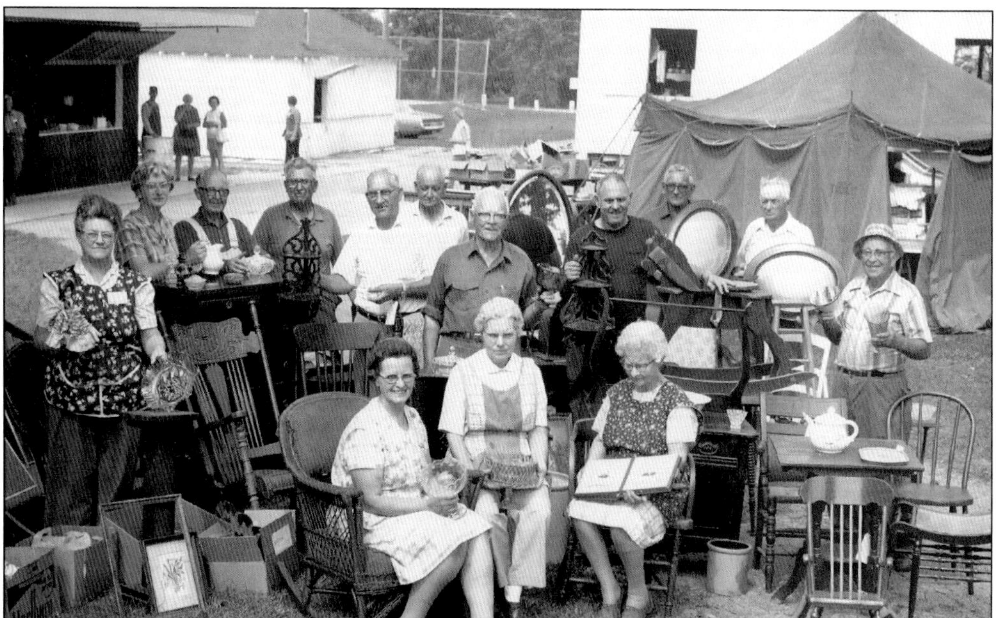

BETHESDA COUNTRY STORE. Originally at Discher Park, Bethesda moved its business to the Dodge County Fairgrounds before opening its shop at 104 Clinton Street on May 6, 1989. A nonprofit organization that sells everything used, including the kitchen sink, it serves the community with proceeds benefiting the developmentally disabled, whether mentally or physically challenged. (Courtesy Horicon Reporter.)

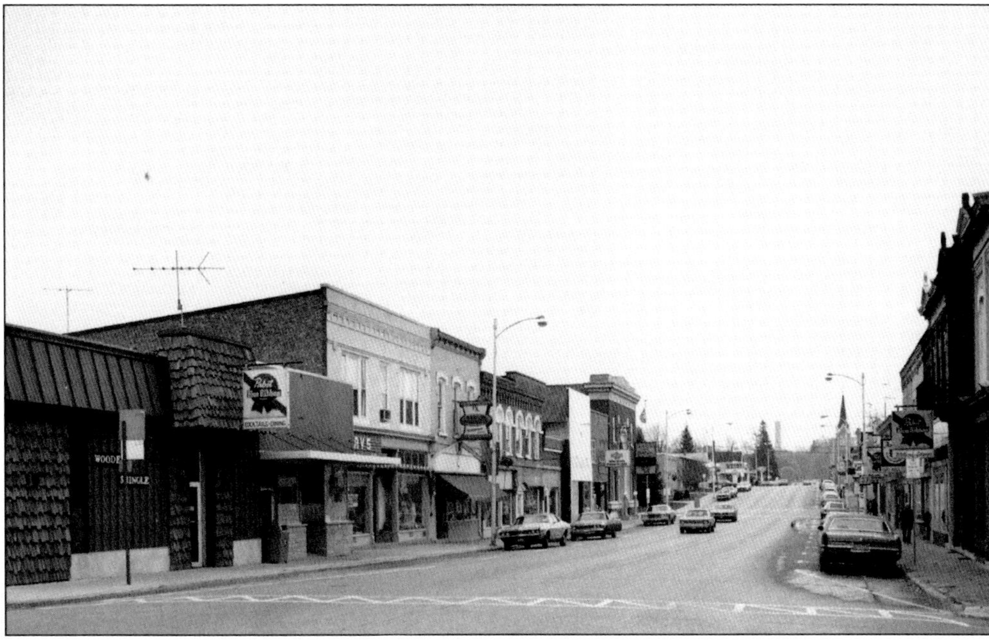

CORNER OF LAKE AND VINE STREETS, 1970S. Since the 1970s, the face of East Lake Street has changed little. Most notably, the buildings standing next to Horicon State Bank on the left side of this photograph have been razed to make way for parking and a modern, one-story office building that is home to attorney Douglas Plier. (Courtesy Fred Schwertfeger.)

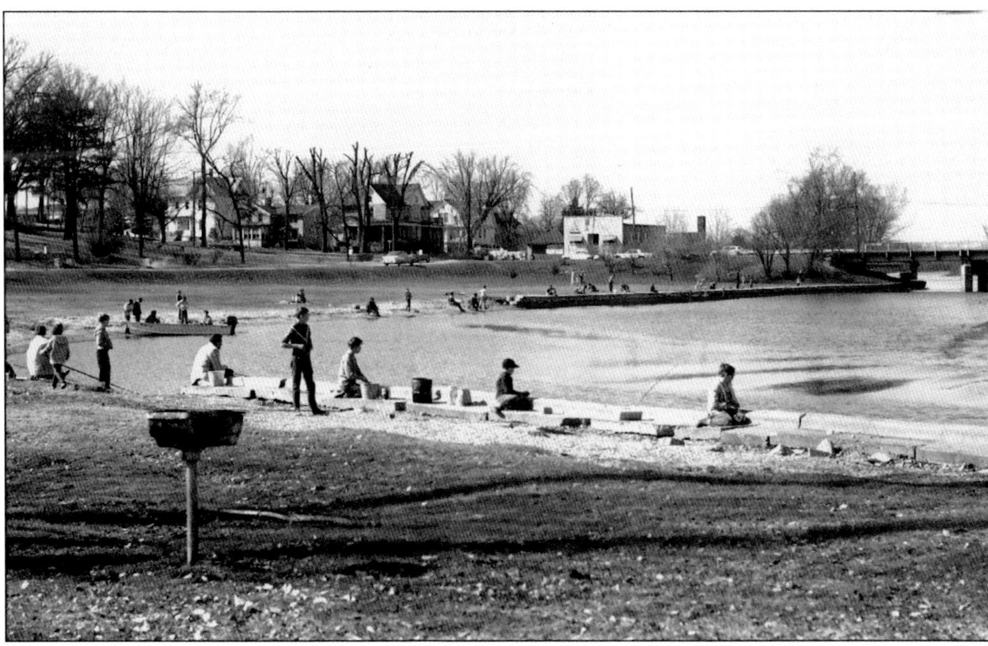

FISHING AT BOWLING GREEN PARK. A calm day, fresh air, and room to let the children run turns into a wonderful combination to fish for bullheads at Bowling Green Park. Because of the bountiful waters in Horicon, not only did fishing provide plentiful food for the family, it also gave residents the chance to chat with the neighbors. (Courtesy Horicon Historical Society.)

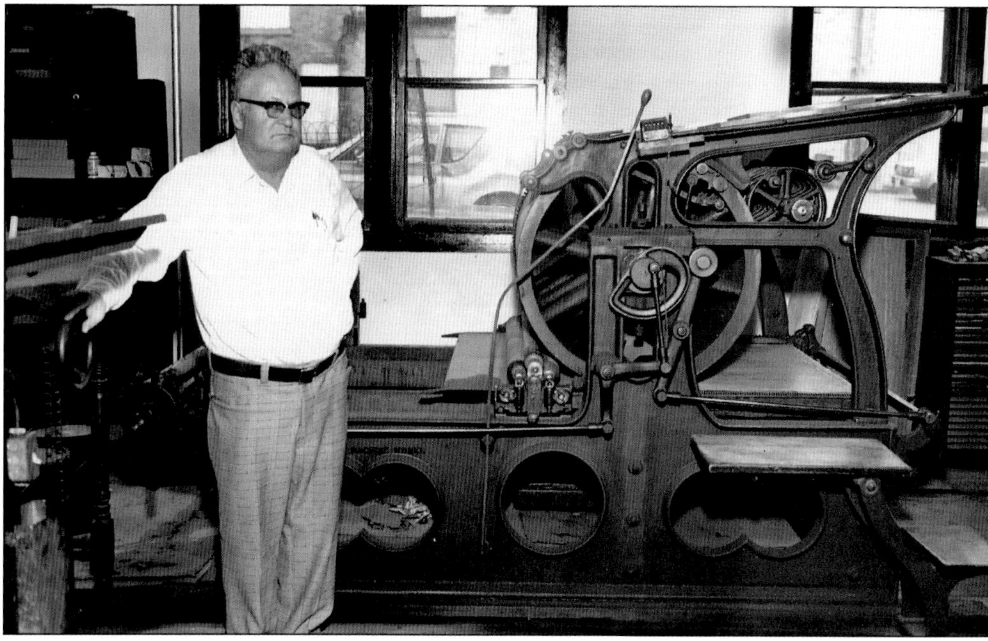

Ed Marolla, 1960s. Standing next to the old sheet-fed press used in the early 1900s at the *Horicon Reporter* is a former owner of the business. The charismatic and sometimes controversial Ed Marolla utilized the equipment until 1967, when the offset printing was then performed at Ripon Community Printers. Marolla brought his boys Ed Jr. and Julius into the business at an early age. Recording history from 1958 to 1989, Ed Sr. continued to write the "Hello Horicon" section of the paper even after his retirement in 1976 until Andrew Johnson bought the paper in 1989. Ed Sr. promoted city projects, including the new post office, the golf course, and the new high school. (Courtesy Julius Marolla.)

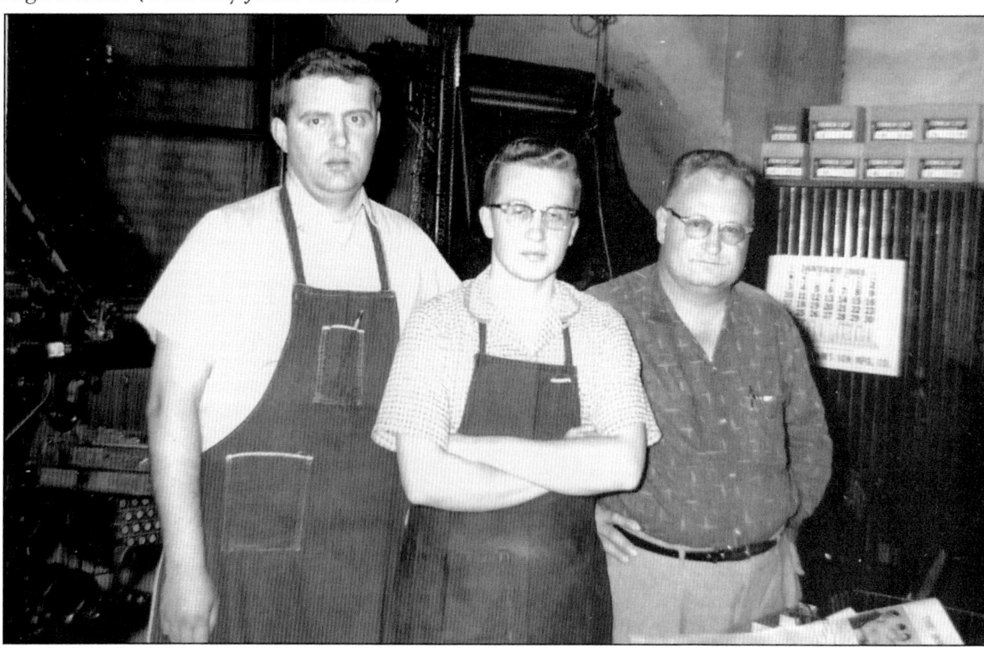

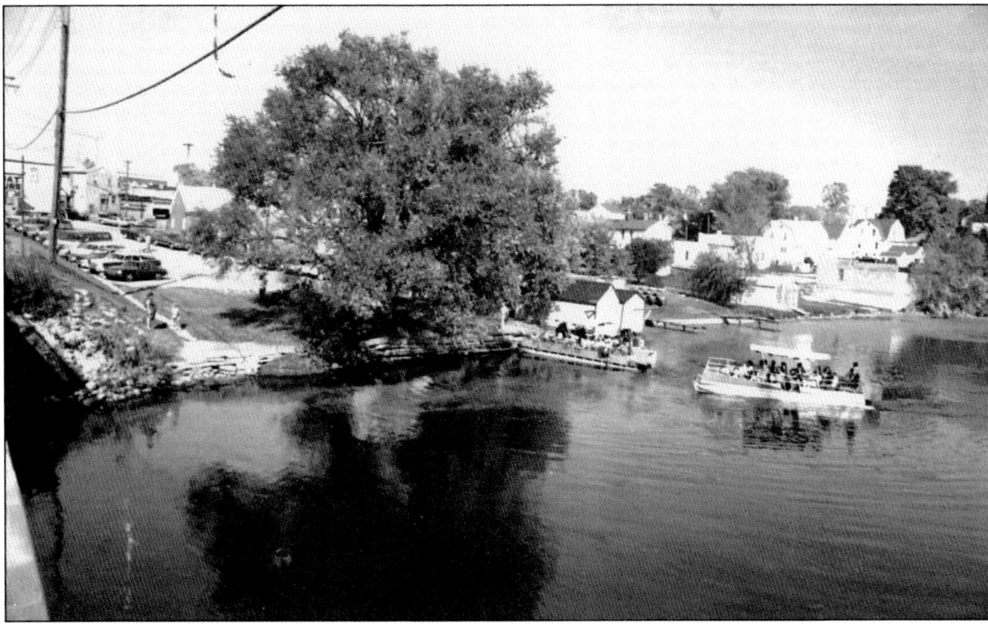

BOAT TOURS, 1960S. Established in 1963 by the Roland Zuelsdorf family as Horicon Marsh Boat Tours, boat tours up the Rock River and Horicon Marsh are the perfect way to experience the area's natural beauty. Located at Mill Street on Highway 33, the business began with a small pontoon boat for 8 with the addition of larger 24-passenger boats shortly thereafter. Roland's son Marc, along with his family, continue to run the tour company. In 1984, the business purchased the Canoe Outfitters property, changed the company name to Blue Heron Landing, and began renting canoes. Kayak rentals were offered in 2001. As the tour company's name suggests, it is not uncommon to see blue herons at rest along the shoreline. (Courtesy Horicon Reporter.)

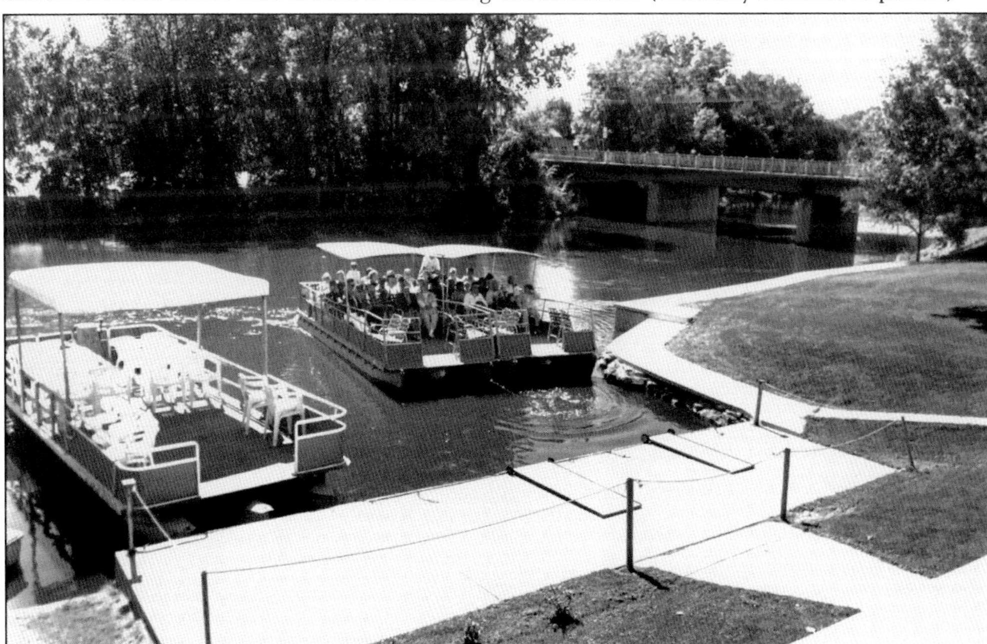

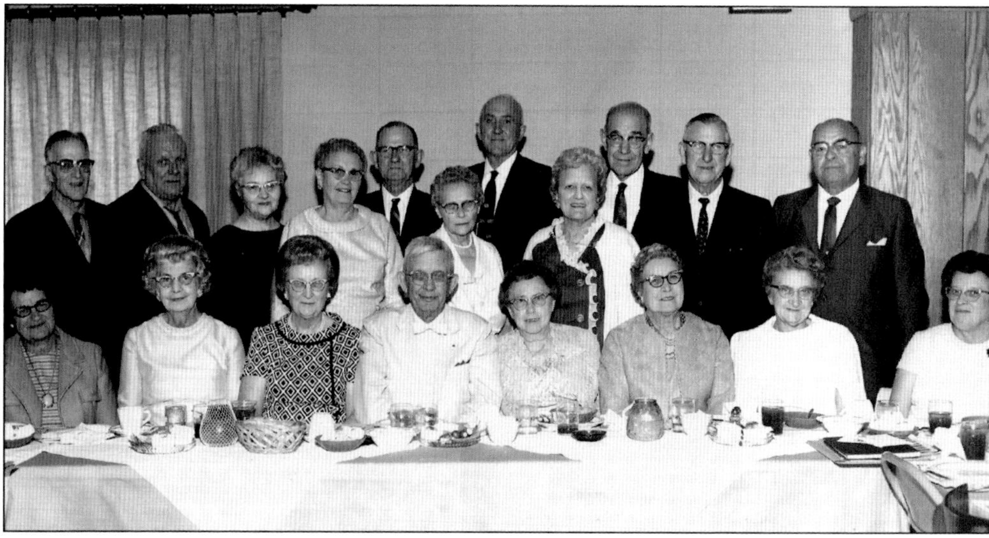

A 50th Class Reunion, 1969. The Horicon High School class of 1919 includes, from left to right, (first row) Elizabeth Lange Redding, Evelyn O'Rourke, Irma Helbing Morse, W. R. Bussewitz, Marguerite Hintertheur Lehman, Lillie Zieschke Tietz, Helen Henning Goodrich, and ? Gurske; (second row) Wilton Erdman, Clyde Huffman, Lillian Stueber Heublein, Elvira Raasch Kohlman, Chester Strehlow, Lettie Schroeder Schneider, Nathan Goodrich, Mildred Raue, Lother Raue, Ben Tietz, and Alfred Gurske. (Courtesy Horicon Historical Society.)

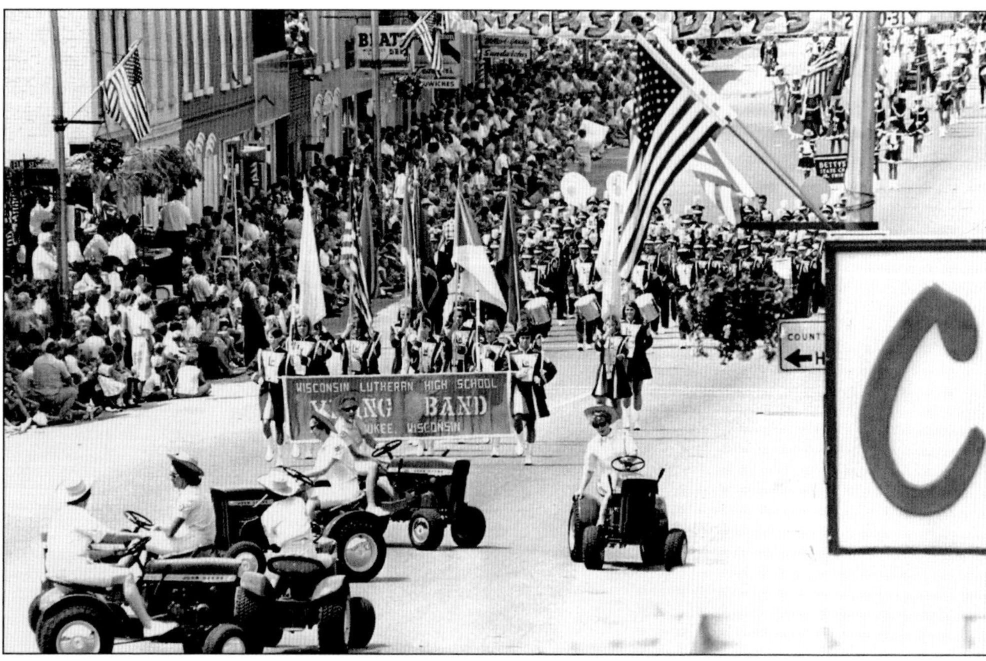

Marsh Day Parade, 1970. Hundreds came from miles around to participate in the festivities and watch the parade. With John Deere Horicon Works looming in the distance, it was only fitting for women to take the riding mowers for a twirl in the yearly event. Unfortunately, the last parade was held in 2006 as Marsh Days was discontinued the same year. (Courtesy Horicon Reporter.)

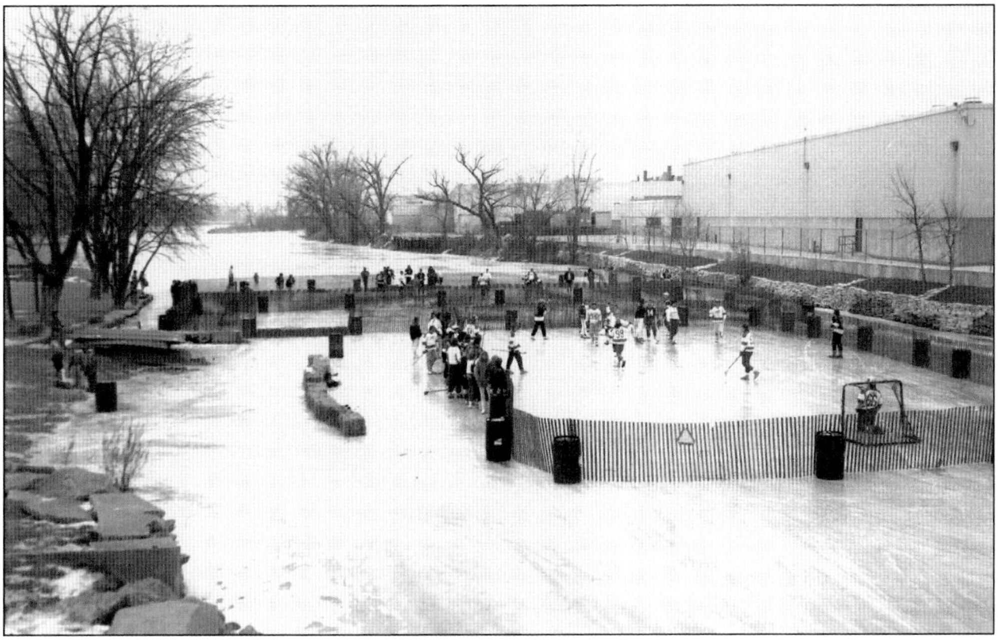

ICE HOCKEY LEAGUE, 1970S. The first Marsh Cup Broom Hockey Tournament was held on March 11, 1973, with two rinks on the Rock River. The annual tournament was held throughout the 1970s at both Kiwanis Park and near the Lake Street Bridge. Today the city's youth can be found playing pickup games of ice hockey at a seasonal rink in Discher Park. (Courtesy Horicon Reporter.)

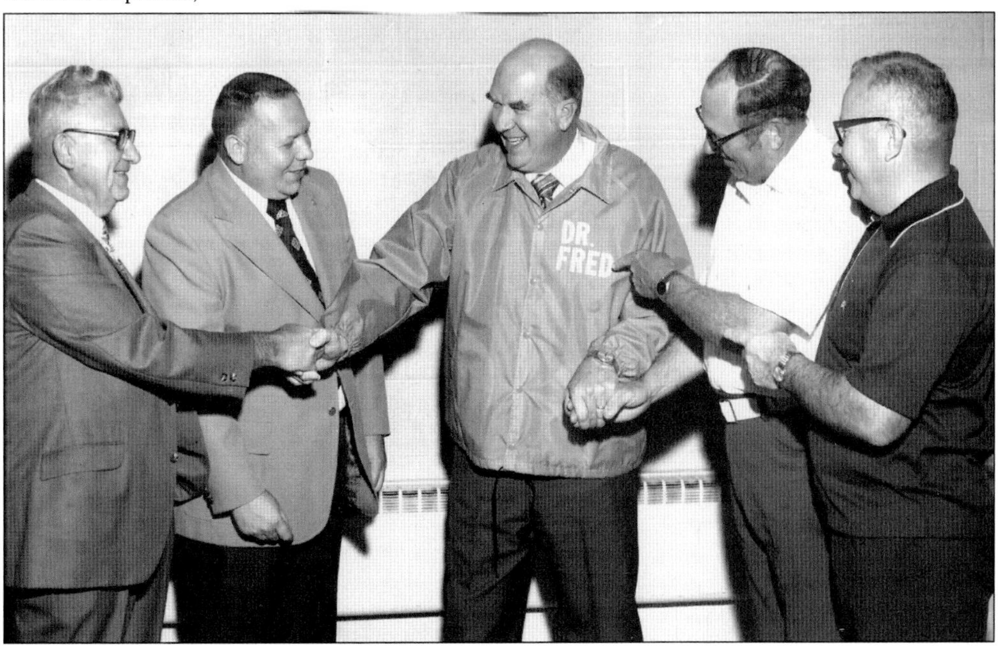

DR. FRED KARSTEN, 1970S. Being a third-generation doctor for the town, like his grandfather Adrian Karsten and father John Karsten before him, Dr. Fred was known to show up whenever called. Here the fire department is shown honoring him with his own bright orange jacket with "Fire Department" emblazoned on the back. (Courtesy John Karsten family.)

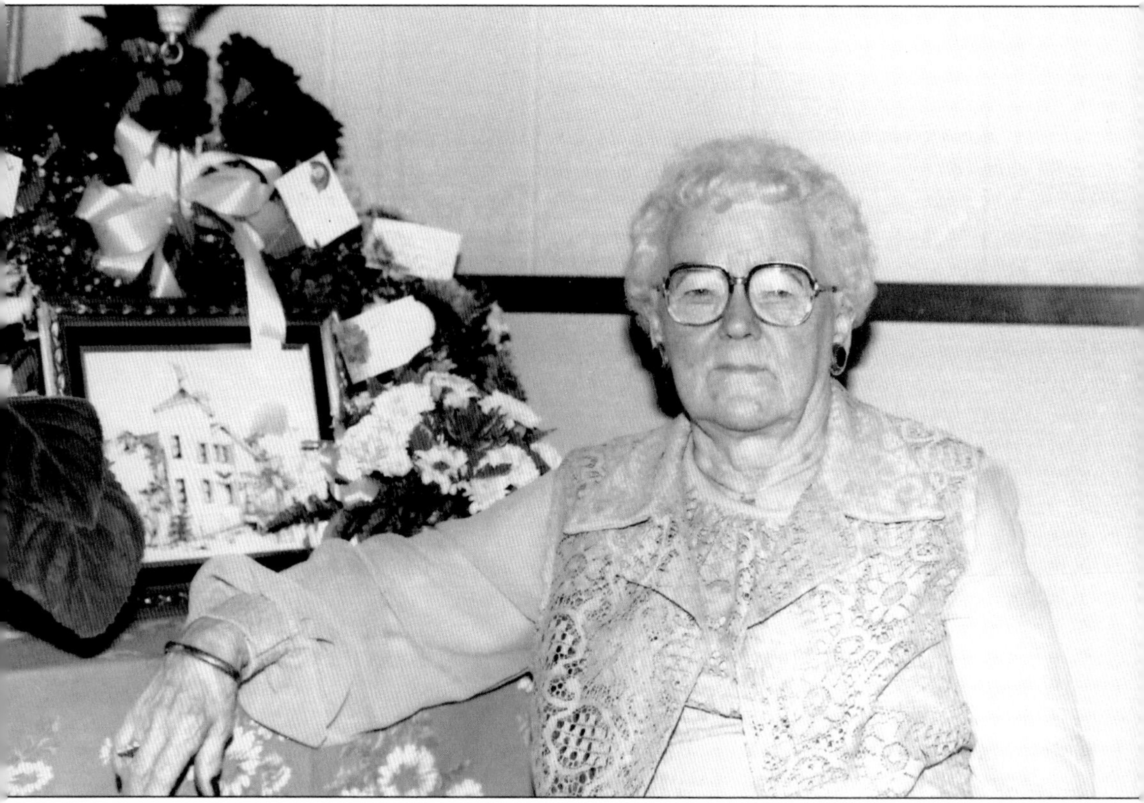

Bobby Burrow, 1983. Celebrating 50 years in business at Eagle Hill Tavern, Bobby Burrow was asked the secret of her longevity. She replied, "If I have to tell the truth, I think it is because I drink a shot of whiskey every day. I believe in that. My dad always took a kummel. And he lived to be 75." Bobby and her husband, Lee "Pappy" Burrow, purchased and moved the old Presbyterian church, which had been used as a Socialist political club, to their property overlooking the marsh. Although it had no living quarters, no electricity, and no water, they were able to turn the church into a home and tavern. Known as the "Old Clubhouse," Eagle Hill Tavern was used as a meeting hall for the U.S. Air Force Reserve, the Horicon Rod and Gun Club, and the Horicon American Legion Post 157 before they each built their own clubhouses. Pappy trapped on the marsh for more than 40 years and in earlier years would host trappers and fur traders doing business at their tavern. (Courtesy Charlotte Burrow.)

Four

EDUCATION AND RELIGION

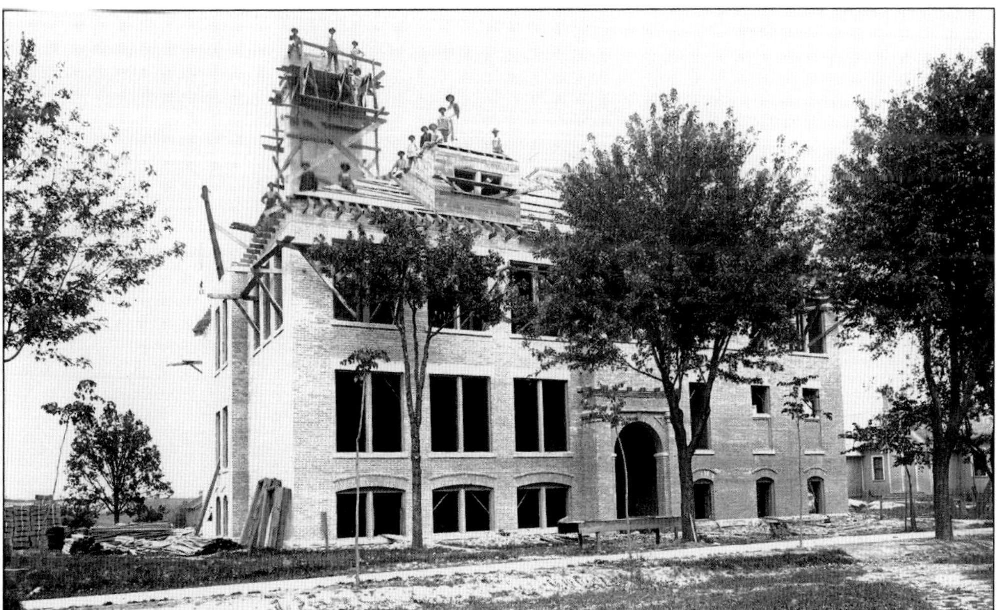

HORICON UNION SCHOOL, 1905. The original building opened for students on April 20, 1857. After several additions, once again the school was in need of facilities for its growing student population. This wing was added and opened for use in 1906, and two smaller buildings were removed. The building was immediately filled to capacity, and discussion abounded as to the need for more classrooms. (Courtesy Fred Schwertfeger.)

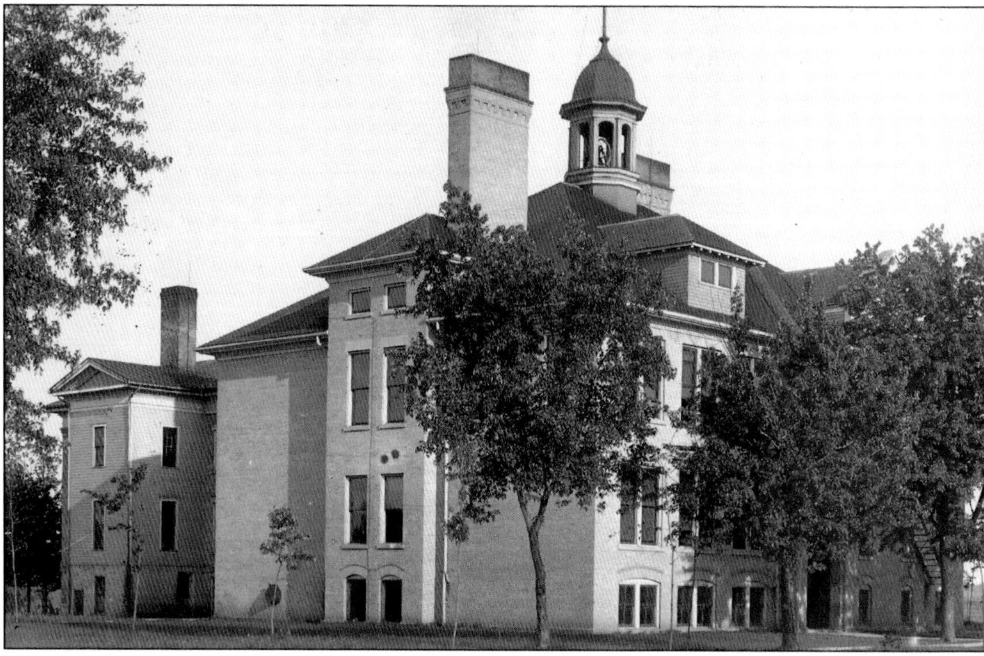

HORICON UNION SCHOOL, C. 1910. Known as "Academy Hall," this building was designed to accommodate 400 students and prepare them for colleges and universities. With three stories and a basement, it quickly outgrew the needs of the community, and in 1906, a brick wing was added. In 1920, a two-room primary building was completed at a cost of $9,000. (Courtesy Horicon Historical Society.)

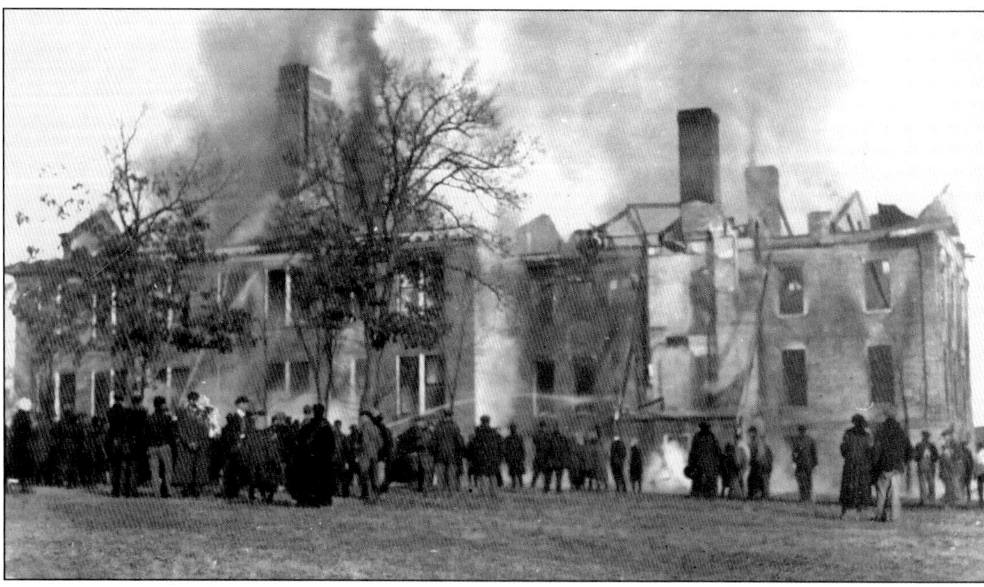

SCHOOL ON FIRE, 1920. On November 17, 1920, smoke began belching out from under the roof of the school, and the city alarm sounded. The furnace overheated during the morning's firing, and the ventilation system carried the smoke and fire rapidly throughout the building. The townspeople watched in horror and amazement while the building went up in flames. Very little was salvaged from this disastrous inferno. (Courtesy Horicon Historical Society.)

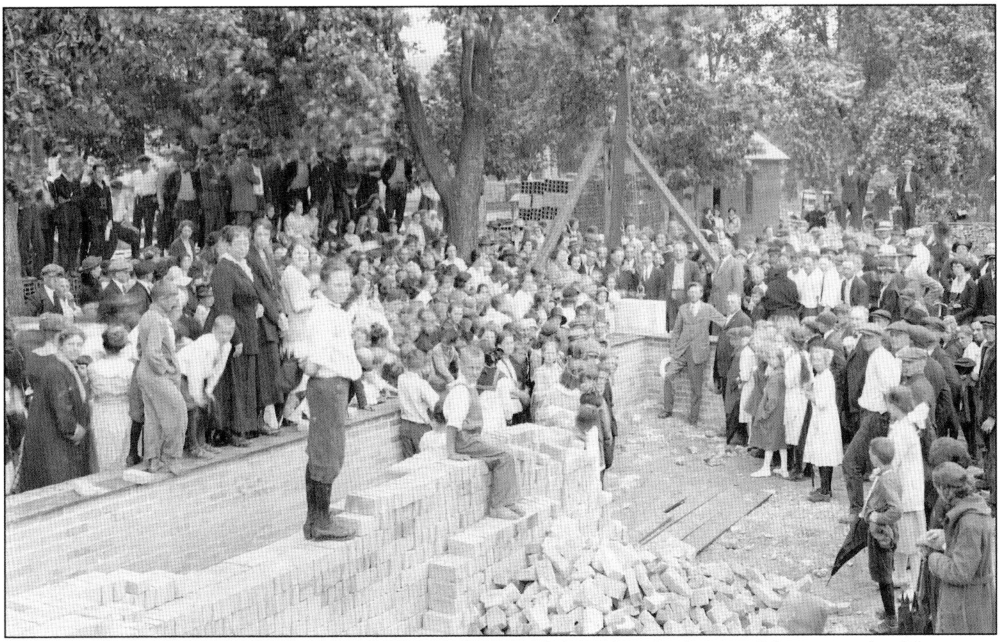

CORNERSTONE FOR SCHOOL, 1921. With the loss of the school, the need for a new building was dealt with immediately. Mary Eichelberger donated $75,000 for the construction of Van Brunt Memorial School in memory of her brother-in-law and sister, Daniel C. and Martha L. Van Brunt. Arthur W. Wilcox donated $25,000 toward a gymnasium in memory of his wife, Hattie Van Brunt Wilcox, a week later. (Courtesy Paul Kruel.)

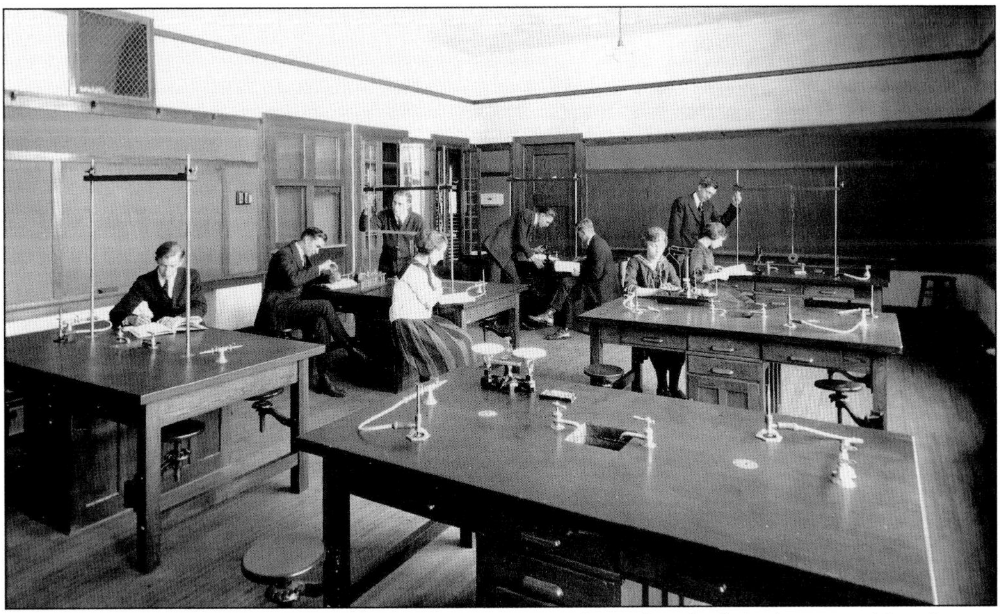

CHEMISTRY LAB, 1920S. Designed by Parkinson and Dockendorf Architects of La Crosse, no expense was spared to build an educational atmosphere for the students. The committee that took on the task included wonderful science and chemistry labs. It is reported that this lab looked nearly the same in the 1960s when students there took classes. (Courtesy Horicon Historical Society.)

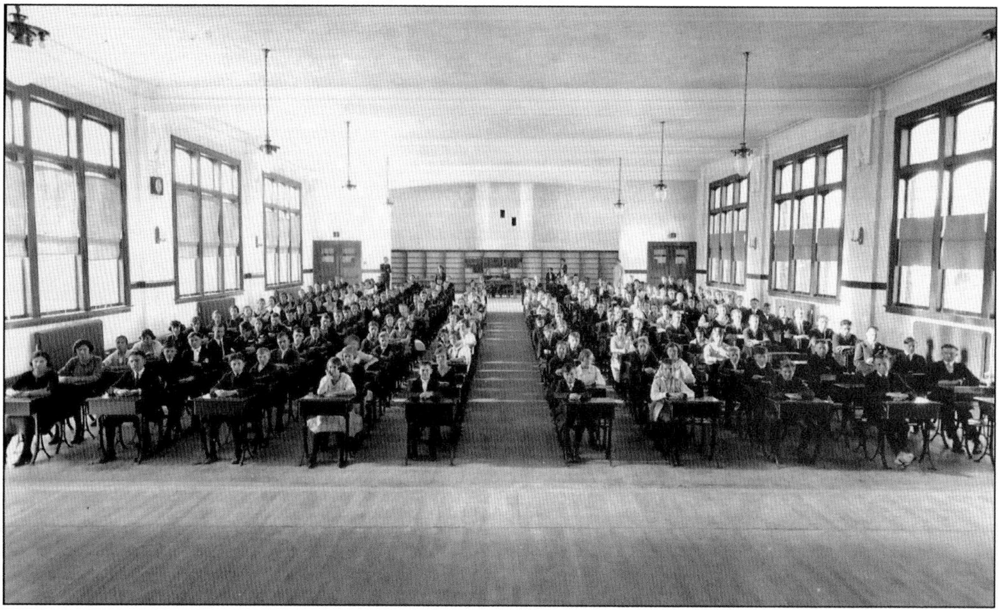

Assembly Room, early 1920s. The newly completed Van Brunt Memorial School accommodated the lower grades on one side of the building and the upper grades on the opposite side with a large assembly room between the two, giving the appearance of an H. The connecting room was also used for study hall. (Courtesy Horicon Historical Society.)

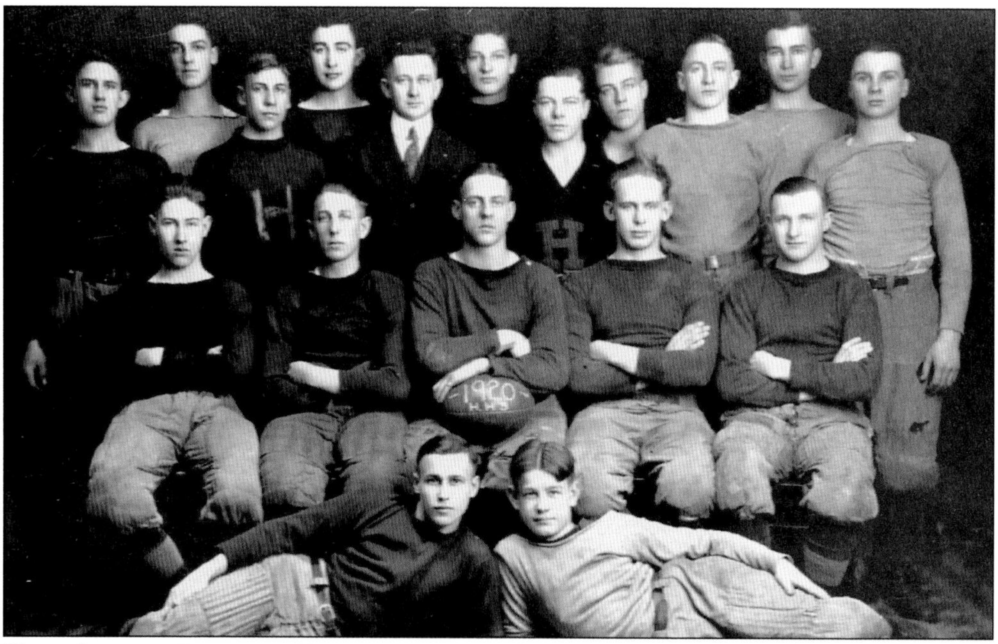

High School Football Team, 1920. Seen here are, from left to right, (first row) Carl Firehammer and Alex Mellenthien; (second row) Charlie Laupp, Erwin Beske, Percy Sellick, Richard ?, and Carl Schultz; (third row) Jay Warden, Ben Marks, Ray Lindemann, Byron Goodrich, Mr. Barta, unidentified, ? Frienwald, Ervin Henkel, Robert Erdman, Lawrence Hintz, and Ray Winkelmann. (Courtesy Horicon Historical Society.)

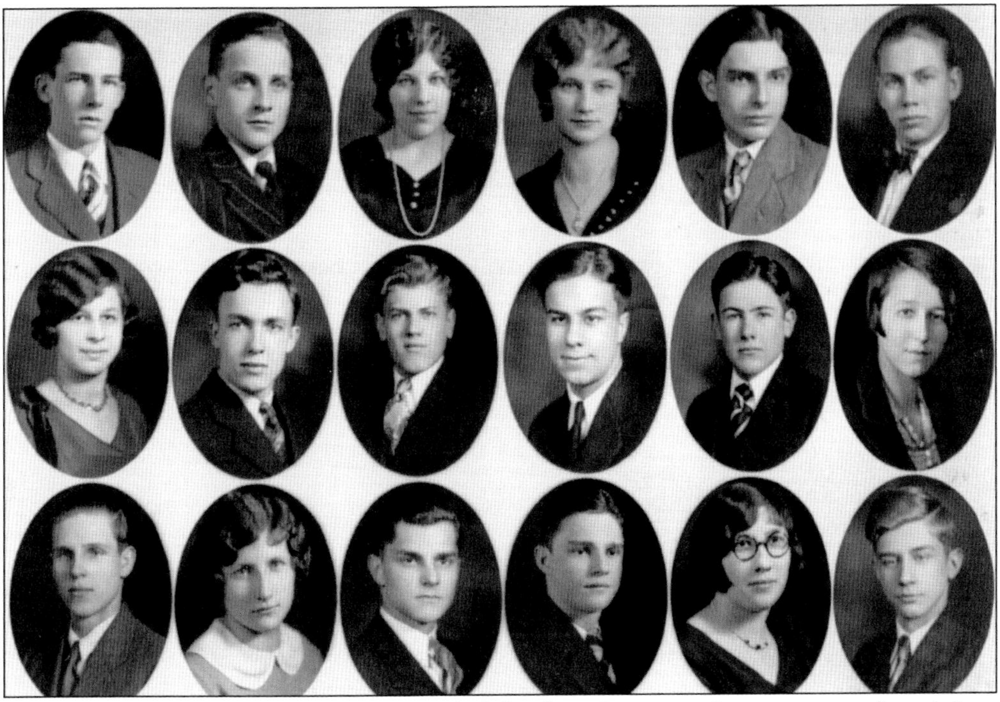

GRADUATING CLASS, 1929. Horicon High School graduates in this image are, from left to right, (top row) Ray Lockwood, Richard Helbing, Elizabeth Weber, Edna Oberdiek, Ralph Her, and Hilbert Hoppe; (second row) Elvira Gishkowsky, Earnie Zarling, Orin Rex, William Washburn, Russell Young, and Gladys Rohloff; (third row) William Voss, Pearl Wagner, Clarence Bennett, Floyd Williams, Gladys Berndt, and Clarence Schmidt. (Courtesy of Horicon Historical Society.)

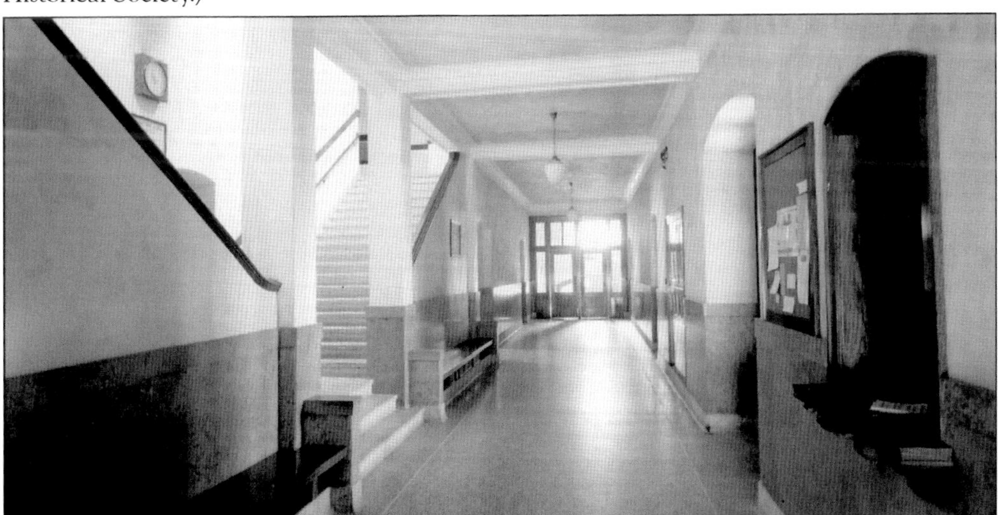

HIGH SCHOOL INTERIOR, 1930S. During the years that the building housed the high school, the bench on the left was where students would wait to see the principal in his office, located across the hall on the right. The classic and sleek lines of the architecture are clear to see in this photograph and remain largely intact on the second floor of the Van Brunt Elementary/Middle School today. (Courtesy Horicon Historical Society.)

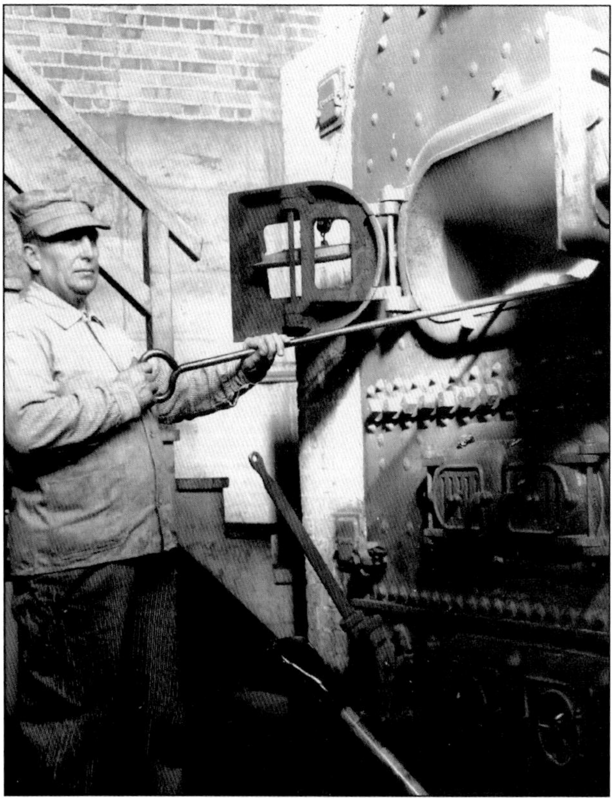

JOHN RECHNOR, 1935. Known affectionately as "Boss," John Rechnor maintained his position as the school janitor for 23 years before illness caused him to resign his post. His duties included keeping the building heated, cleaning the facility, and keeping up with repairs. Even today many former students have a Boss story to share. (Courtesy Horicon Historical Society.)

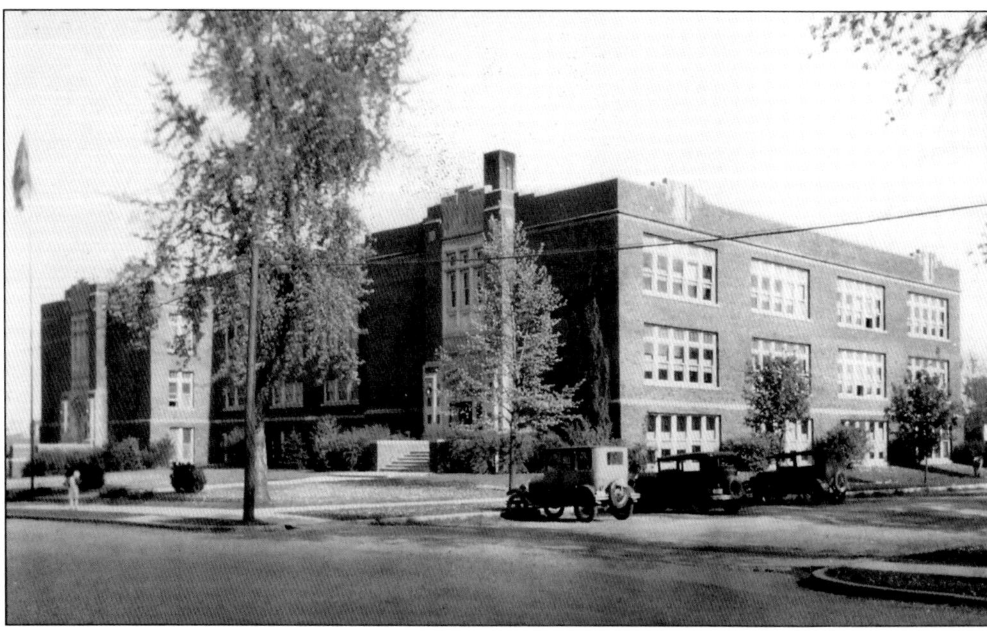

OLD HIGH SCHOOL, 1930S. With the population continuing to grow, a new high school was added in town in 1964 on Gray Street. However, this classic two-story, H-plan brick building designed by La Crosse architectural firm Parkinson and Dockendorf still stands at 611 Mill Street and now serves as the local elementary and middle school. (Courtesy Buzz Vanderhei.)

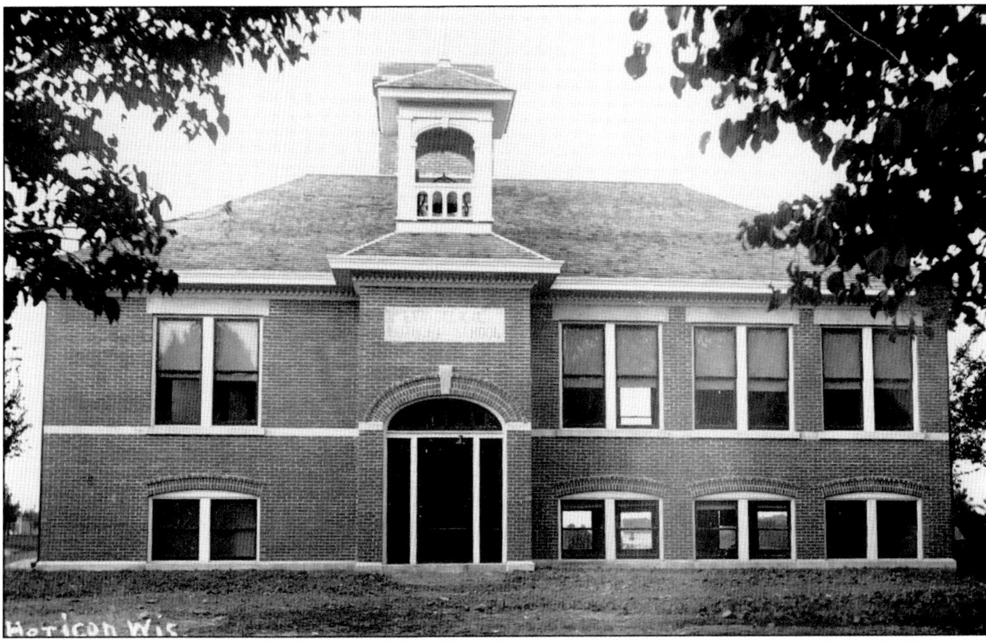

ST. STEPHEN CHRISTIAN DAY SCHOOL, 1940S. Erected in 1913 at a cost of nearly $10,000, this grand building remained a teaching ground for many years. With the new facility on North Palmatory Street opening in 1956, this structure later housed Bemus Printing. It still stands on Maple Street and is used for commercial purposes. (Courtesy Horicon Historical Society.)

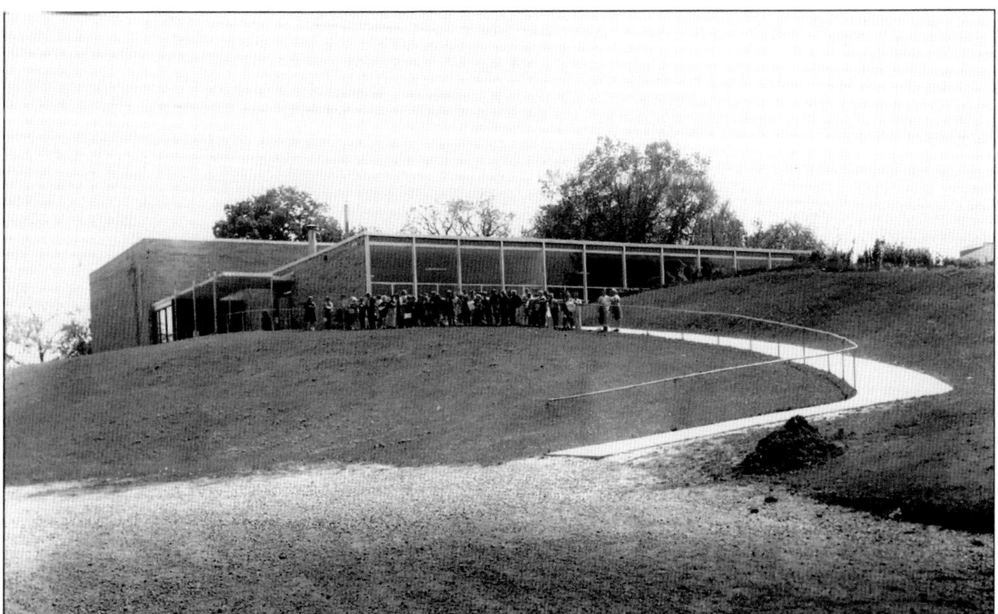

ST. MALACHY'S CATHOLIC SCHOOL, 1950S. Catholicism was prominent, and many children attended St. Malachy's on Valley Street. The rectory was next door to the school, and the church was but a short walk away. No longer functioning as a school, the building is empty, and the rectory is now a private home. The old St. Malachy's Church is now home to Amazing Grace Community Church. (Courtesy Horicon Historical Society.)

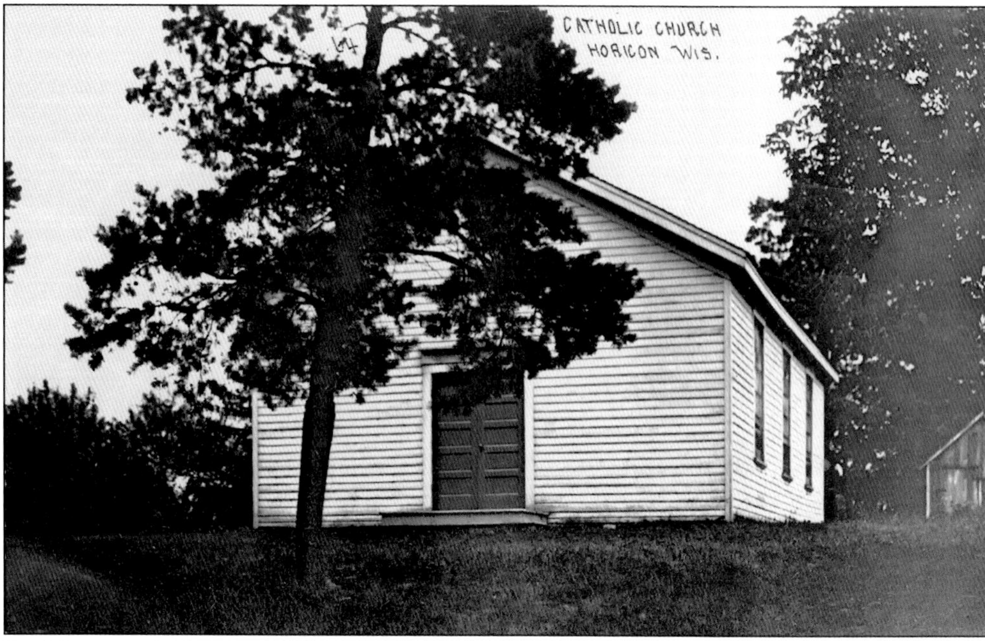

ST. MALACHY'S ORIGINAL CHURCH. Dedicated in May 1856, this building was located on the grounds of St. Malachy's cemetery. The mother of Judge Charles H. Larrabee donated the Valley Street site to the church. As the church grew, a new facility was required, and this building was razed. The new church's cornerstone was laid in 1914 at the corner of Barstow and Vine Streets. (Courtesy Horicon Historical Society.)

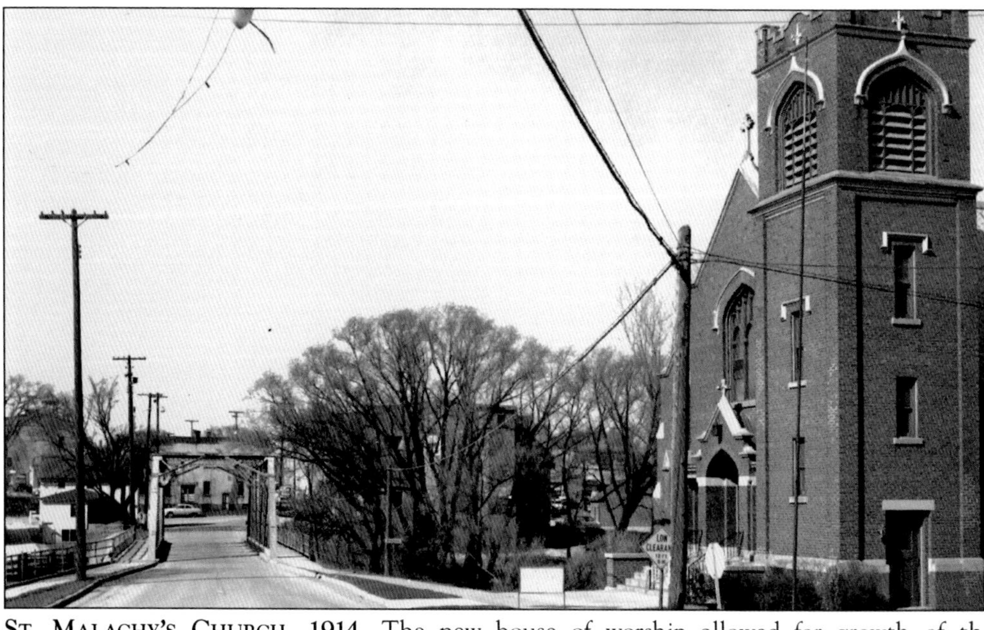

ST. MALACHY'S CHURCH, 1914. The new house of worship allowed for growth of the parishioners. After remaining at this site for more than 75 years, the congregation once again needed larger quarters. Combining St. Malachy's Parish and Immaculate Conception of Juneau, the new facility, which opened in 2001, is located at the western edge of the city on Washington Street and is called Sacred Heart Parish. (Courtesy Horicon Historical Society.)

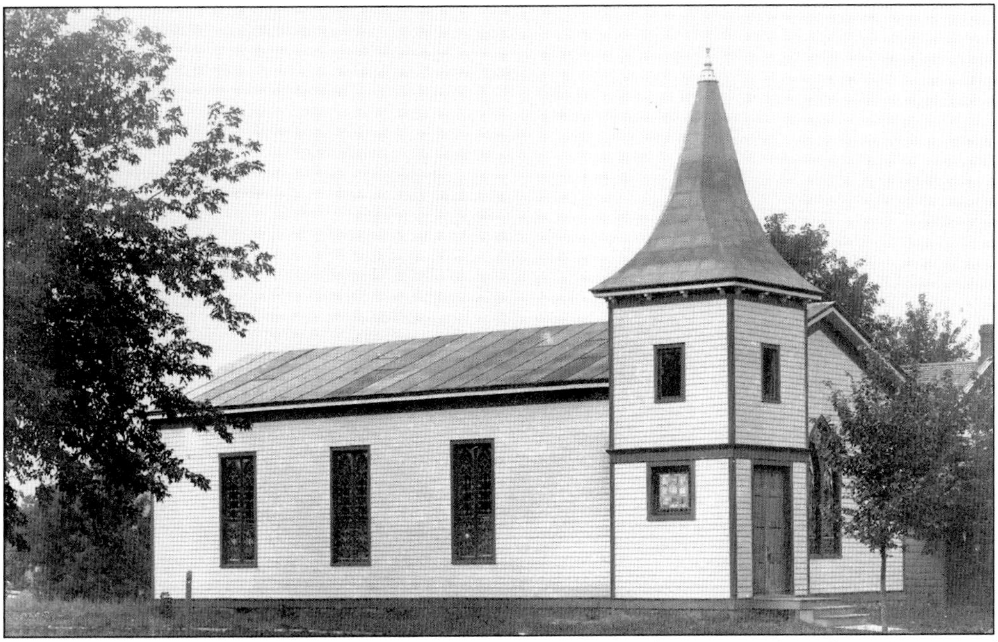

ORIGINAL PRESBYTERIAN CHURCH. Dedicated on September 28, 1856, after 10 years of services, this building was utilized until early in the first decade of the 20th century, when the South Cedar Street lot was cleared, and a new brick structure was constructed. The new facility, dedicated in May 1917, combined Old World architecture and modern design. Lee and Bobby Burrow later moved this building to Eagle Hill and ran it as a tavern. It is now a private home. (Courtesy Charlotte Burrow.)

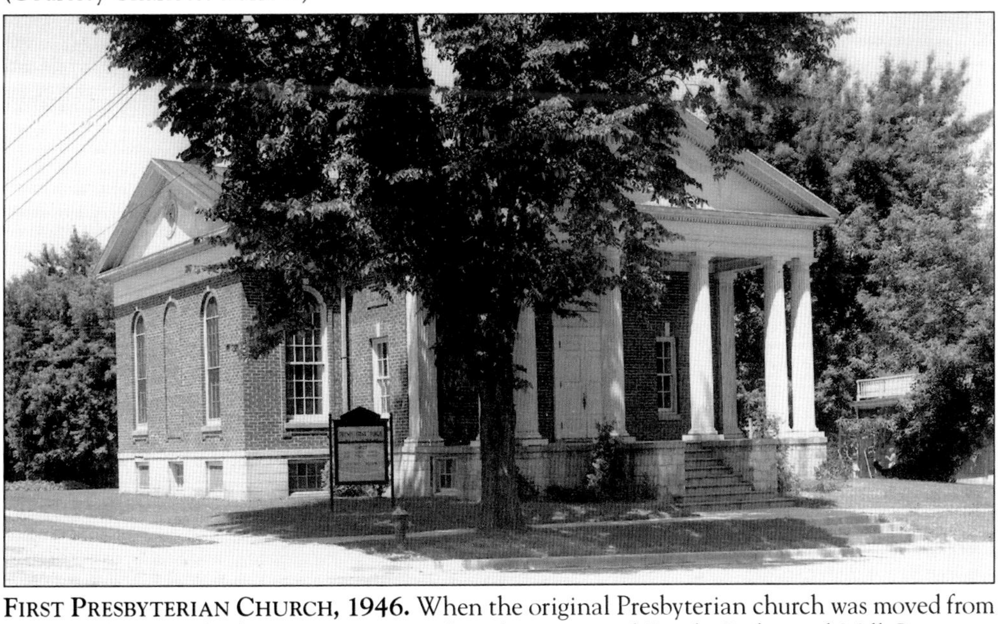

FIRST PRESBYTERIAN CHURCH, 1946. When the original Presbyterian church was moved from the site, this new facility was constructed at the corner of South Cedar and Mill Streets to take its place. Its 1917 dedication provided more room for the growing congregation. In the 1940s, it was redecorated and a new Hammond organ was installed. The church's centennial was observed in April 1946. (Courtesy Horicon Historical Society.)

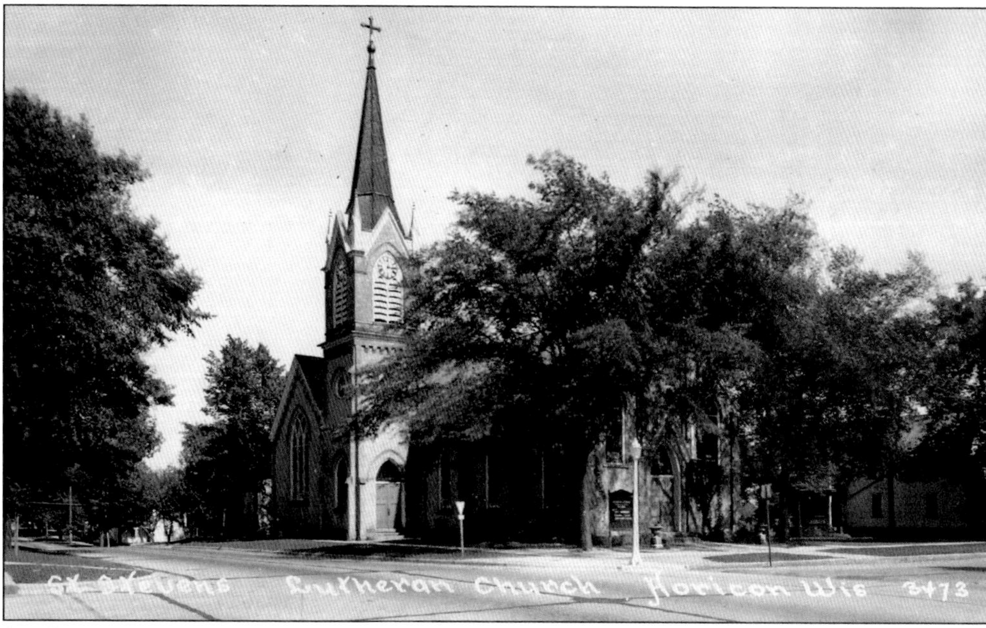

ST. STEPHEN LUTHERAN CHURCH, 1930S. In 1867, this new facility was constructed at the corner on South Cedar Street and served as both church and school. Additions over the years included an expansion (1905), a clock tower (1912), and a freestanding school erected on Maple Street (1913). Due to the church's growth, St. Stephen built a new church on Palmatory Street, and this building now houses MarshView Ministries. (Courtesy Horicon Historical Society.)

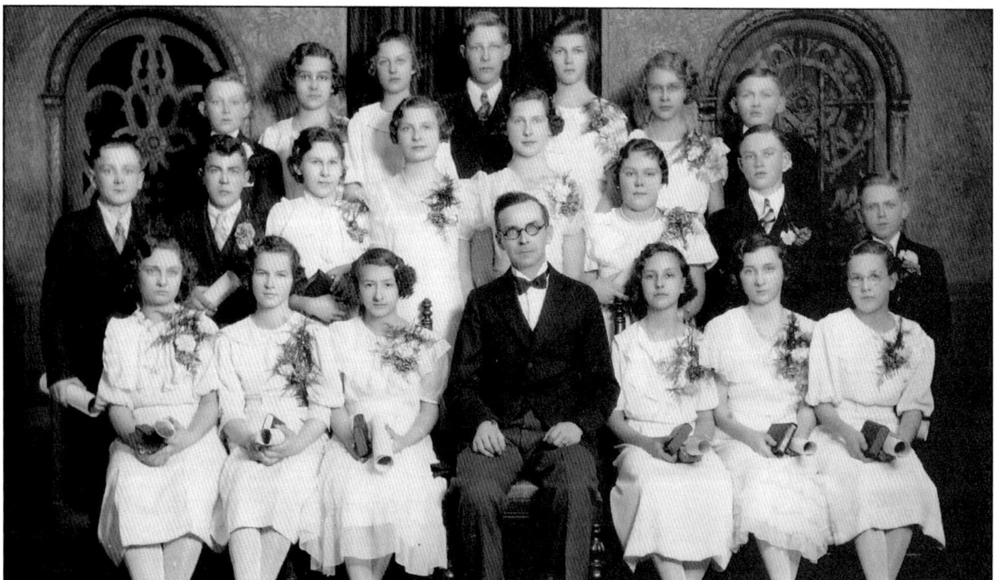

ST. STEPHEN CONFIRMATION, 1935. Students are, from left to right, (first row) Florence Heintz, Florence Utteck, Ruth Pegelow, Pastor Fred Schwertfeger, Marion Wille, Mildred Schoppe, and Virginia Selchert; (second row) Marvin Baerwald, Roy Bodga, unidentified, Kordula Marquardt, Geri Bentz, Bernice Kirchoff, Palmer Werner, and Alvin Bunkoske; (third row) Quinton Neitzel, Doris Brandt, Meta Schmude, Preston Lehman, Evelyn ?, Laura Kurtz, and unidentified. (Courtesy Bob Blankenheim.)

EMMANUEL EVANGELICAL UNITED BRETHREN CHURCH, 1930S. Dedicated in December 1899, this church was also known as the German Methodist Church with services conducted in German. Children of other faiths came to learn German, but classes were discontinued in the 1920s. The Evangelical Church and the Church of the United Brethren in Christ merged in 1946. Today the church is called Emmanuel United Methodist Church and is part of the Shared Covenant Ministries of Horicon, Juneau, Lowell United Methodist Churches. (Courtesy Horicon Historical Society.)

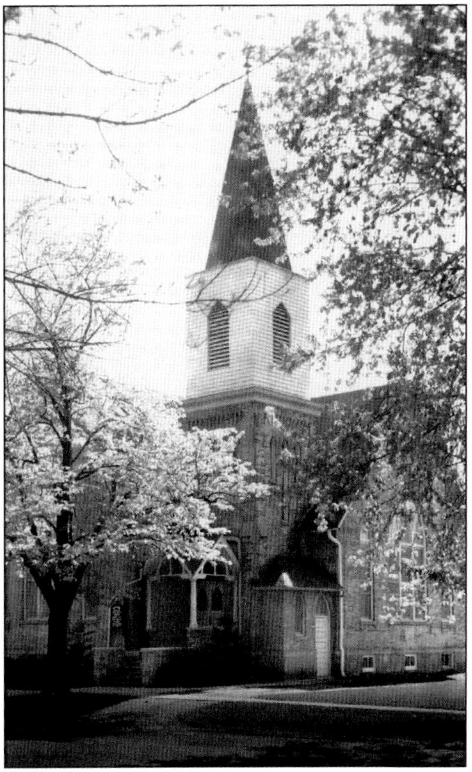

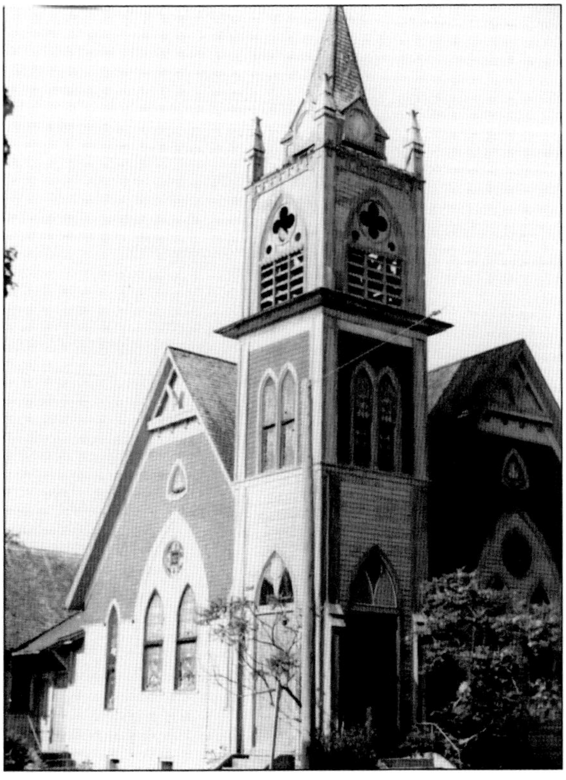

METHODIST EPISCOPAL CHURCH, 1935. Original facilities were located in a redbrick church on the corner of Cedar and Maple Streets, with dedication occurring in 1856. Because of growing membership, this new building was dedicated in 1894 and stood on the corner of Walnut and Elm Streets until it was razed in 1938 due to dwindling membership. Contractors salvaged the lumber for other building projects. (Courtesy Horicon Historical Society.)

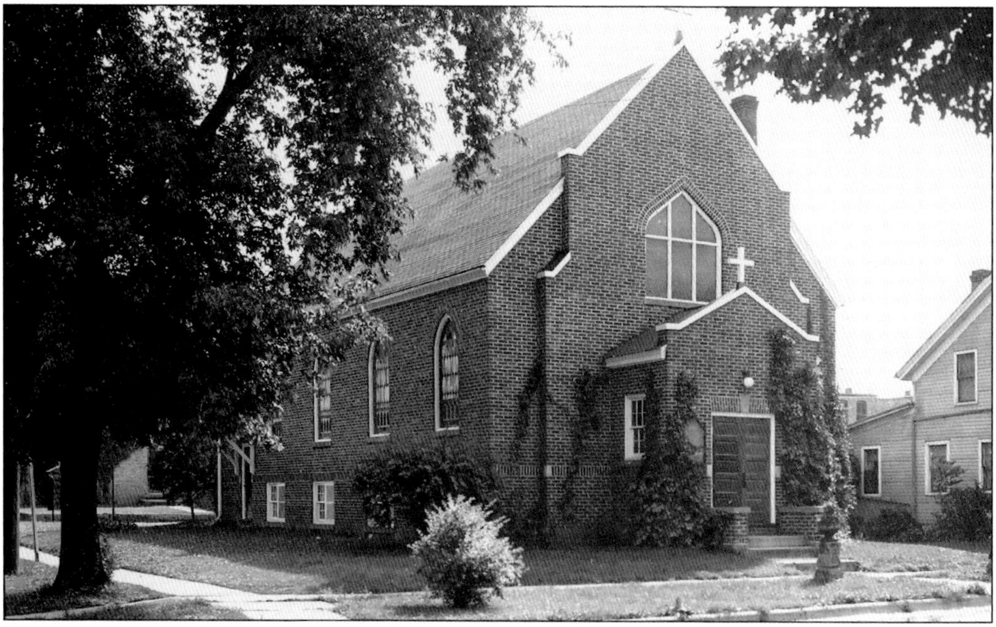

ZION EVANGELICAL LUTHERAN CHURCH. Organized in 1917, the new facility for parishioners was ready for services by Christmas of 1918 with dedication of the building taking place in January 1919. In 1954, the church was expanded to its current cruciform plan. The church is located on Walnut Street and continues to meet the needs of the congregation today. (Courtesy Horicon Historical Society.)

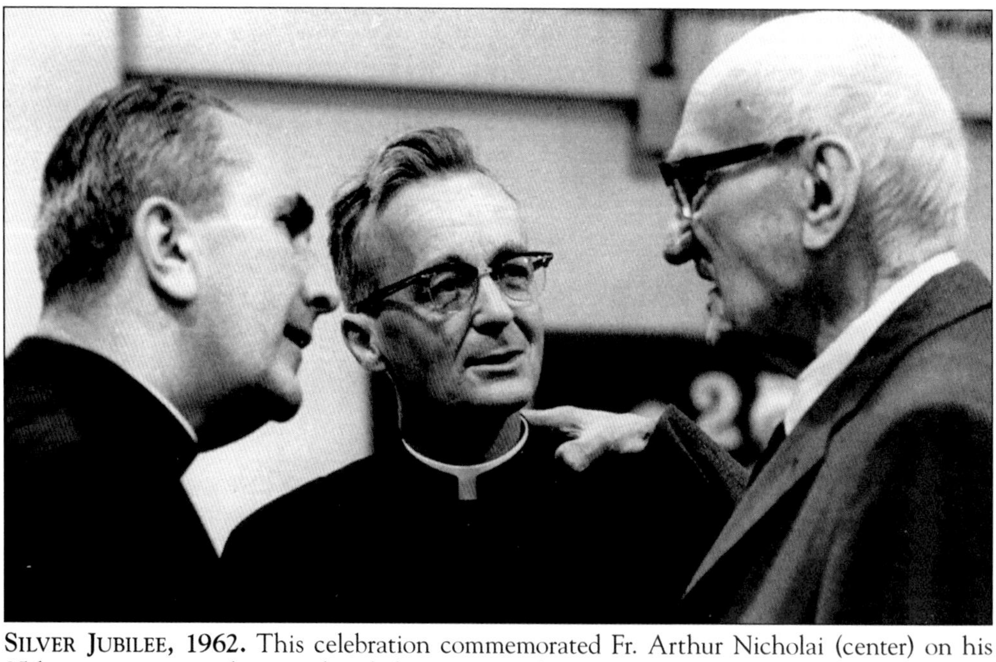

SILVER JUBILEE, 1962. This celebration commemorated Fr. Arthur Nicholai (center) on his 25th anniversary in the priesthood the very year he arrived at St. Malachy's. On the left is Fr. Anthony Zukaitis, a visiting priest from St. Kilian, and on the right is Frank Bodden, age 96, one of Horicon's oldest residents, who operated a fuel business in Horicon for many years. (Courtesy Horicon Reporter.)

Five

The Horicon Marsh

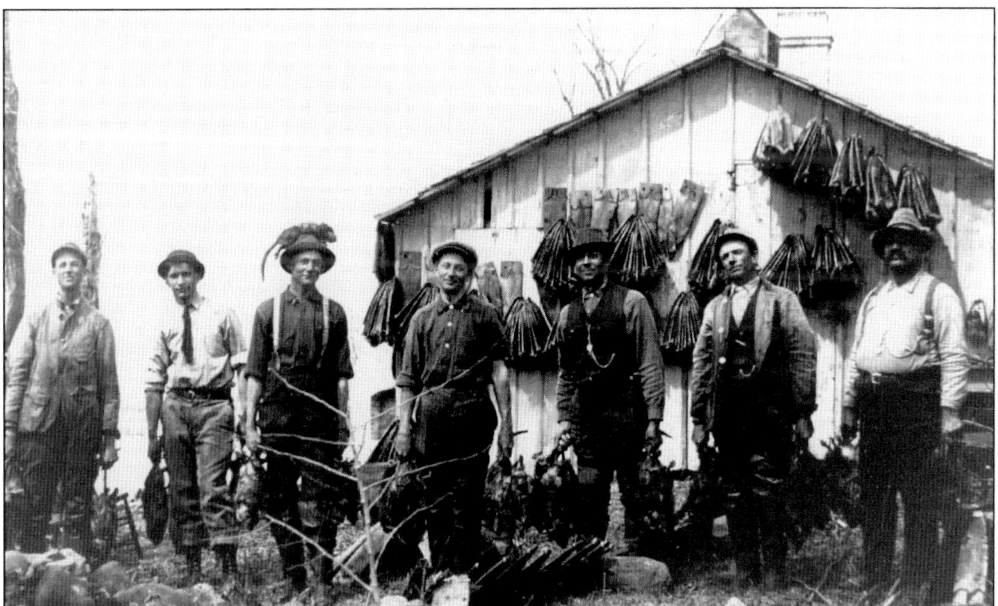

Muskrat Harvesting, Late 1800s. Muskrat, better known as the poor man's mink, was well harvested in the Horicon Marsh in light of nonexistent regulations during this era. In this photograph, from left to right, F. Dahms, E. Pagel, F. Winters, E. Miescke, F. Hoschild, C. Lauer, and L. Reynolds are shown with muskrats and stretching boards after a successful day of trapping. (Courtesy Buzz Vanderhei.)

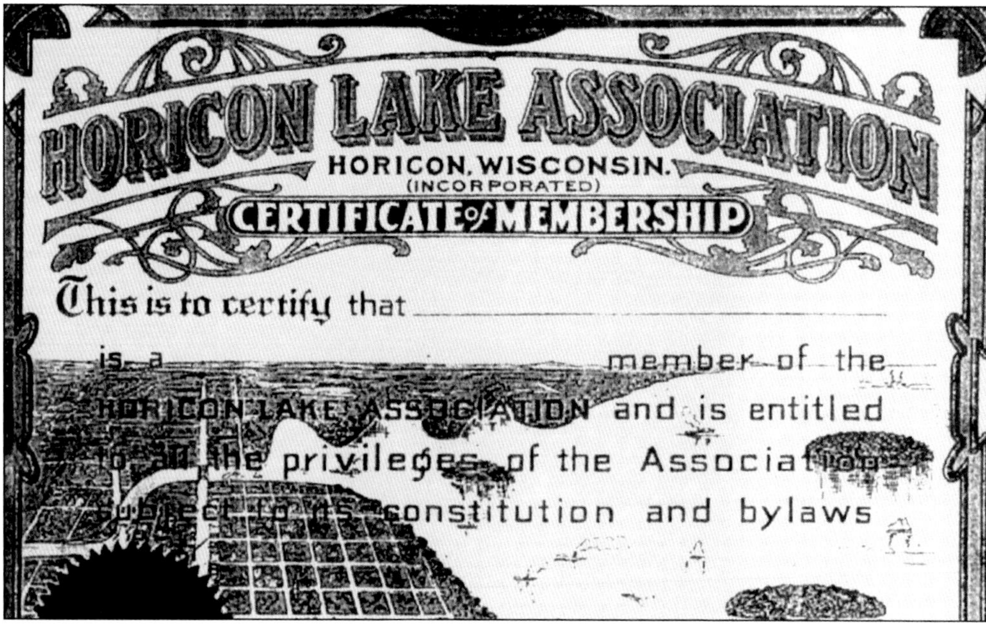

HORICON LAKE ASSOCIATION, 1868. Those who wished to have the marsh revert to native habitat were opposed by members of the Lake Association. Despite many who wished to maintain Lake Horicon and all the businesses whose survival depended on the waters, they were defeated, and the dam that created the artificial lake was removed. (Courtesy Horicon Historical Society.)

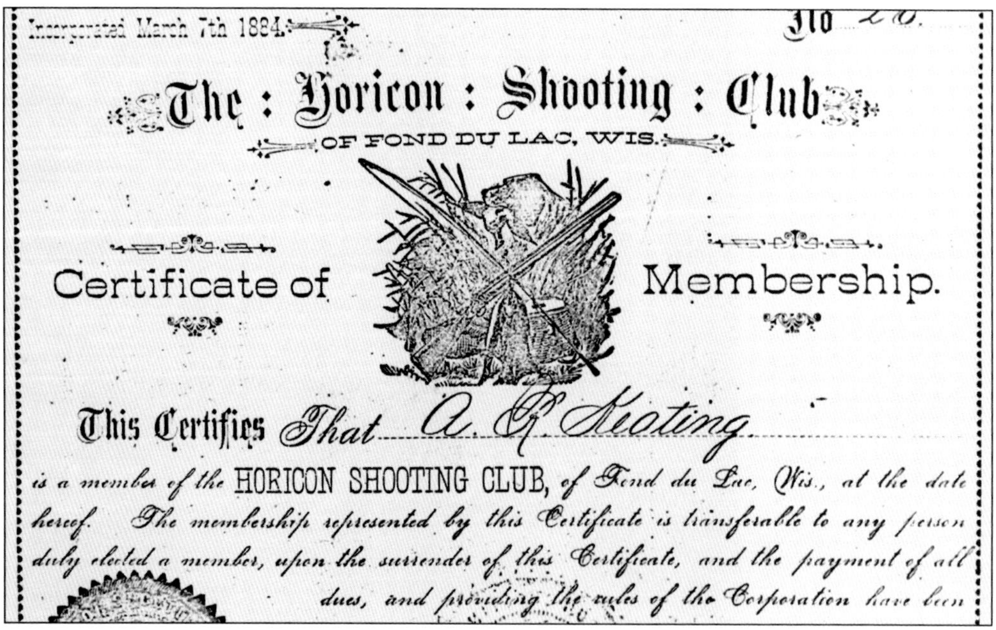

HORICON SHOOTING CLUB, 1892. Among the major hunting clubs on Horicon Marsh were both local hunting clubs and out-of-towner clubs. The local clubs, such as the Horicon Shooting Club, catered to area hunters and oftentimes limited the number of members to relatives and close friends. The out-of-towner clubs limited membership as a result of steep membership fees, which most of the locals could not afford. (Courtesy Horicon Historical Society.)

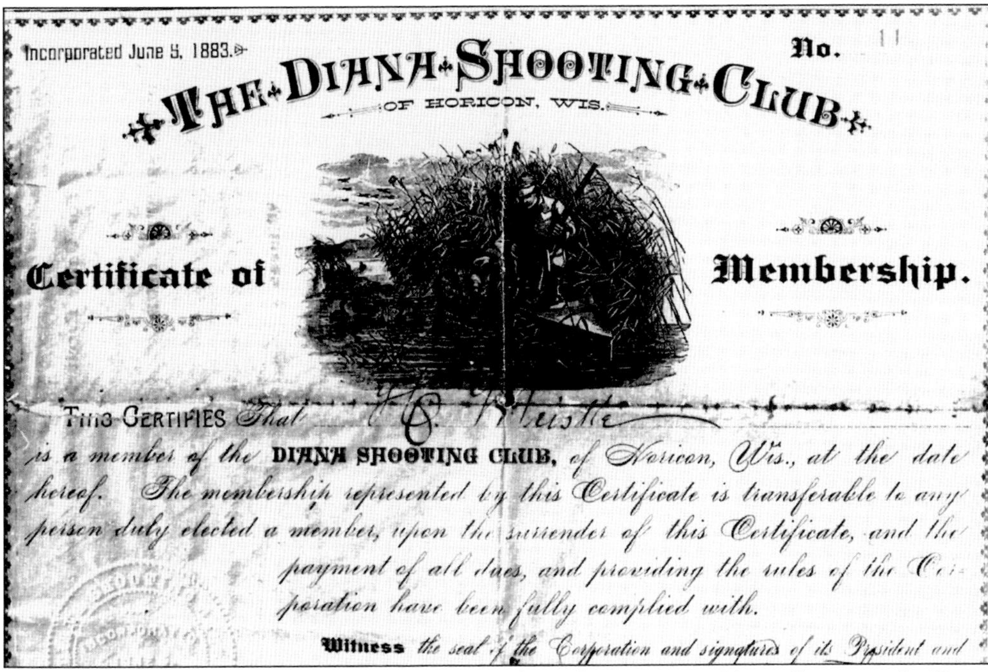

Incorporated June 5, 1883.

No. 11

The Diana Shooting Club

OF HORICON, WIS.

Certificate of Membership.

This Certifies That [illegible] is a member of the DIANA SHOOTING CLUB, of Horicon, Wis., at the date hereof. The membership represented by this Certificate is transferable to any person duly elected a member, upon the surrender of this Certificate, and the payment of all dues, and providing the rules of the Corporation have been fully complied with.

Witness the seal of the Corporation and signatures of its President and

DIANA SHOOTING CLUB, 1883. Taking its name from the Roman goddess of hunting, the Diana Shooting Club was the largest of the hunting clubs on Horicon Marsh, catering primarily to well-to-do local businessmen and out-of-towners from Milwaukee, Madison, and Chicago. Bylaws of this club stressed that members would shoot for sport and not for "big bags" and that they were unanimously opposed to shooting during the mating and breeding season. Interestingly, the Diana Shooting Club had its own railroad stop along the Chicago, Milwaukee and St. Paul Railway line, which would stop along Swan Road on the west side of the marsh to let hunters off for the weekend and then pick them up again for their travels back home. (Courtesy Horicon Historical Society.)

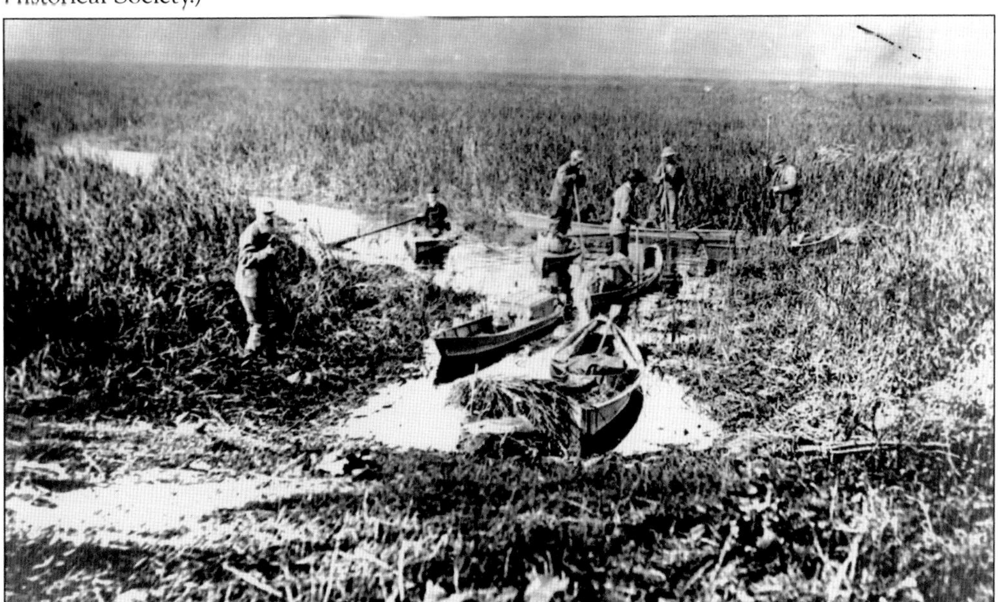

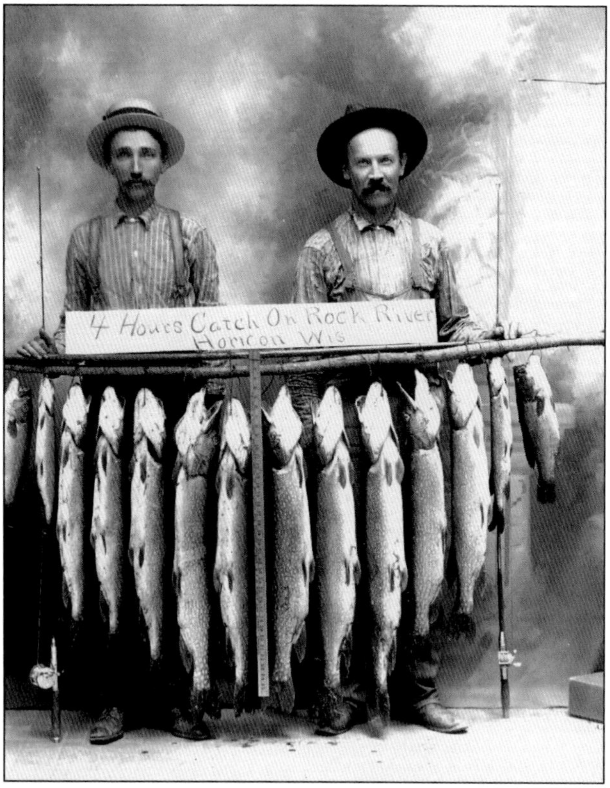

WILLIAM AND FRED BERGEN. The Rock River once supported abundant pan fish and game fish, such as this four-hour catch of large northern pike and bass. Note the yardstick in the middle of the photograph indicating the size of the fish—something that the present condition of these waters no longer supports. (Courtesy Horicon Historical Society.)

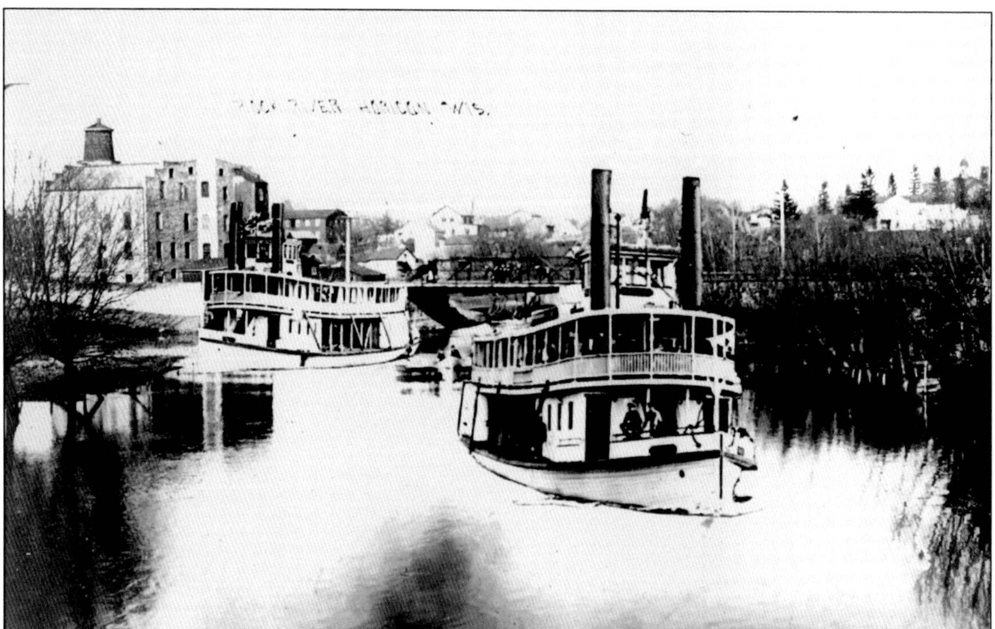

STEAMBOATS ON LAKE HORICON. During the time that Lake Horicon was in existence, five steamboats plied the waters of this man-made lake, carrying timber, farm products, and tourists. When the Horicon Dam was ordered to be removed in 1869, the lake and the boat traffic it supported both disappeared. (Courtesy Horicon Historical Society.)

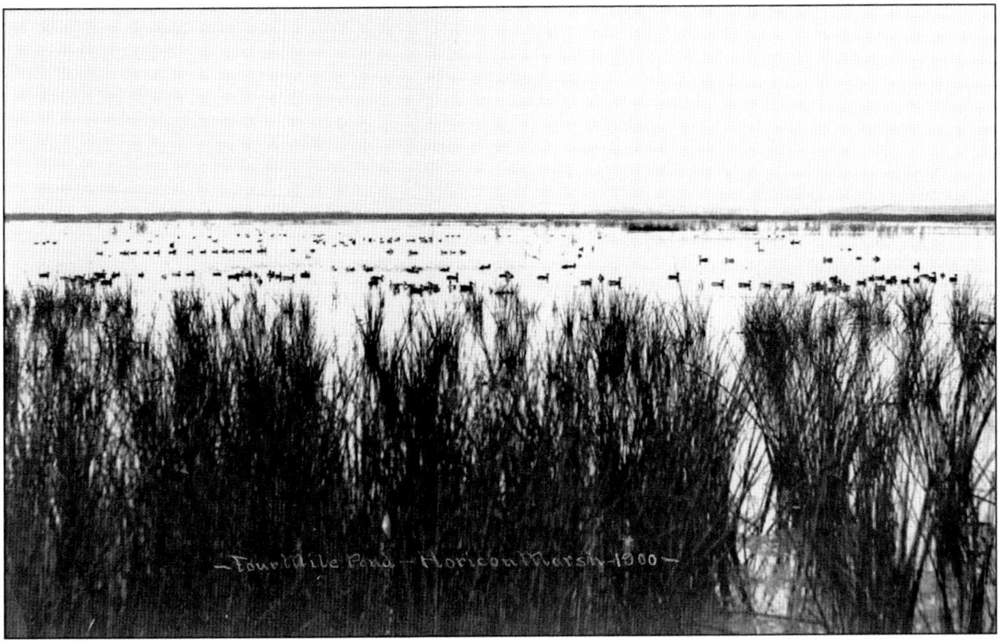

FOURMILE POND, 1900. Horicon Marsh originally consisted of stands of wild rice and other wetlands plants interspersed with pools of open water. Fourmile Pond is one of many of the well-known "potholes" that attracted abundant wildlife and waterfowl hunters. (Courtesy Horicon Historical Society.)

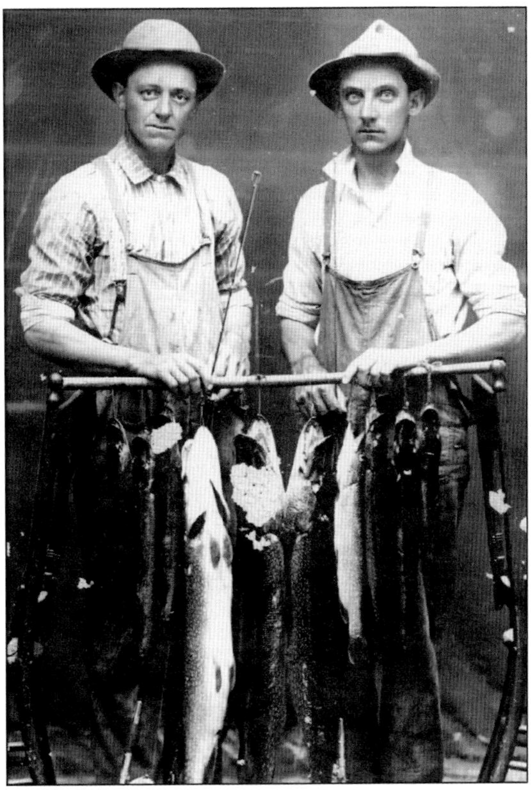

LAST AND GADOW, 1907. The Rock River has always been a source of food and sport for the residents of Horicon. Because Sunday was considered the day of rest and one to be spent with the family, if one was caught fishing on that day in 1857, a $2 fine would be issued. Shown here are Louis Last, on the left, and Ed Gadow, local fishermen. (Courtesy Horicon Historical Society.)

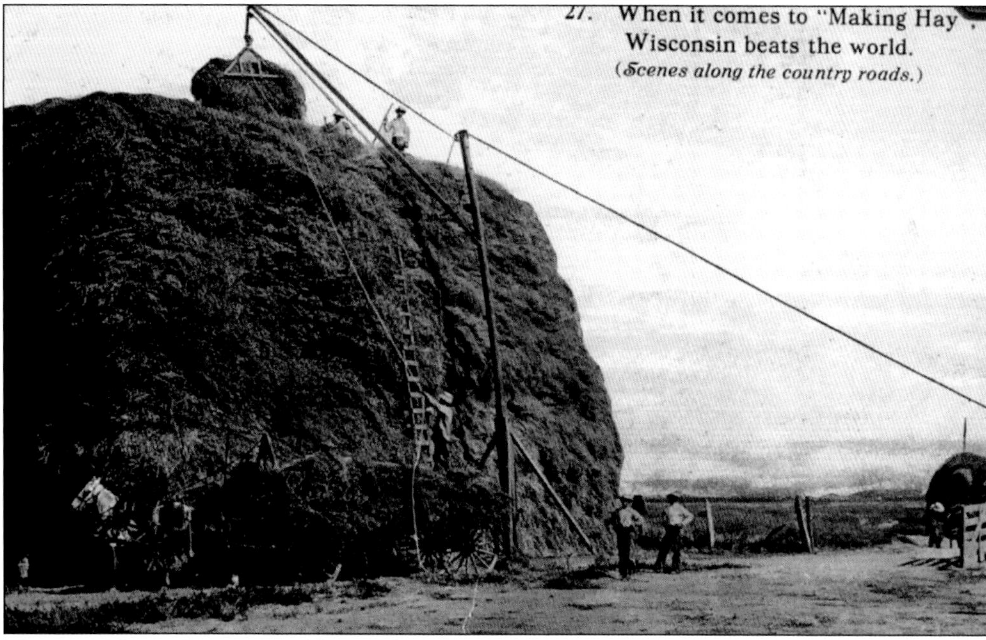

Making Hay. This postcard boasted "When It Comes to 'Making Hay,' Wisconsin Beats the World." While farming of the marsh for onions and other crops was not successful, the moist soil grew abundant stands of canary grass. The great harvest of marsh hay provided bedding for livestock and was used as packing material for a variety of products. (Courtesy Paul Kruel.)

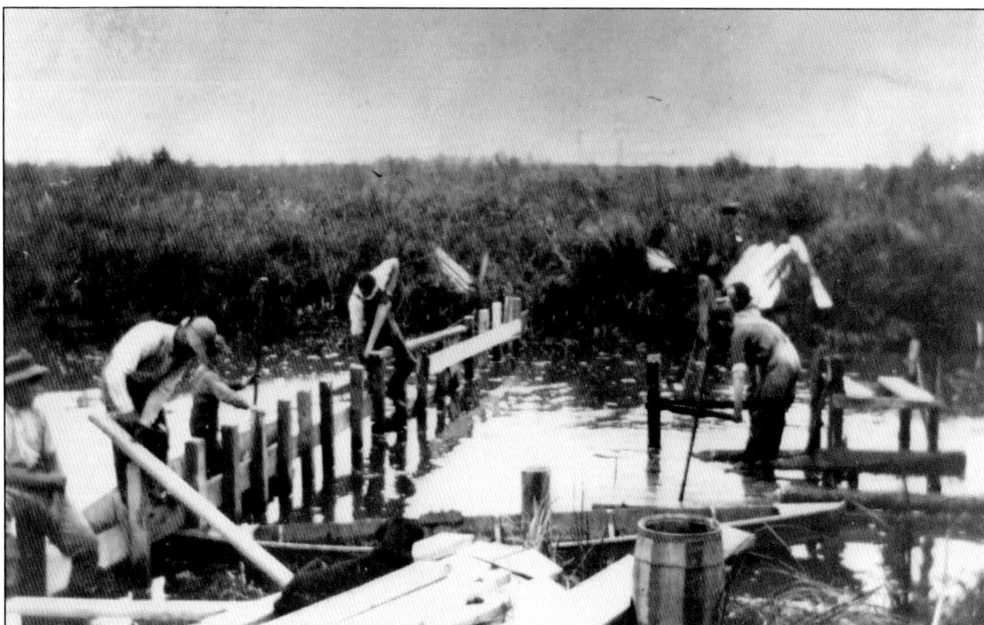

Strook's Club Dam Construction, c. 1910. Members of the Strook's Club constructed a private dam in Horicon Marsh to improve their duck hunting opportunities. The Diana Shooting Club had built a dam on the west side of the marsh, but by the time the Strook's Club dam was completed, draining of the marsh had begun, undermining their efforts. (Courtesy Horicon Historical Society.)

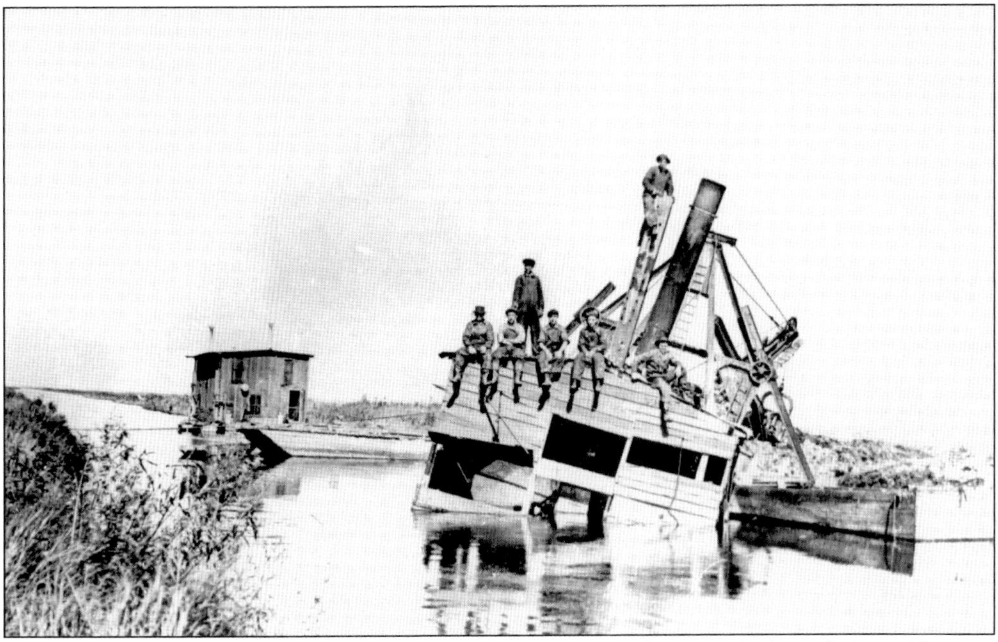

START OF THE DREDGING. Running from 1910 to 1916, efforts to ditch and drain Horicon Marsh for agricultural purposes created a 14-mile-long ditch down the entire length of the marsh and around the first bend of the Rock River. It required four years to dig the main ditch and two more years to excavate the lateral ditches. In the photograph below, the Old Marsh Road was constructed across Horicon Marsh, connecting the towns of Chester and LeRoy. Where it crossed the main ditch in the center of the marsh, a bridge was constructed. Here the marshland has been plowed by tractor to the point of this bridge on the west side of the ditch. (Above, courtesy Horicon Historical Society; below, courtesy Paul Kruel.)

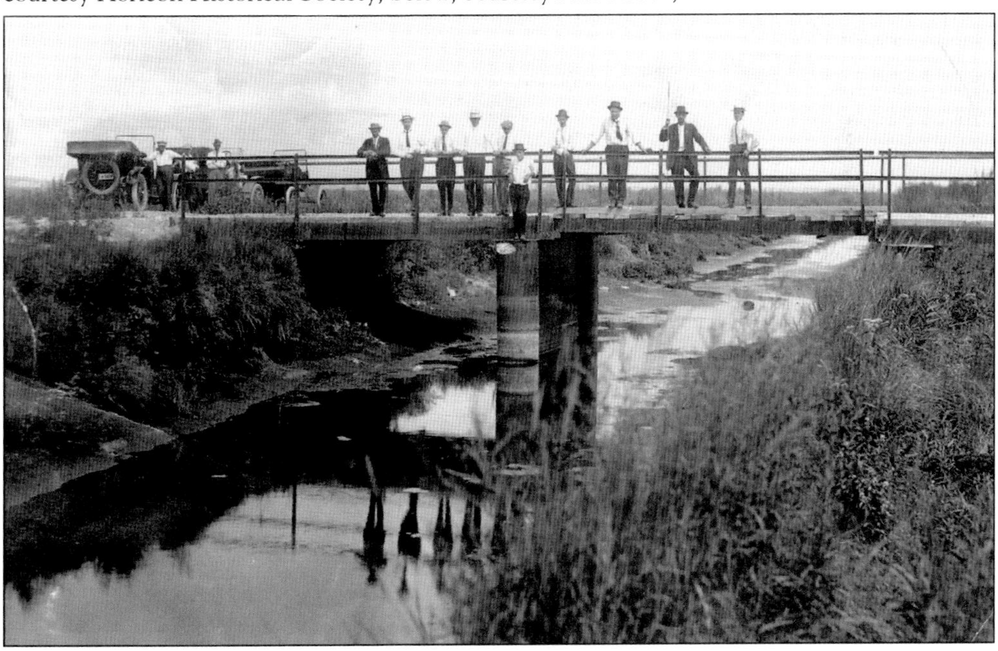

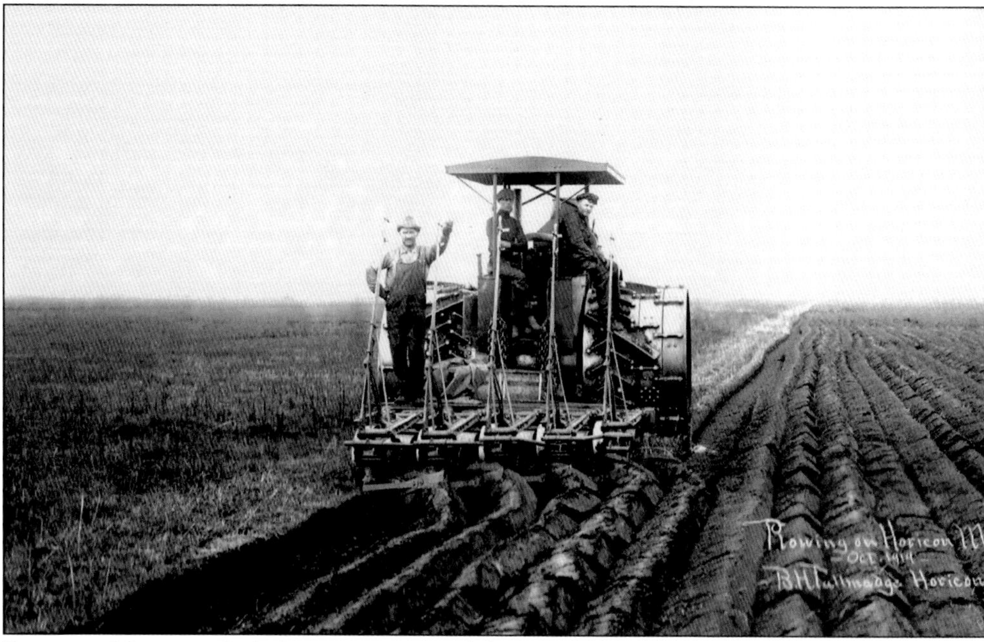

PLOWING MARSH, 1914. As construction of the main ditch was nearing completion, farming efforts began to encroach on the marsh soils. The black peat soil held lots of hope for those who wished to reap abundant crops. Unfortunately, for a variety of reasons, that did not result. The peat soil of Horicon Marsh, comprised of the undecomposed plant material that had built up over thousands of years, was soft and readily absorbed moisture. In order to work the soil and not get stuck, tractors with large steel wheels were used and horse teams were outfitted with marsh shoes. Fastened to the horse's hooves, the marsh shoes acted much like snowshoes, keeping the animals from getting stuck in the marsh. (Courtesy Paul Kruel.)

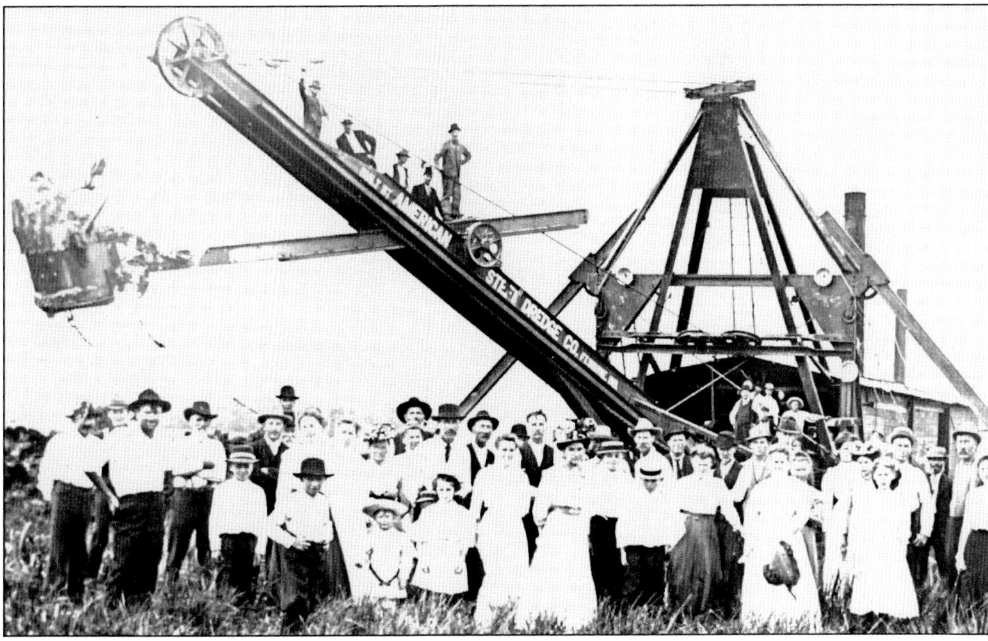

DREDGING THE MARSH, 1911. The dredge coming down the Rock River was cause for an outing. Starting in 1910 on the north end of the Horicon Marsh near the town of Chester, this floating steam shovel continued down to Horicon, forever changing the area's landscape. Although its promoters stated dredging the marsh would create fertile farmland, growing crops for consumption proved an unsuccessful venture in the peat soil. (Courtesy Buzz Vanderhei.)

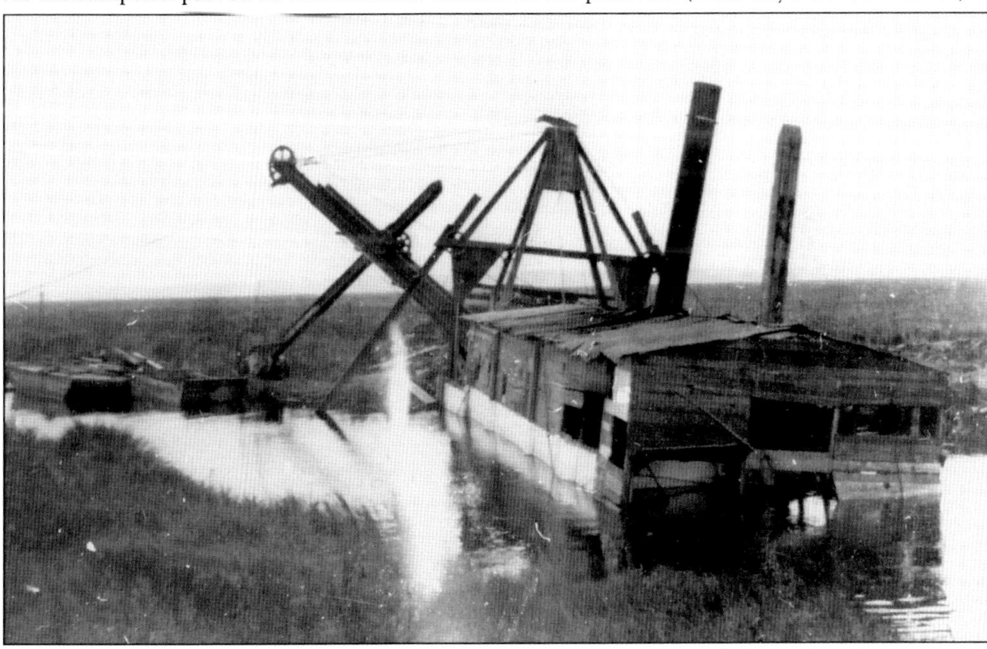

HORICON DREDGE. The Horicon Dredge was built in Chicago and shipped to East Waupun where it was transported and erected on the marsh. The job of the dredge was to dig a ditch 8 feet deep, 60 feet wide, and 14 miles long in an effort to drain Horicon Marsh for agricultural purposes. (Courtesy Horicon Historical Society.)

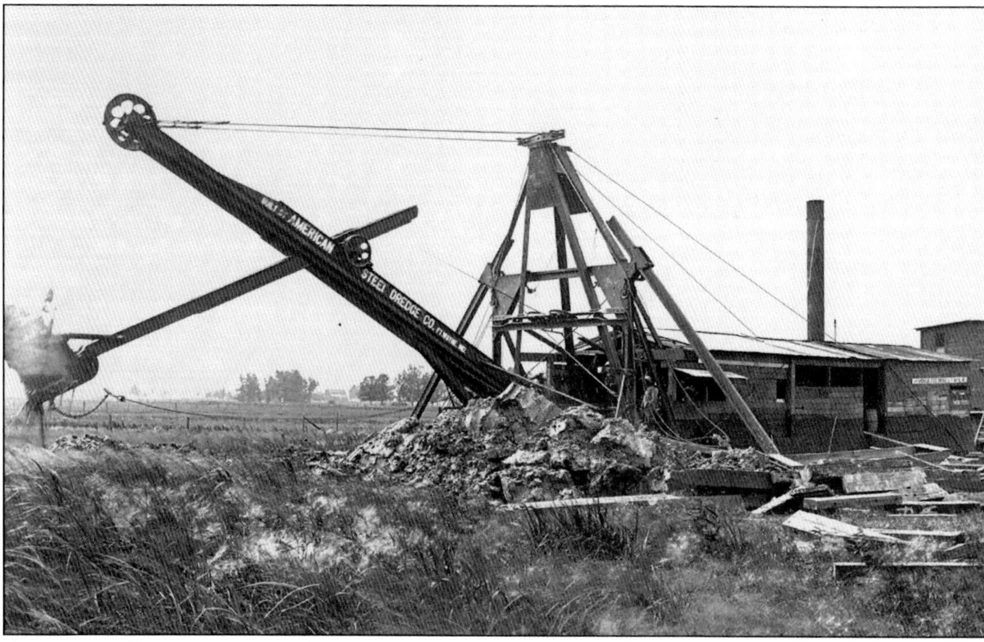

AMERICAN STEEL DREDGE COMPANY. It required four years to dig the main ditch down the entire length of Horicon Marsh and around the first bend of the Rock River through the city of Horicon. Dredge spoils were dug out of the marsh to construct the ditches and the material simply piled along the edge. The ditches and dredge spoils still remain throughout the marsh today. (Courtesy Horicon Historical Society.)

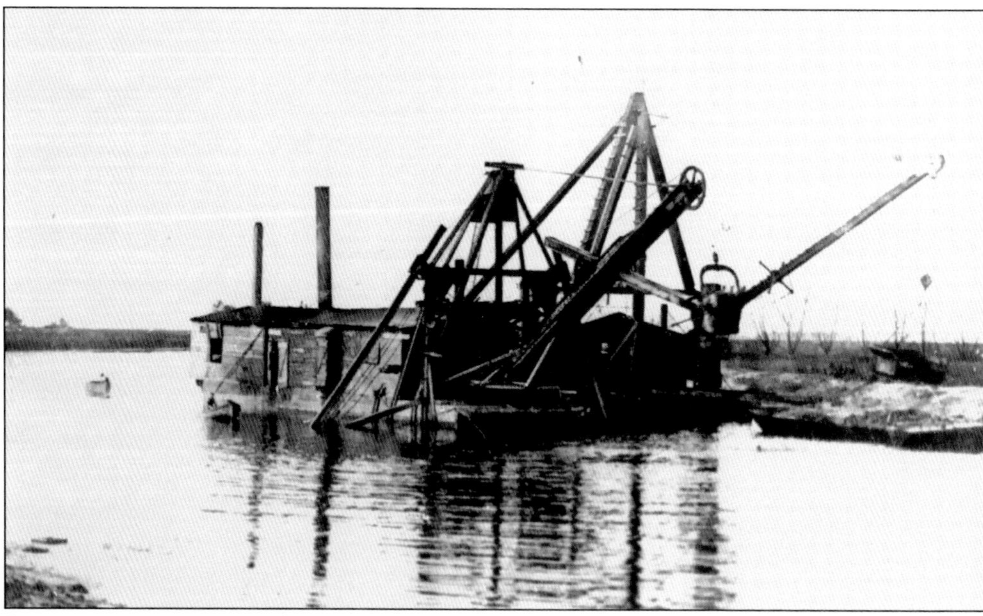

DREDGING THE RIVER. The main ditch was cut from north to south along the axis of the marsh. As it approached the city of Horicon, the ditch was angled toward the river outlet of the marsh. A second dredge was brought in to help hurry along the work of this major undertaking. Together they dredged the Rock River to increase drainage and then finished work on the lateral ditches. (Courtesy Horicon Historical Society.)

TRAPPING SHACK. Many of the local trappers maintained shacks on Horicon Marsh where they could store their equipment and prepare the hides they harvested. Some of these also served as second homes during the week for many trappers. They would live on the marsh during the fall trapping season before heading home on weekends. (Courtesy Horicon Historical Society.)

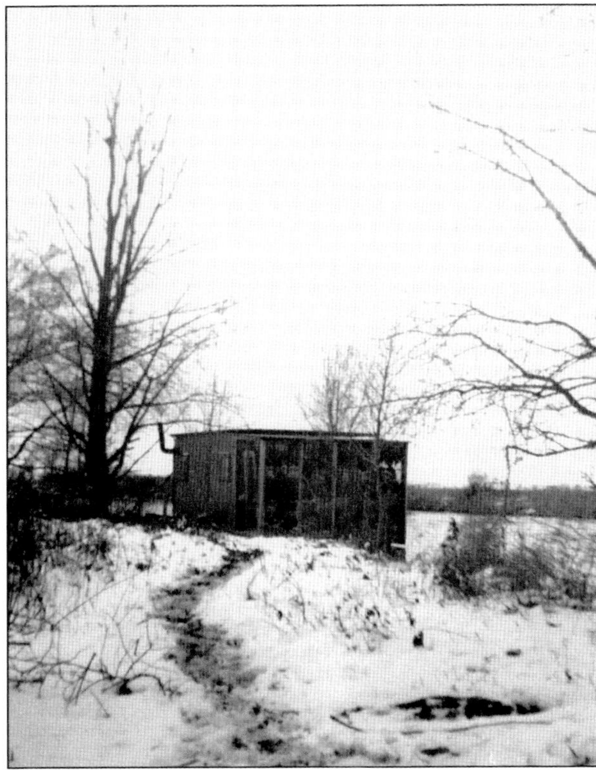

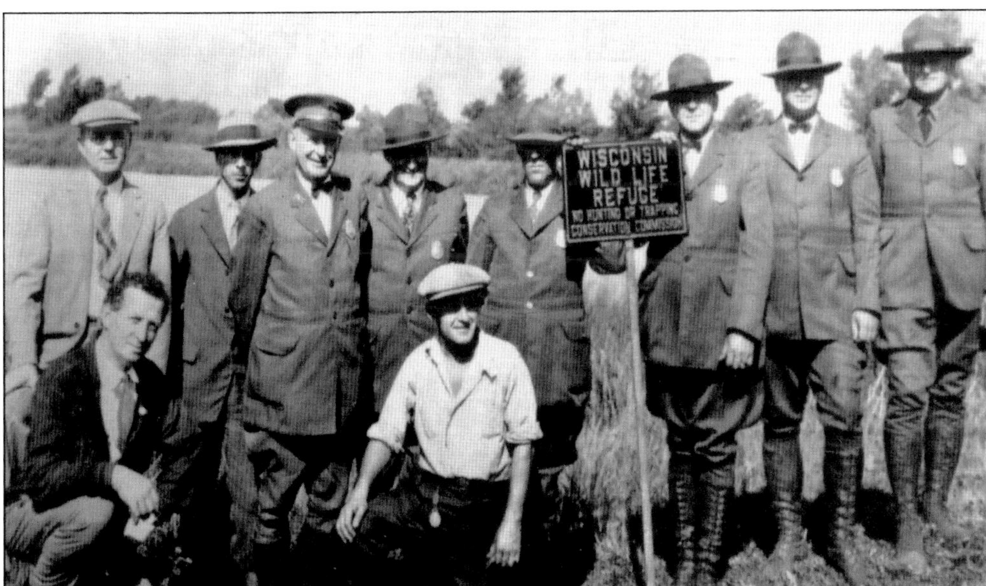

MARSH WARDENS, 1927. The Izaak Walton League played a leading role in the revitalization of the Horicon Marsh. Standing are, from left to right, Adam Port and Judge H. Washburn, both officers of the Horicon Chapter of the league; and wardens W. H. Riebe, W. H. Mackenzie, Harry Hosford, Arthur Tie, A. J. Robinson, and K. C. Jakoubek. Kneeling are officers of the league, from left to right, Louis Radke, who spearheaded the chapter, and Earl Snyder. (Courtesy Buzz Vanderhei.)

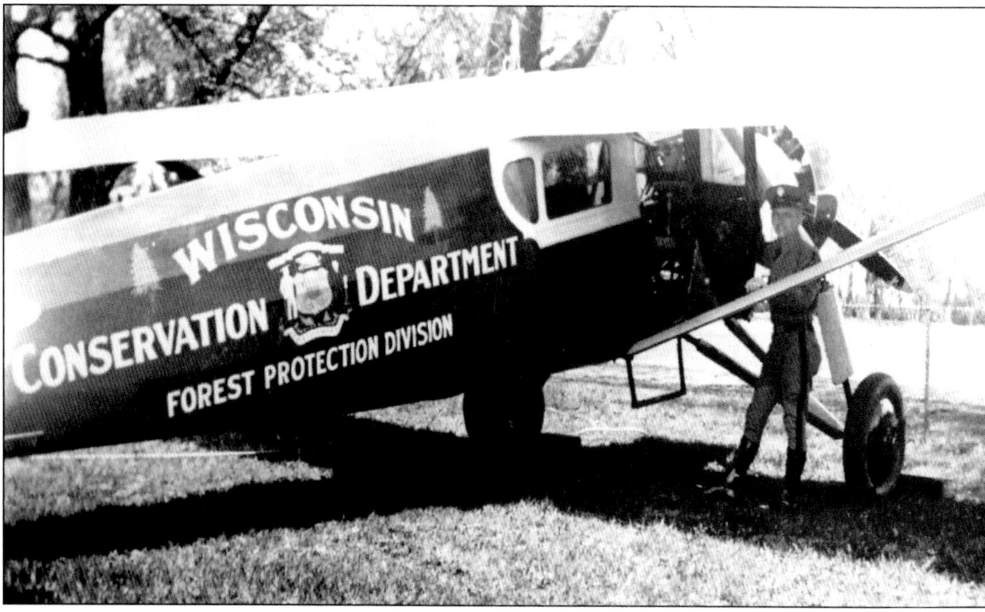

CONSERVATION AIRCRAFT, 1930S. Beginning in 1915, Wisconsin became the first state to use airplanes for detecting forest fires. By the 1930s, aircraft were used regularly by the Wisconsin Conservation Department for fire detection and reconnaissance during fires. In 1938, the Federal Communications Commission approved the use of ultrahigh-frequency radios, and they were immediately installed in the aircraft. Radios were also provided to primary fire tower crews and rangers' vehicles. (Courtesy Buzz Vanderhei.)

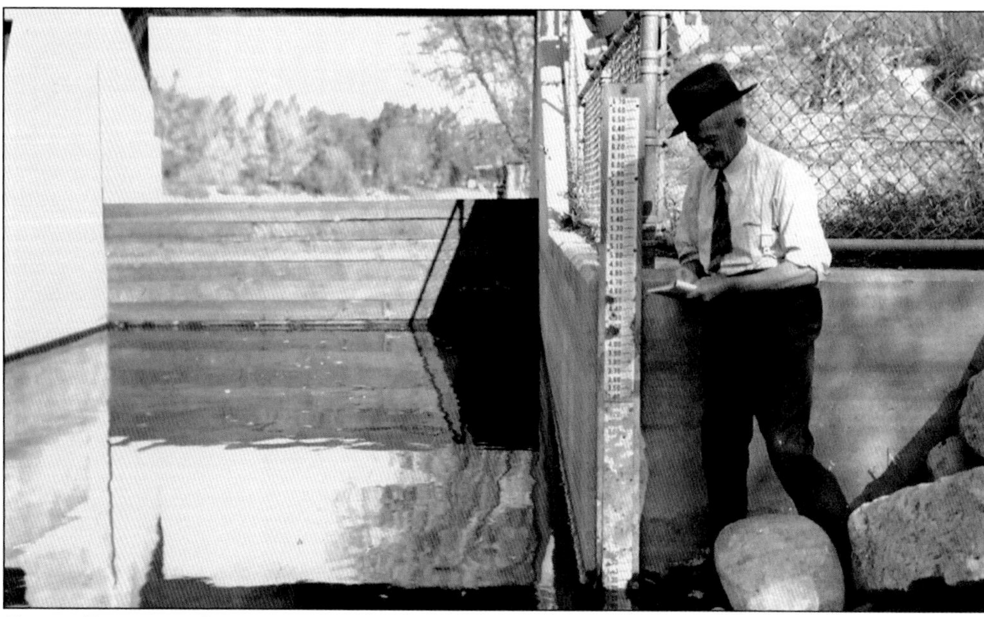

GAUGE READING, OCTOBER 11, 1934. With Horicon Dam construction completed, water levels returned to the original benchmark surveyed for Horicon Marsh prior to draining. The state, convinced of its legal right to reflood the marsh by constructing a dam, essentially plugged the ditch that was dug to drain the marsh, and legal challenges followed. Here William Snyder reads the gauges at Horicon Dam. (Courtesy Wisconsin Department of Natural Resources.)

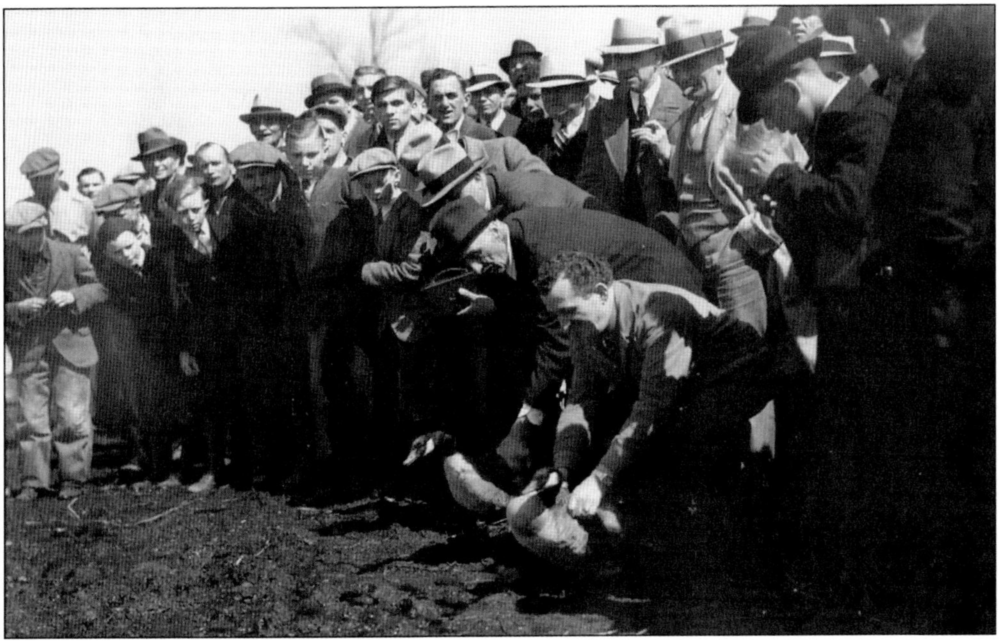

DUCK LIBERATION DAY, 1935. Led by Louis "Curley" Radke, the State Conservation Commission agreed to lend support to the "planting" of domestic ducks on the marsh to attract wild birds on their spring migration through the area. Ducks were sold for $1 each, and men banded the 1,180 domestic ducks and two wild Canada geese before their release in order to track the success of the event. Approximately 5,000 people came from all over to bring ducks and join in the merriment. Gen. Ralph Immel, head of the State Conservation Commission, attended the ceremony and expressed his approval of the experiment of having the domestic birds draw the wild birds to the marsh. (Courtesy Wisconsin Department of Natural Resources.)

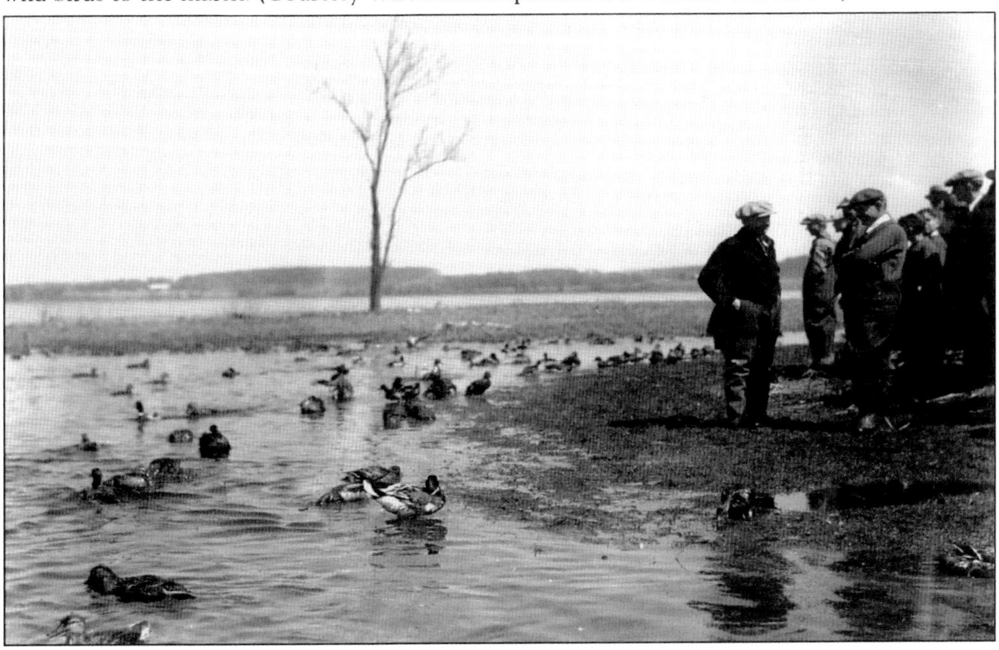

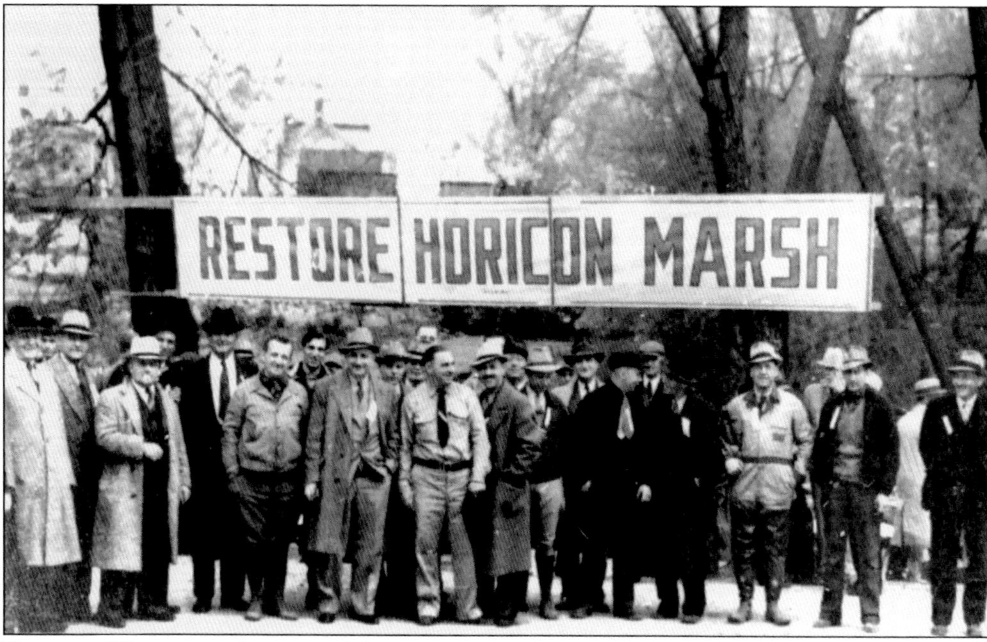

RESTORE HORICON MARSH. Celebrating Duck Liberation Day, a parade was led through the city leading up to "Conservation Hill" on the north end of Palmatory Street and then down to the marsh where the donated ducks were released during a public ceremony. While most of these domesticated ducks lived a short life, the event did more to garner public interest and support for managing Horicon Marsh as a wildlife area. Joe Penner, a radio comedian, promoted the event held on April 20, 1935, with his pet phrase "Wanna buy a duck?" Glenrose Armstrong-Borden and Theodore John Erdman were two who attended that day to watch the release of the ducks into the wild. (Courtesy Horicon Historical Society.)

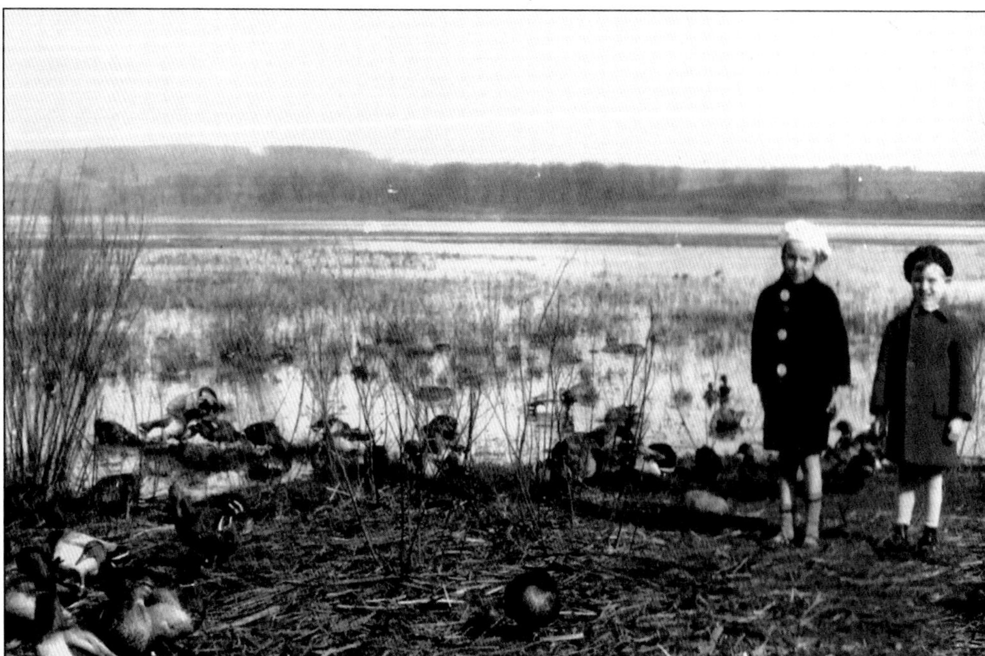

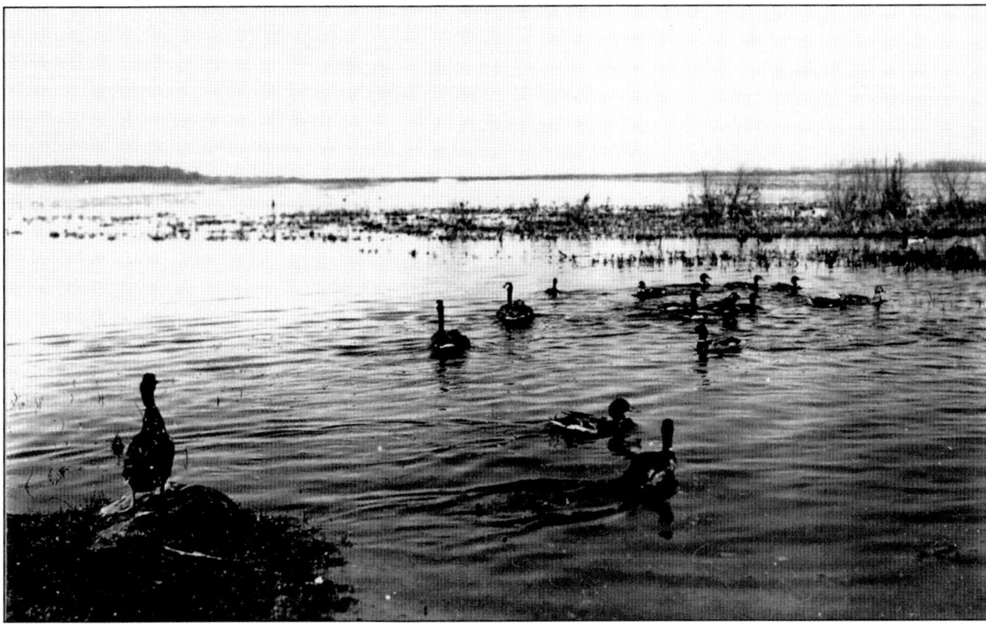

RELEASE OF DUCKS. With the ducks enjoying the waters of the marsh, all deemed the day successful in bringing the waterfowl back to the marsh and in obtaining the public interest in conservation. J. N. (Ding) Darling, head of the United States Biological Survey in Washington, D.C., took an interest in the proceedings occurring that day. Being a talented artist, he designed the first federal duck stamp. (Courtesy Wisconsin Department of Natural Resources.)

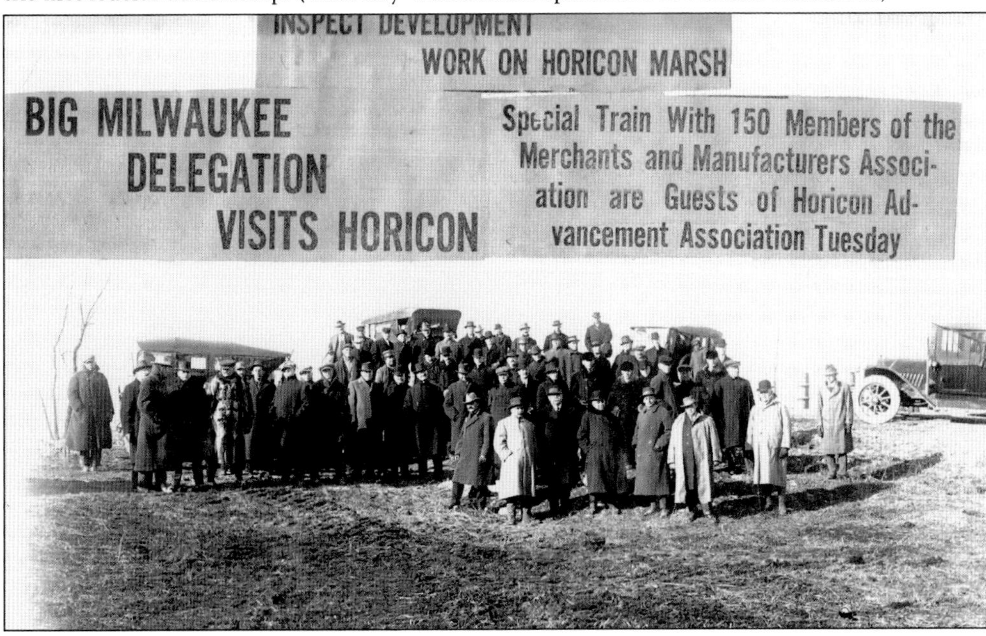

DELEGATION AT HORICON, 1939. Those opposed to reflooding the Horicon Marsh mounted lawsuits challenging the state over construction and operation of the dam at the outlet of the marsh. Newspaper accounts reported, "A battery of over 30 automobiles conveys delegations on thirty mile trip on Big Meadow-visitors much impressed with future prospects of both the Big Marsh and this City." (Courtesy Paul Kruel.)

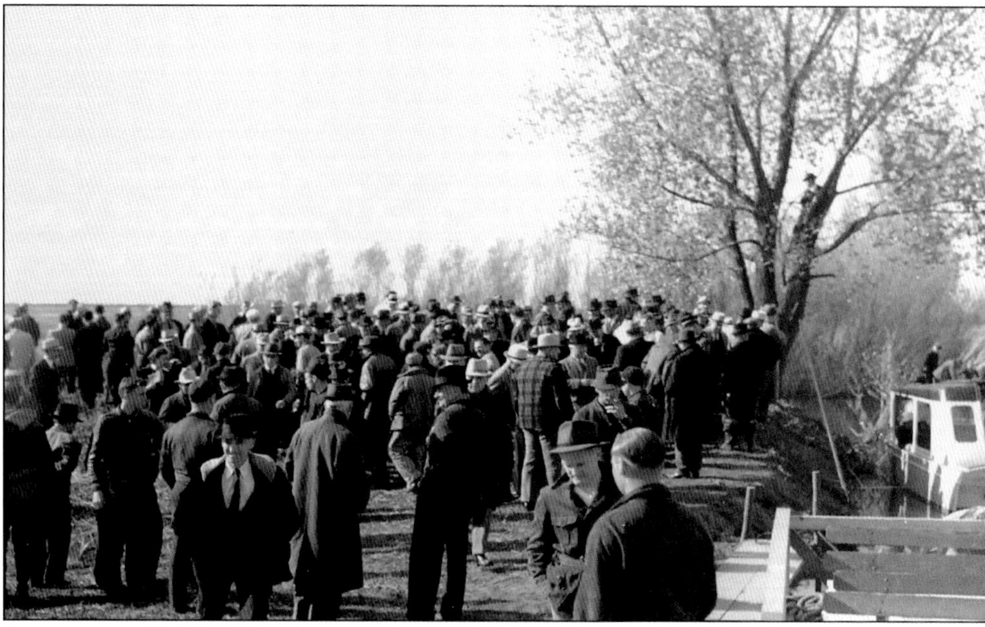

LEGISLATIVE INSPECTION, MAY 1939. The controversy over reflooding of the marsh led to the legislature touring the Horicon Marsh for an on-site inspection. Legislative inspection of Horicon Marsh was conducted by providing a series of floating platforms for the legislators to stand on while being towed by this boat to give them a first-hand look at the marsh restoration issue. The tour allowed for legislators to inspect the dam and allowed them to experience the wealth of wildlife being attracted to the newly reflooded marsh. The outcome of this battle was that the state and the courts concurred that Horicon Marsh, as a previously navigable waterway, could be reflooded to its original water level but not held above that point. This ruling still dictates the operation of the Horicon Dam today. (Courtesy Wisconsin Department of Natural Resources.)

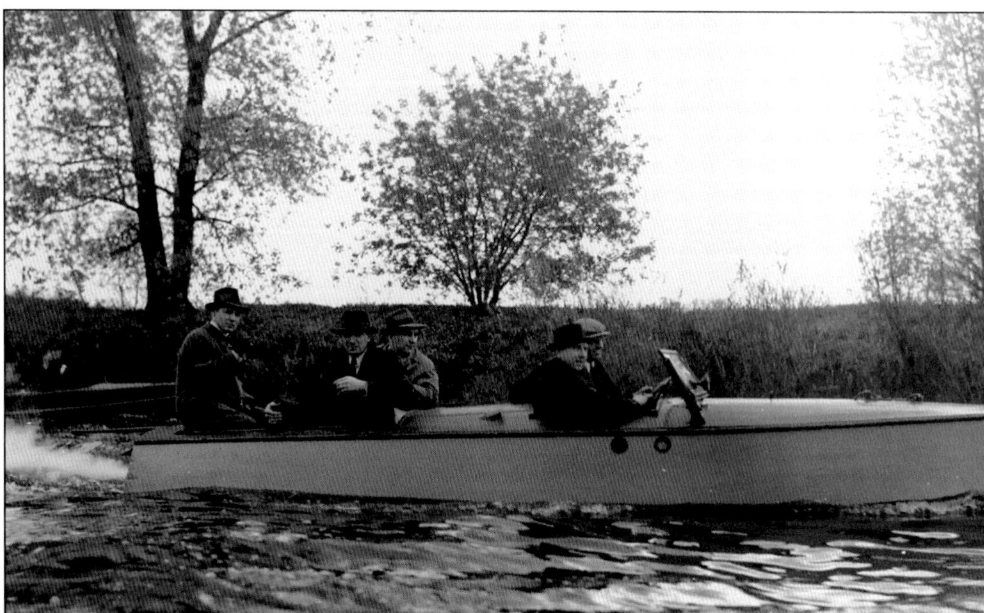

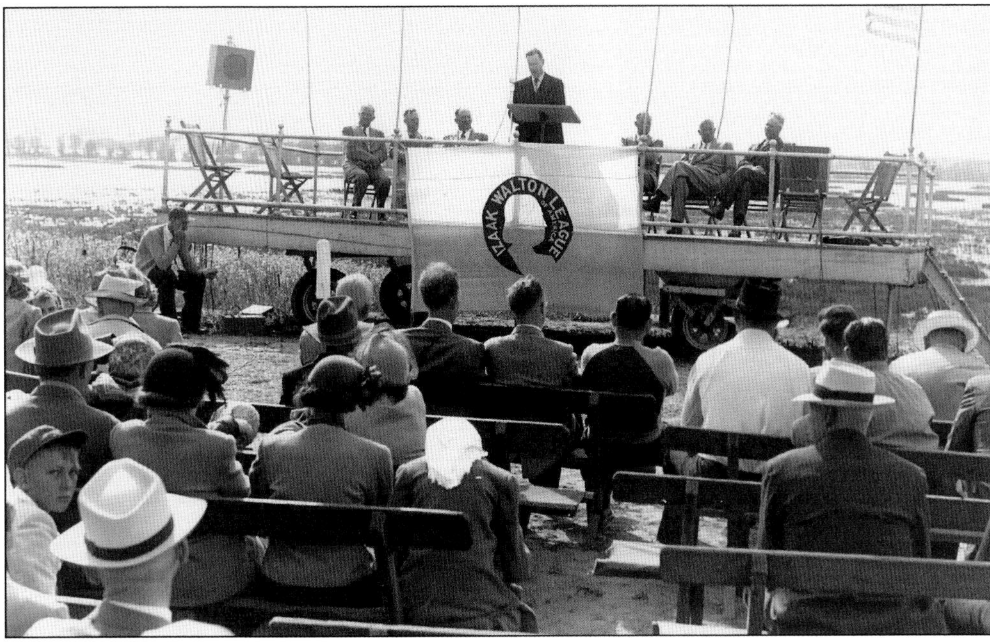

RADKE MEMORIAL DEDICATION, 1950. Following his passing in 1948, a monument was erected memorializing the work and vision of Louis "Curley" Radke. In the photograph above, Wilton E. Erdman, chairman of the Radke Memorial Committee-Wisconsin Division of the Izaak Walton League of America, presented at the dedication of the monument for Radke. Seated on the platform are, from left to right, William J. P. Aberg, Ernest Swift, Sen. Frank Panzer, William Voigt Jr., V. J. Muench, and Max Elsinger. In the photograph below, Sarah Ulmer, granddaughter of Radke, unveiled the memorial for her grandfather, fittingly with a beautiful view of the marsh he worked so hard to preserve. The memorial is located at what is now the Department of Natural Resources' facility overlooking the Horicon Marsh. (Courtesy Horicon Historical Society.)

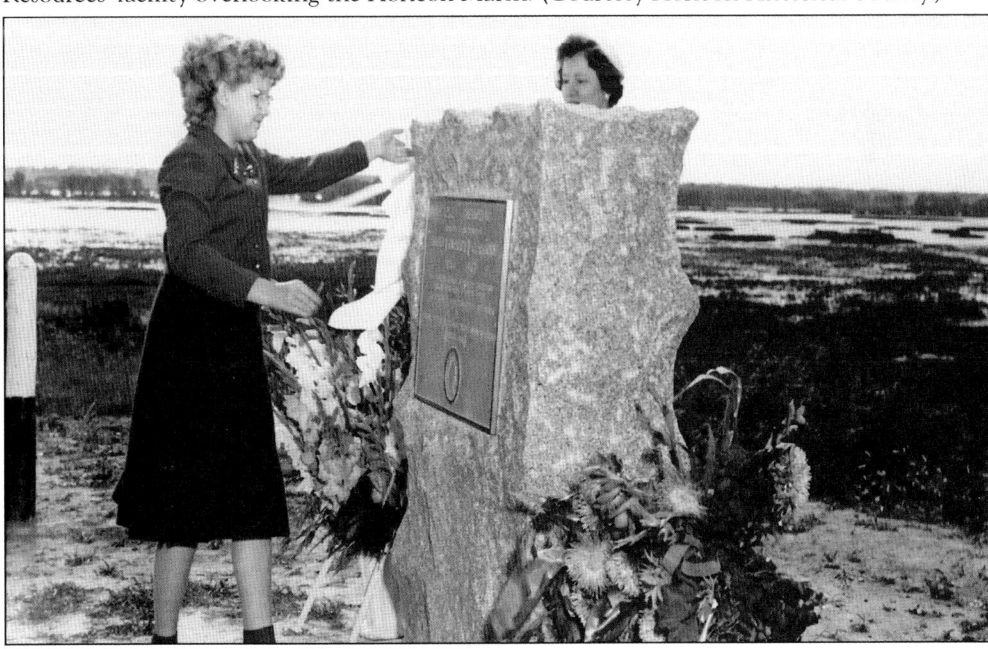

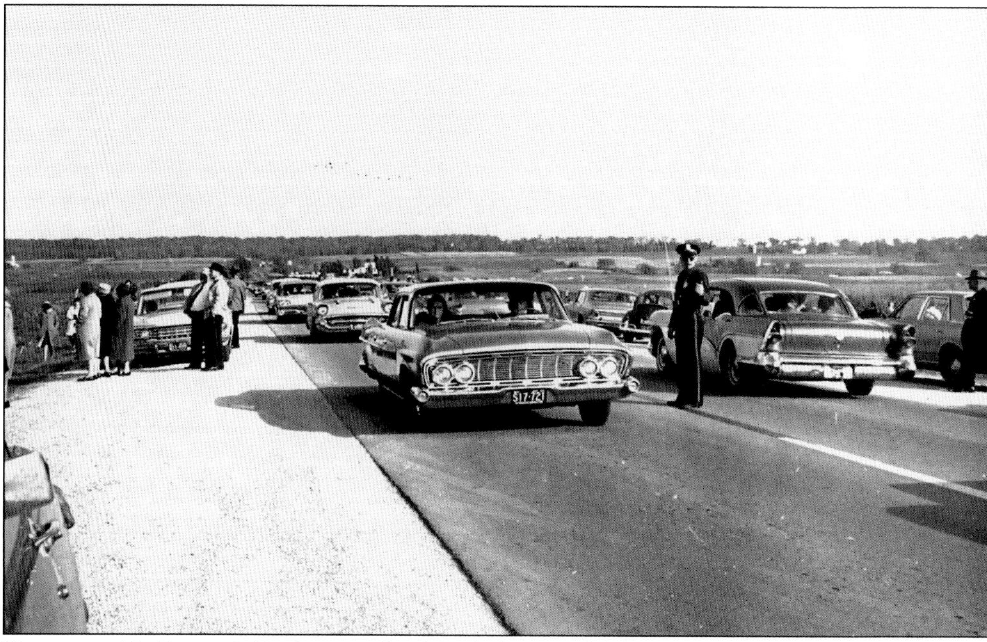

HIGHWAY 49, FALL 1964. As a result of food plots established along Highway 49 in the 1960s to try and keep Canada geese on the marsh and reduce crop damage on nearby farmland, the outcome was more of a lure, bringing even more geese to the area and creating an unequaled wildlife viewing experience. Thousands of people came by car to watch the spectacular fall gathering of nearly 250,000 geese feeding and resting just off the highway. This also created incredible traffic jams, which tied up the highway, leading to traffic control on fall weekends. The famous photograph, below, by Edgar Mueller, provided an opportunity to forever depict one of those days at the height of the fall migration on film. (Above, courtesy Wisconsin Department of Natural Resources; below, courtesy Horicon Historical Society.)

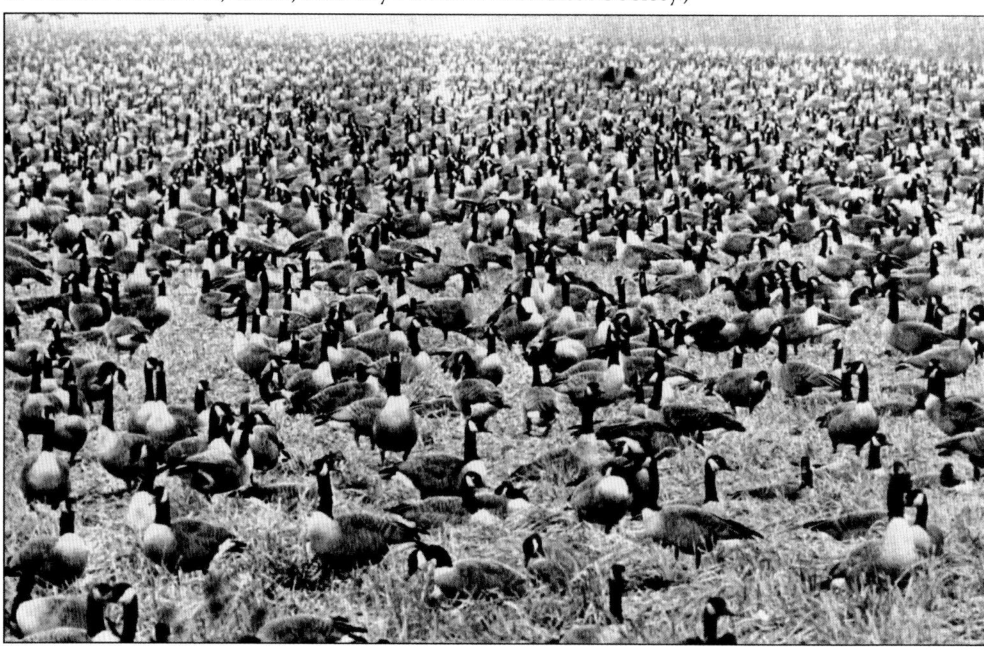

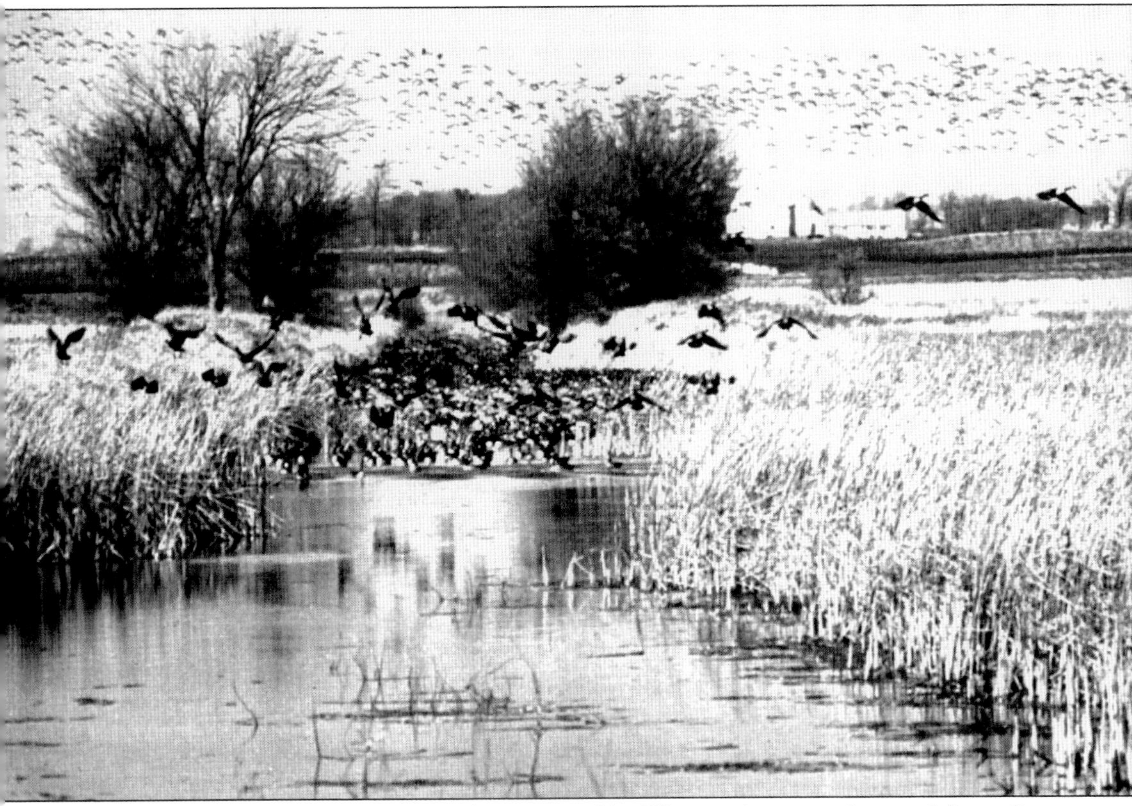

THE RESTORED MARSH. Horicon Marsh, an area of 31,653 acres, became a haunt of the earliest Native Americans. A dam was built in 1846 that created Lake Horicon, which was believed to be the largest artificial lake in the world. The lake promoted lumbering, transportation, and agriculture, causing Horicon to become one of the most important cities in Wisconsin. Dam removal was ordered in 1869, beginning the restoration of the marsh, which was subjected to various development schemes that changed its character. After a 20-year struggle by conservationists, led by Louis "Curley" Radke, the Horicon National Wildlife Refuge was established on July 16, 1941. With the purchase of the marshland by the state government in 1927 and the federal government in 1941, Horicon Marsh was coming back to life as the area was reflooded and plant life became established in the shallow waters. The marsh responded quickly and began to lure wildlife back to this land. Today the success is evident, as nearly 300 different varieties of birds have been recorded on the marsh. (Courtesy Buzz Vanderhei.)